# 500 Questions & Answers from the BIBLE

## Mark Fackler, Editor

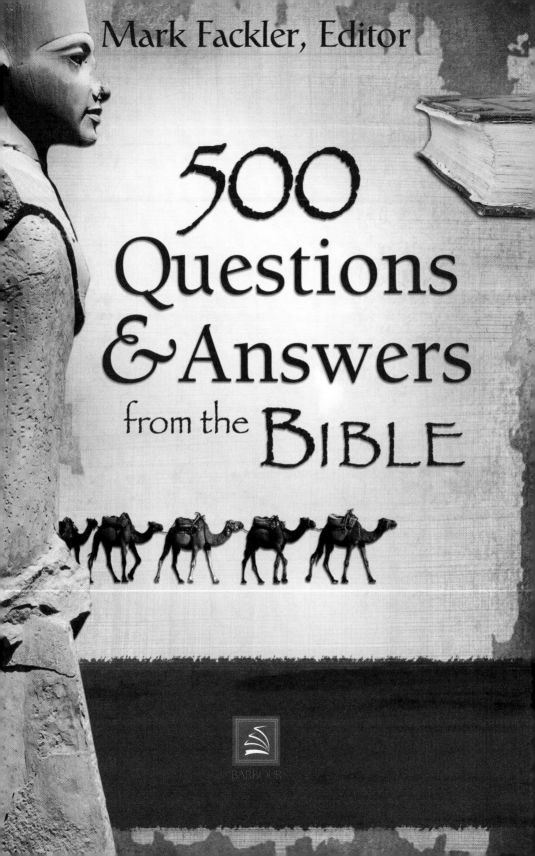

Mark Fackler, Editor

# 500
# Questions
# & Answers
## from the BIBLE

General Editor:  Dr. Mark Fackler
                 Calvin College (Grand Rapids, Michigan)

Contributors:    Sandy Beelen
                 InterVarsity Christian Fellowship—Great Lakes West Region (Carol Stream, Illinois)

                 Jack Crabtree
                 Long Island Youth for Christ (Huntington Station, New York)

                 Mark Fackler
                 Calvin College

                 Kent Keller
                 Kendall Presbyterian Church (Miami, Florida)

                 Neil Wilson
                 The Livingstone Corporation (Carol Stream, Illinois)

                 Len Woods
                 Christ Community Church (Ruston, Louisiana)

Produced by The Livingstone Corporation, (www.Livingstonecorp.com). Project staff include: David Veerman, Dana Veerman, Kirk Luttrell, Joel Bartlett, and Mary Horner Collins.

Cover images © istockphoto.com and Getty Images

Published by Barbour Publishing, Inc. P.O. Box 719, Uhrichsville, Ohio 44683, www.barbourbooks.com

*Our mission is to publish and distribute inspirational products offering exceptional value and biblical encouragement to the masses.*

# Introduction

The fact that you are reading the words on this page indicates that you have interest in the Bible. Maybe you grew up with the Bible, or perhaps you've just been introduced. Maybe you believe every word of scripture, or perhaps you admit to skepticism. Maybe you fall somewhere between those extremes.

Whatever your perspective, you can probably agree that. . .

♦ the Bible is a very large book.

♦ the Bible contains some rather confusing passages.

♦ the Bible's people acted in ways that we in the twenty-first century find strange.

*500 Questions & Answers from the Bible* was written to help you make sense of this best-selling, ancient, sometimes perplexing, and yet vitally important Book. The approach is popular, rather than scholarly—attempting to answer questions that anyone, with a background in the scriptures or not, might ask.

The material is presented in biblical order—that is, it starts with the book of Genesis and continues through the Old Testament; then it picks up with the New Testament and ends with the Bible's final book, Revelation. A scripture reference accompanies each question, telling you where to find the background material in the Bible itself. Then the question is answered in an easy-to-read manner, providing a helpful explanation based on sound Christian doctrine and belief.

As you read, you'll learn about the origins of the Bible, God's character, puzzling biblical practices, ancient cultures, and much more. Full-color illustrations throughout bring the text to life, promising an educational and entertaining reading experience.

You can access this book in several ways, of course. You might want to read straight through, from the first question and answer in Genesis to the last pair in Revelation. Or you could skim the list of questions in the table of contents until you see one that catches your attention—perhaps something you've always wondered about—and then flip to the right page and read the answer. Or you could use this book as a resource for a personal or group Bible study. In that case you would check out the questions and answers in a specific passage that you're studying.

Regardless of your approach, if you have questions about what's in the Bible, this book has answers.

# Contents

- Why do people regularly fail to listen to God?
- Are malnourishment and dehydration really spiritual problems at the core?
- Does God become so angry as to refuse to listen to prayers?
- Would God really punish people, with no chance for an appeal?
- Is poverty, at the core, ever a spiritual problem?
- Is ignorance, at its core, a spiritual problem?

- Why does an all-powerful God allow children to suffer?
- Is it okay to complain to God in prayer?

- What do these "wheels" tell us about God?
- What does "son of man" mean?
- Why would Ezekiel—or anybody—speak truth to stubborn people who refuse to listen?
- What are cherubim?
- Why was Ezekiel told not to grieve the death of his wife?
- "Dem bones, dem bones, dem dry bones," the song goes. What message lies hidden in the dry bones?

- Why did Daniel make such a big deal over his diet?
- Are some of Daniel's visions of the future still pending?
- Why did God use dreams and visions to communicate with so many people in the Bible?
- Why didn't Shadrach, Meshach, and Abednego bow down to the golden statue?
- Does trusting God mean nothing bad will happen to us?
- Who was the fourth person in King Nebuchadnezzar's furnace?
- Why did King Nebuchadnezzar lose his mental health?
- Why did Daniel ignore the law criminalizing prayer?
- How did Daniel survive the lions' den?

- Is the story of Gomer and Hosea real history or an allegory?
- Why would God tell a spiritual leader to marry a woman who would cause him heartache and embarrassment?
- Was the prophet Hosea the real father of Gomer's three children?

- If God chose Jehu to destroy the house of Ahab (2 Kings 9:7), why was Jehu condemned by Hosea for the massacre of Ahab's house?
- When God spoke to Hosea about Israel's various "lovers," to what did this term refer?
- Why the frequent references to prostitutes and prostitution in the book of Hosea?
- What's the meaning of Hosea's reference to "half-baked cake"?
- What is the connection between the terms *Ephraim, Jacob, Judah,* and *Israel*?
- Does God have mood swings?

- Are natural disasters like floods, locusts, drought, and earthquakes God's methods of punishment?
- How does Joel's message to Israel apply to anything today?
- What is repentance?

- What is a Nazirite?
- Who are the "fat cows"?
- What are Sakkuth and Kaiwan?

- What does friendship require?
- If God will judge whole nations, what good is individual virtue and obedience?

- How can a person survive seventy-two hours inside a fish?
- What explains a pagan king's eager repentance?

- Why should people listen to God against their personal wishes?
- Is the Old Testament always worried about ceremonial purity and ritual?

- What's so important about the prediction of Nineveh's downfall?

- Why does God make us wait for the answers to our prayers?
- Was God's reputation tarnished when the Israelites were defeated and humiliated by other nations?

# GENESIS

*All of the big questions about life and truth start with the Bible's first words. Where did we come from? Who made all this stuff? Why did Eden disappear? For the Bible's key truths, start your quest here.*

## GENESIS 1:1

### Where did the universe come from?

Who has not heard a child ask that question? Unfortunately, we have no eyewitnesses around to answer it. We do have a record, however. Genesis 1 is the story of God's creation of the world and its heavens. Genesis does not intend to be a comprehensive, detailed account of how God created all there is. The story moves in wide, sweeping strokes. Yet it does answer two fundamental questions about *when* and *who*—in the beginning, and God.

Most religious faiths recognize that the world could not have created itself. For the universe to do that, it would have to exist before itself, which is logically impossible. Something else outside of and existing prior to the universe must be responsible for its creation. That something, the Bible tells us, is Someone—God.

Nothing forced God's decision to create. The decision was an expression of God's character: creative, relational, loving. God created the world to say something about Himself, to extend His relational nature to embrace beings who bear His image, and to communicate with them.

Genesis does not provide a scientific record of how and when the universe was created. Christians who wish to argue with science about these matters become caught in the give-and-take of empirical data and scientific inference, a debate that the book of Genesis was not intended to solve. (Recall that not long ago Christians firmly believed that a biblical view of creation required that the earth was the center of the universe and all other heavenly bodies revolved around it. Nowadays, thanks to scientific measurement, only crackpots make such an argument. Christians can and should learn from science.)

Genesis teaches that the universe sprang from God's nature and will. The mechanics that God employed to give expression to His will are the important domains of science (physics, chemistry, biology), which like other fields of study has sometimes, regrettably, forgotten about God. But each source—the Genesis account and science—plays a vital role in our understanding of God's creation. Genesis identifies the God whom we should praise, and science employs God's gifts of intelligence and curiosity to uncover clues concerning the mechanics of God's work.

## GENESIS 1:26

### What's important about being made in God's "image"?

Humans are not replicas of God, but we do share certain common characteristics with God. God is all-knowing, all-powerful, all-present, perfectly good, holy, and loving. We are not. But like God, we are spiritual, rational, emotional, communicative, and moral beings. We have dignity, purpose, and meaning. And we can experience the bonds of personal relationships.

God created human beings in His image.

## GENESIS 1:27

### How were humans created?

The Bible records the origin of the human race in the familiar story of Adam and Eve. Equally familiar to most people is the seemingly contrary story offered by the natural sciences, namely, the evolution of the human race from simpler organisms, ultimately from a single living cell spawned in the earth's primeval oceans. Two accounts explaining the same result could hardly be more different. The debate surrounding which account is the better explanation has often put Christians on the defensive, seemingly out of touch with the modern world and defending an ancient story uncorroborated by scientific evidence outside

of itself. Christians, believing strongly in the integrity of God's Word, have argued that the real existence of Adam and Eve is important not only to the Old Testament but also to the New Testament, where Adam figures prominently in the gospel story as a prototype of all people in the story of salvation (Romans 5:14).

Finding a scientific basis for the Genesis story of Adam and Eve has been the project of a group of theologian-scientists operating under the label "creation science." This loose coalition of scholars marshals data to argue for a young earth (biblical genealogies also seem to point to the earth's recent origin) and the first humans as the product of a special act of creation not preceded by any genetic development. There are also strong proponents of "intelligent design," who argue that the complexity of creation points to an intelligent creator.

On the other extreme, scientist-theologians faced with strong evidence of genetic linkage between *Homo sapiens* and other primates have generated a theory called "theistic evolution." This says that the development of human beings progresses much along the lines described by natural science, but at a particular point in that development, God imbues humans with the mark that sets them apart from all other species—the image of God (conscience, will, the capacity to reflect, the desire to belong to God and praise God).

In the middle, not straddling but grappling with data of both scientific and biblical research, are Christian scientists who believe that the intention of Genesis is to teach that human beings: (1) are indeed set apart by the special gift of God's image, mysterious as that is; (2) are morally responsible and accountable, unlike any other species; (3) show strong genetic similarities to nonhuman species that must be accounted for in any explanation of origins. They also believe that the earth's age is certainly ancient (unless God placed evidence of ancient origins in a "young earth"). It is noted by all contenders that the link between humans and nonhumans (hominids, humanlike ancestors that predate the gift of God's image) remains undiscovered and, in any case, given the immense implications at stake, will likely never be established with compelling certainty. The study of these matters continues with intensity on all sides.

## GENESIS 2:2

### Why did God need to rest on the seventh day of creation?

The Bible does not say that God needed to rest, as if from exhaustion, but only that God did rest. God does not lack energy or become fatigued from hard work, as we do. But using the seventh day for rest tells us that rest itself is good. God's rest also helps us understand our own needs for a Sabbath (Exodus 20:8–11). God gave us the fourth commandment for our own benefit, but God also put a divine seal of approval on observing a day of rest by doing so Himself.

The earth and the moon.

## GENESIS 2:8–14

### Where was the Garden of Eden?

No one knows for sure, but the Bible seems to locate the garden near the conjunction of the rivers Tigris and Euphrates, the Fertile Crescent of ancient days. Today that area is in southern Iraq.

## GENESIS 2:17

### Where did moral rules come from?

For Adam and Eve to live as full human beings, they would need to obey God. That would require moral limitations, boundaries that they would carefully observe and not trespass, as a sign of obedience. God applied one restriction on their use of creation— one tree whose fruit they could not eat. It was that same tree, of course, that provided the proverbial apple that has gone down in history—the agonizing first taste of human sinfulness.

## GENESIS 2:18–24

### What is the importance of marriage?

God's creative work was not complete until He made woman. And then marriage and family became the basis of society—the central organizing unit. God could have made woman from the dust of the ground as He had made man. God chose, however, to make her from the man's flesh and bone. In so doing, God illustrated that in marriage man and woman symbolically become one flesh. This is a mystical union of the couple's hearts and lives. Throughout the Bible, God treats this special partnership seriously. If you are planning to be married, are you willing to keep the commitment that makes the two of you one? The goal in marriage should be more than friendship; it should be oneness.

## GENESIS 5

### Why did people in the Bible live so long?

Throughout the book of Genesis, people are routinely reported to have lived remarkably long lives, even hundreds of years. Adam died at age 930, and the most famous senior citizen in history, Methuselah, lived until the age of 969.

With fewer people occupying the world and a greater need to bear and raise offspring, God may have extended these early lives for very pragmatic reasons. At the same time, war, famine, disease, and crime were not as "institutionalized" as today. Another possibility is that these numbers are symbolic rather than literal. Bible writers often used numbers symbolically, and they rounded numbers off liberally. This does not suggest inaccuracy, but only that they used numbers differently than we do today.

## GENESIS 9:13

### Why did God use a rainbow as a sign of the covenant with Noah?

Perhaps God chose the rainbow because it appears after a rainstorm, an appropriate reminder of the great flood and of His promise not to destroy the world again. Note also that the rainbow curves downward at each end. God's "bow" rests pointing away from the earth, away from people. God has in effect hung up His bow; it no longer points menacingly toward the sinful earth.

## GENESIS 14:18

### Who was Melchizedek?

His name means "king of righteousness." He was king of Salem, an early name for Jerusalem, a Canaanite city in the time of Abraham. Melchizedek worshiped the true God, though we have no idea how he discovered the truth. He was a priest as well as king, and in Hebrews 7, he becomes a sign or prototype of the great high priest-king, Jesus.

## GENESIS 15:6

### Why did God choose Abraham as the father of the "chosen people"?

Not because Abraham was perfect. Just like us, Abraham was skillful in using deception to save his skin, as just one example of his humanity reveals (see Genesis 12:10–20). Imperfect as he was, however, Abraham had faith, and this quality made all the difference. Abraham's faith would be tested severely, but in the testing, his faith would become stronger.

Noah and his family leave the ark after the flood. God used a rainbow as a sign of His covenant to never again allow floodwaters to cover the entire earth.

## GENESIS 15:9–20

### Why did Abraham kill and dismember animals in a covenant ceremony?

In the ancient Near East, people commonly entered into treaties or agreements by establishing a blood-bond, a pledge not to be broken. Such agreements were certified by sacrificing animals, then cutting each carcass into two pieces. The covenant participants would walk between the pieces to signify that if either broke the agreement, he would be dismembered like the animals. Abraham was frightened at the prospect of walking between the pieces of his own covenant bond. Instead, God walked through in the form of a smoking firepot and flaming torch. God thus promised Abraham that the promised blessings would indeed belong to his descendants.

## GENESIS 22:2

### Why did God ask Abraham to sacrifice Isaac?

The Bible does not explicitly give God's reasons. Child sacrifice was common among the pagan Canaanite religions of the time. In this case, however, it was a test of faith, never an intention to eliminate a child's life (Genesis 22:12). It was also a unique test that has not been used since and likely will never be used again. The test carries significance for us because it prefigured the act of God Himself offering His own Son, Jesus, as a sacrifice for us.

## GENESIS 25:23

### Why did God favor Jacob over Esau?

The Bible does not often tell us why God does what He does. In this case, God's favoritism preceded the birth of these twins, so it could not have been merit-based. Rather, we must rest in the confidence that God chooses what He will and that God's plans are good. Jacob and Esau become examples of the biblical doctrine of election, which teaches that God chooses to use whom He will for His own purposes. Those purposes may not always make sense to us, but we don't have to understand—only submit to His loving sovereignty.

## GENESIS 28:12

### What's the point of Jacob's dream of a stairway of angels?

In Jacob's region of the world, places of worship were often built as ziggurats—stair-stepped pyramids. Usually the top of the ziggurat had a small shrine where worshipers would pray and make sacrifices. In Jacob's dream, God assured him of prosperity and

In his dream, Jacob's stairway (some Bible translations say "ladder") reached from the earth to heaven.

life purpose—Jacob's difficulties would count for something. Here was a special promise: Jacob's descendants would inherit the land God had promised to his grandfather Abraham.

## GENESIS 37:4

### Why did Joseph's brothers resent him so much?

Joseph was clearly his father's favorite. Joseph knew it as did all his brothers. To make things worse, Joseph told his brothers about a dream in which God had told him that he would rule over his brothers someday.

Since God was in charge of all these events, it is difficult to draw lessons on raising families here. Clearly, however, father Jacob let his preferences show. And Joseph was not taught to be discerning on what he knew, especially when blabbing his knowledge would inflame those around him.

## GENESIS 41:40

### How did Joseph become second-in-command in Egypt?

Through a series of circumstances that God arranged, Joseph found himself in an Egyptian prison. While there, God blessed him with unusual wisdom and an ability to interpret dreams. When Pharaoh wanted a reliable interpreter, Joseph was summoned. Such was his wisdom that Pharaoh made Joseph the chief executive officer of his great country.

# EXODUS

*The Old Testament story of the Israelites' escape from oppression in Egypt is a metaphor for everyone's spiritual journey. Through Christ we are delivered from the bondage of sin and enter a land of promise. Along the way, we have much to learn.*

## EXODUS 1:15-16

### Why did Pharaoh order all male babies to be killed but female babies saved, as a way of dealing with the growing population of Israelites?

Pharaoh did not have a coherent strategy. His kingdom enjoyed the slave labor of Hebrew men who yielded an immense boost to the Egyptian economy, yet he intended to exterminate an entire generation of them. He worried over increased Hebrew birthrates, yet he would spare the female babies. It seems apparent that Pharaoh intended to assimilate the Hebrew women into the Egyptian population. They could bear the children of Egyptian men and thus increase Pharaoh's kingdom. Removing the "seed" of Israel would, in Pharaoh's estimation, exterminate the entire lot without the violence of a bloodbath.

Pharaoh did not calculate the strength of the interpersonal bond between midwife and mother. His patently unjust order would spare soldiers from violence, while placing the burden of genocide on female caregivers. Such foolishness backfired when the caregivers continued to give care and lied to cover up their refusal to comply with the new edict.

## EXODUS 2:11-17

### Is violence okay when fighting violence?

Moses learned an important lesson about violence and anger here. In the first case, he observed violence against a fellow Israelite and responded by killing the perpetrator. Clearly, other options were open to him: reporting the misdeed, using his position to bring the power of the state to bear against the perpetrator, advocating a change in state labor laws. In the second case, he intervened when some annoying shepherds pestered a group of young women. This time he did not kill but simply drove off the nuisances.

The lesson he learned was how to respond appropriately. Surely in the latter case, some force was involved (why else would the bullies retire?). Moses was getting a grip on his own temper, restraining his sense of outrage, and calculating his response to achieve just results without escalating into a vengeance situation.

That principle works just as well between states as between people. If you would reduce violence, keep your response to it firm, calm, and under control.

## EXODUS 3:5–6

### Is there an appropriate personal distance between humans and God, a space we cannot invade?

As God confronts Moses in the burning bush, He warns Moses not to approach any closer. Moses has come close enough to feel fear, and apparently God also wants to keep some space between Himself and the created order.

This kind of physical distance that an Old Testament theophany (divine appearance) required disappears completely in the New Testament. Jesus lived and worked very closely with His disciples. At one point He invited them to touch Him in order to satisfy curiosity concerning His resurrection body. Certainly God invites close interpersonal relationships between all believers. The common New Testament phrase "in Christ" suggests very little spiritual distance at all between almighty God and His children. Through Christ the necessary distance between holiness and human sin has collapsed, enabling people today to draw much closer to God than Moses ever dared.

## EXODUS 3:14

### What did God mean by identifying Himself to Moses as "I AM WHO I AM"?

When you ask for someone's identity, you normally get a name. Names distinguish individuals from other people. Jane differs from Sarah and from Jennifer, who are all women, similar in many ways yet distinct. But God has no similar others; thus God has no name.

God describes Himself to Moses not by a name but by a declaration of essential character. The verbs in this quotation are common imperfect tenses of the verb "to be," suggesting continuing unfinished action. God is neither past tense "was," future tense "will be," nor static present tense "is." God is ongoing present active: the Is-ing One. What better description of the eternal, living God than this! God is the One who is, always and forever, living and active, not Is-ness (a state of being) but Is-ing (living Being).

## EXODUS 11:10

### Why was Pharaoh so stubbornly resistant to what God told him through Moses?

Because his heart was hardened. That then begs the question, "Why would God harden Pharaoh's heart, as the verse says?" Moses and Aaron had warned about what God would do if Pharaoh didn't let the people go, but Pharaoh was stubborn, hardening his own heart. He continued to harden his heart throughout the first six plagues—saying he would let the people go and then changing his mind once the plague was stopped. Then after the sixth plague, when it became evident that Pharaoh wouldn't change, God confirmed Pharaoh's decision. God didn't *make* Pharaoh reject Him; instead, God had given Pharaoh every opportunity to change his mind and trust in the one true God. But Pharaoh refused.

## EXODUS 16:2–3

### Why did the Israelites complain so much?

It makes you wonder, doesn't it? They've just been brought through the Red Sea and saved by miracle after miracle, then a month into the wilderness they decide that they want to go back to Egypt. "At least there we had food," they whined. "Out here we'll starve to death." Never mind the flawed thinking that

God would save them from the Egyptians and then starve them in the wilderness. And never mind the fact that they seemed to have forgotten that they were *slaves* in Egypt!

The Israelites' complaining may not seem so unusual, however, if we really think about our own responses to stressful situations and difficult times. How often has God miraculously brought you through a tough time only to have you complain and worry and whine when the next difficulty comes? The Israelites complained for the same reasons we all do. They were human.

## EXODUS 20:1–17

### Should people obey the Ten Commandments today?

Certainly no Christian today observes all the regulations and laws of the Old Testament. The ceremonial law was made obsolete in the once-for-all sacrifice of Jesus Christ. The behavioral law was summarized by Jesus in

Moses descends from the mountain with the Ten Commandments.

the two great commands, namely, to love God and other people (Matthew 22:37–40). What remains, then, of Old Testament law that deserves our attention today?

Jesus, who fulfilled the law, answered that question. He warned His followers not to disregard God's law, which remains true and obligatory until the end of time (Matthew 5:17). He also warned us not to follow the Pharisees' self-righteousness and their narrow interpretation of the law. If murder is forbidden, Jesus taught, then "murder" by slander is also a violation (Matthew 5:21–22). Fulfilling the law is a matter of the heart first, and then the will. The Ten Commandments have not been rescinded; they are meant to be followed today as evidence of a grateful heart, not to showcase moral rectitude.

## EXODUS 20:7

### Why do people misuse God's name so much if such misuse is against God's law?

The name of God used as an expletive is so common today that it is possible for people to hear God's name repeatedly but never in reverence or respect. Such use is wrong. God's name is always to be held in highest honor.

Christians should be careful about using casual slogans that sidestep the direct misuse of God's name through altered sounds or spellings but with the same intention and meaning as a curse. The misuse of God's name signals disrespect for God and His creation. Who would want to explain such misuse of God's name to God's face? When you must express anger or frustration, find another way.

## EXODUS 20:8-10

### Should people work on Sunday?

God's intention since the creation of the world is that one day a week should be set aside for rest and worship. The person who works seven days a week is cheating himself or herself out of this opportunity and frustrating the worthy goals to which his or her work is directed. For most Christians, Sunday is observed as that day of rest.

Some people must work on Sunday, however: hospital staff, ministers, military personnel, and emergency repair workers, to name a few. Jesus taught that our devotion to Sunday rest should not be slavish and nitpicking, as the Pharisees had made it, but free and joyous (Matthew 12:1–14). When Sunday work is required, the Christian should set aside some other day for rest and meditation.

In a secular culture where worship is, at best, an afterthought or casual ritual, one must guard against the encroachment of recreation and other worthwhile pursuits as substitutes for worship. That encroachment in America is most frequently encountered in organized sports, professional and amateur.

## EXODUS 20:12

### Should children obey parents, even when parents are wrong?

The principle articulated in the fifth commandment is to honor and respect parents, not to obey them blindly when their advice contravenes some established principle of faith and conduct. The burden of proof should fall on children who choose to avoid parents' directives. In no case is disrespect warranted.

Parents are imperfect, however, and sometimes downright wrong. The child of an alcoholic is not obliged to follow such a parent's wisdom or to participate in or condone the fits of rage that accompany alcoholism. Still, the impetus of the fifth commandment requires as much loyalty as possible, as much submission as is appropriate to the child's own personhood and growth. As children mature, they assume leadership, even at times "parenting" their aged parents who need care. Still, the commandment requires respect and esteem for one's parents, age notwithstanding.

In the rare case when a child must side with law enforcement or spiritual elders in dealing with a wayward parent, still the child's attitude should exhibit compassionate care, not hatred or vengeance.

## EXODUS 20:13

### If murder is wrong, should anyone join the armed forces or police, where lethal force may be required?

Some Christians, notably the Mennonites, have refused military service or any profession where the killing of people is taught as one's duty or might be required on the job. Other Christians have placed this sixth commandment in the context of biblical teaching

The Battle of the Pyramids; July 21, 1798.

concerning justice and judgment and have concluded that a "just war" warrants the taking of life according to certain rules that restrict the brutality of killing and retard the acceleration of cruelty under conditions of war.

The first group of Christians teach that sacrificing one's own life is always preferable to taking another. The latter teach that protecting one's own life and the lives of those under one's care may require a level of force that, at the extreme end, justifies homicide.

# EXODUS 20:14

## Does the seventh commandment permit sexual activity, as long as adultery is avoided?

The spirit of the seventh commandment is taught by Jesus in Matthew 5:27–30. Looking lustfully at a member of the opposite sex is an action far short of intercourse. Yet Jesus warns that this common daily occurrence violates the intentions of the commandment. Men are hormonally wired for frequent sex with multiple partners. God's commandment is to direct that appetite into a faithful, monogamous, heterosexual marriage, a relationship endorsed throughout the Bible (Genesis 2:23–24).

Popular culture offers multiple opportunities for exciting lustful desires, for enhancing the adulterous imagination, and for testing and breaking the rules of common morality and biblical teaching. The seventh commandment advises everyone to focus sexual pleasure in one's marriage and to avoid other sexual appetites.

# EXODUS 20:16

## Is it ever okay to lie?

To be entirely and blatantly truthful in everything we say could unnecessarily hurt a lot of feelings and create a lot of worries. Thus, in everyday conversation we say "white lies" about someone's appearance or even about our own state of health. Doctors withhold information based on an argument that their first obligation is the best interest of a patient. Police agencies send an officer undercover (assuming a false identity) based on the argument that the good to be realized in catching a criminal warrants a well-directed lie.

Moses carries the tablets containing the Ten Commandments.

Some Christians believe that all lying is wrong but that some lies are more serious than others, the worst being the lie that leads a soul to hell (false religion), the least wrong being the lie that affords a moment of relief from pain or anguish (a placebo). Other Christians allow that some lies do not violate the ninth commandment: lying to Nazi agents about Jews hiding in the attic; the lie of Rahab concerning the Hebrew spies in her house (Joshua 2). These lies must be justified on moral and biblical grounds. When they are, the telling of a lie will sometimes be what morality demands, not merely a moral option.

All Christians agree that truth telling is the first requirement. Justifying a lie can never be the private business of the individual but must always be based on arguments open to public inspection.

## EXODUS 21:23–25

### Was the ancient "eye-for-an-eye" punishment more effective then than now?

Eye-for-an-eye punishment has certain social disadvantages. The punishment is usually irrevocable. Mistakes in judgment cannot be entertained. Corrections cannot occur. Hostility and vengeance are the only courts of appeal. As vengeful social forces grow, standing government must be more and more repressive to retain control. Social control deteriorates into the question of whose army is bigger. Law is defined by who owns the guns.

Many Christians today are worried, nonetheless, about a criminal justice system that fails to punish adequately and thus fails to deter criminal activity. Indeed, some criminal activity is hardly punished at all, and what punishments are meted out seem to follow the interests of money alone. These Christians talk favorably about the recovery of eye-for-an-eye punishment as a better deterrent than the current system.

Indeed, criminal justice systems are always imperfect and in need of reform. In only one court will perfect justice be meted—God's final judgment. All other courts must reckon with biblical mandates for mercy, justice, fairness, compassion—the balancing of which is always tainted by political interests and greed.

Strict eye-for-an-eye punishment would lead to social ruin, as the population would be largely maimed and handicapped, unable to work, lead normal lives, or defend territory from invasion. Yet casual treatment of crime leads to anarchy, another form of social ruin. Finding the balance should be the ongoing work of Christians called to be missionaries in the social geography of God's world that we call criminal justice.

## EXODUS 34:5–7

### What does God's glory look like?

Moses had asked to see God's glorious presence (Exodus 33:18). God responded by passing in front of Moses with all His glory. What is God's glory? It is His character, His nature, His way of relating to His creatures. Notice that God did not give Moses a vision of His power and majesty but, rather, of His love. God's glory is revealed in His mercy, grace, compassion, faithfulness, forgiveness, and justice. God's love and mercy are truly wonderful, and we benefit from them. We can respond and give glory to God when our character resembles His.

# LEVITICUS

*Most readers pass over the Bible's third book because its
ancient rules and laws seem unimportant today. Use the
following questions to lead you into a deeper exploration
of this God-given book.*

## LEVITICUS 1:1–2

### Why did God give Moses and the Israelites so many rules to follow?

God's holiness requires that those who serve and worship Him do
so with great care. God's laws point to God's purity: "You must be
holy because I, the LORD, am
holy. I have set you apart"
(Leviticus 20:26). God wanted
the redeemed Israelites to
stand out and be different from
pagan nations around them. By
carefully adhering to the standards of God's covenant, Israel
would be a light to the rest of the
world, demonstrating the blessing
of knowing and serving Yahweh
(the Old Testament name for God).
Many of the rules were given to
protect the people from harm,
such as laws regarding sexual
purity, and to provide them a
life full of good things.

Moses receives the tablets of the
Law from God on Mount Sinai and
explains them to the Israelites.

## LEVITICUS 1:4

### How are we made right with God?

The Bible teaches that being right with God requires *atonement*,
which means "to cover." It is the same word used in Genesis 6:14,
where Noah sealed the ark with pitch. Just as the pitch covered the
ark and provided protection from the deadly floodwaters, so the

blood of Christ's sacrifice covers and protects us from the righteous wrath of God.

The theological sense of the word conveys the idea of satisfaction—satisfying the payment for sin. God covered the peoples' sins until a final, acceptable sacrifice would remove those sins completely. Leviticus 16 tells about the high and holy day of atonement. On that somber occasion each year, the high priest washed himself and made a sacrifice for his own sin. Then to atone for the sins of the nation, he would obtain two goats, one to slaughter as payment for sin and the other to become a "scapegoat." The priest laid hands on this second goat to symbolically transfer the sins of the people. The goat was then taken and released in the wilderness, representing the removal of guilt. Thus, the way of approaching a holy God through sacrifice would remain open for another year.

In the New Testament, atonement is fully accomplished in the crucifixion of Christ for the sins of all God's people, past and present.

## LEVITICUS 4:2; 5:17–19

### What is the difference between a guilt offering and a sin offering?

Both offerings satisfied God's holiness by covering human sinfulness. However, the sin offering was made when an individual (or whole nation) committed an unintentional offense against God. These were not sins of outright rebellion, just thoughtless or careless acts done out of ignorance or oversight, mistakes or moments of weakness. Nevertheless, such actions offended a holy God and required payment. Making such a sin offering restored fellowship with God.

The guilt offering was more of a compensatory sacrifice. For instance, if a person failed to offer a required tithe, the guilt offering would give

to God His rightful due. Guilt offerings were also made to pay back injured or wronged parties (often with a 20 percent penalty).

## LEVITICUS 4:15

### Animal sacrifice seems barbaric and primitive. Why would God require such an unpleasant religious exercise?

To kill an innocent animal seems quite cruel. Our modern sensibilities are offended by this requirement. But the lesson is this: Sin is serious! It offends a holy God. Human behavior bears consequences for all of creation.

God gave human beings life so that they might worship, serve, and honor Him. When Adam and Eve perverted this gift by rebelling against God, they cut themselves off from the very source of life. They "died" (spiritual separation from God, see Genesis 3), a condition that would have persisted throughout history unless a plan had been enacted to fix the problem. The penalty for sin is death, yet God made it possible under Old Testament law for animals to substitute for people. By giving one life, another could be saved. But this system was instituted only as a short-term arrangement.

At the right time, God sent Jesus Christ, often called "the Lamb of God," to

A lamb is led to be sacrificed on the altar of the Lord.

be sacrificed on a Roman cross as final payment for all sins for all time. Jesus, the perfect substitute, rendered the Old Testament sacrificial system obsolete. Now people can be forgiven and experience spiritual life and union with God, not by killing innocent animals, but by trusting in the crucified Christ as their substitute.

prominently in pagan religious rites. The meat of these animals was not to be eaten.

These dietary laws were suspended in New Testament times (see Acts 10). Jesus told His followers that it is not what goes into a person's stomach that defiles, but what comes out of a person's heart (Matthew 15:10–20).

## LEVITICUS 13:47–53; 14:33–53

### Could leprosy or mildew really infect a house or an article of clothing?

The Hebrew word that is translated as *leprosy* in many popular Bible versions is a broad term that refers to a contagious skin disease or even an infectious mildew. The leprosy implied in these verses is likely some kind of fast-spreading mold or fungus. To reduce the possibility of contact with such bacterial agents, the people of Israel were given specific instructions on how to check their spread. In cases where a fungus had permeated a garment or dwelling, total destruction was warranted.

## LEVITICUS 17

### What's the reason for all the special dietary restrictions of the Israelites? Why do Christians today not observe them?

The restrictions contributed to public health. Many of the forbidden animals were scavengers that fed on decaying and diseased carrion. By not eating such creatures, the Israelites would avoid contracting diseases. Also, these dietary prohibitions would set apart Israel from her neighbors who did not observe these laws. Finally, the laws recognized that certain animals were considered to be symbolic of evil or were featured

## LEVITICUS 18:29

### Why were penalties for sexual sin so severe?

The Israelites found themselves in the midst of a Canaanite culture that was awash in pagan immorality. These heathen nations had merged spirituality with sensuality to create a very alluring and very dangerous combination. To keep His people from joining this around-the-clock celebration of perversion, God decreed severe punishment for those guilty of sexual sin.

All sin is serious, and God hates any deviation from holiness. But sexual perversion is especially insidious. Why? Because it rejects God's original intention in making humans "male and female." It violates the sanctity of marriage and family. It creates addictive and idolatrous behavior, leads to severe emotional problems, and sometimes to disease and death. It elevates physical desire over spiritual priorities. The New Testament adds that believers who sin sexually are sinning against their own bodies (1 Corinthians 6:18). This turns God's residence into a house of ill repute!

## LEVITICUS 21:16–23

### Why are handicapped people kept from temple service?

Prohibitions against disfigured priests were part of Israel's ceremonial law where every article and action was intended to highlight the perfection of God. In the same way that God required unblemished animals for offerings, God stipulated that the priests administering the sacrifices had to be free from physical handicaps. In no way do these laws suggest that handicapped individuals are less valuable to God. In fact, this very passage insists that these Levites share in the priestly food. Handicapped Levites likely performed other important but nonceremonial functions.

## LEVITICUS 23

### What is the significance of the different festivals that Israel was commanded to observe?

In addition to being national holy days set aside for celebrating the faithfulness of God, the festivals (or "feasts" in some translations) often symbolized deeper truths. The one-day feast of Passover (23:5) reminded the people of God's miraculous delivery from Egyptian bondage. The weeklong Festival

Passover was one of the festivals Israel observed. This festival reminded them of their deliverance from Egypt.

of Unleavened Bread (23:6–8) reminded the people of their hurried exit from Egypt. First Harvest (Firstfruits) (23:9–14) was a day set aside during harvest to celebrate God's provision of food and to present back to God the first part of the crops. The Festival of Harvest (23:15–22) was a day marking the

end of the barley harvest and the beginning of the wheat harvest when the people thanked God for their agricultural blessings. On the Festival of Trumpets (23:23–25), the first day of the new year, the people worshiped God and feasted. The Day of Atonement (23:26–32) was a solemn assembly during which the people fasted and the high priest made a sacrifice for the sins of the nation. The Festival of Shelters (23:33–43) commemorated God's protection and guidance during Israel's wilderness wanderings. At this seven-day festival, the people "camped out" in huts or booths made from tree branches and renewed their commitment to God.

These special days were in addition to the weekly Sabbath. The result was an annual calendar in which God was to be regularly worshiped, remembered, and praised. By establishing these holidays, God was saying in effect, "Don't push me to the margins of your lives! Keep me at the very center of your national conscience where I deserve to be, where I can help you and guide you and bless you, and where you can find fulfillment in worship of me."

## LEVITICUS 27:1–7

### Were men more valuable than women in Bible times?

The different amounts paid for males and females who had dedicated themselves to the Lord (50 pieces of silver for young men, 30 for young women; 20 for boys, 10 for girls; 15 for elderly men; 10 for older women; 5 for male babies; 3 for female babies) were probably a factor of physical strength. Simply put, males were able to do more strenuous manual labor. People of both genders were equally loved by God, but laborers in a culture with few labor-saving devices were often considered the more valuable economic resource.

# NUMBERS

*As God's people were numbered and organized themselves for battle, they encountered some bumps along the road to the promised land. But God was faithful.*

## NUMBERS 1:1

### How did God speak to Moses?

The Bible contains many occasions where God spoke and His voice was heard. In this case, perhaps not. If God did provide Moses with an audible message here, it had the unusual quality of detail. Several individuals are named and selected as assistants for the census. Today we might say, "Joe, I believe God wants you to consider missions." And Joe quite correctly may believe that God has spoken to him through that kind of friendly conversation. Perhaps Moses was doing something similar in his recruitment of trustworthy associates. Moses was an unusual person. He was given a very special mission by God, even though he considered himself a mediocre candidate for it. Given his mission, God no doubt communicated with Moses in a way that was clear.

God first speaks to Moses out of a burning bush and calls him to return to Egypt.

God speaks sometimes through a person's conscience, intuition, or emotive longing to know God better. In prayer we commune with God with unusual personal closeness, and we sometimes feel God is speaking to us, though not audibly, as we pray or meditate on His Word. God uses many means. The great Christian leader Augustine believed that God had spoken to him emphatically through the voice of a small child. The result was Augustine's conversion and his considerable influence on the church even today.

The mission of God today is the worldwide announcement that salvation has come in Jesus Christ, His Son. That Good News is conveyed through many channels and means, and it bears implications for every person and profession. It's such an important mission that Christians worldwide testify to the fact that God still speaks, even as He did centuries ago.

## NUMBERS 1:2–3

### Why were women, children, and teenagers omitted from the census?

Israel was a patriarchal culture. Men were leaders, warriors, and priests, while women took responsibility for childrearing and homemaking. Obviously women and children were vital to the survival of the Israelite people and to the conquest of Canaan. Their omission from census numbers does not diminish this importance. But one reason for the count was to see how many fighting men they had for battle.

On a practical level, the technology for counting large quantities was quite unsophisticated in Moses' day, and a census would be easier to produce if certain mathematical assumptions were applied to a head count of adult males only. In Israel's case, since adult males led the clans, it is not surprising that they would count only themselves as a means of calculating the total population.

## NUMBERS 1:51

### Why would people die if they got too close to God?

Old Testament rules of holiness had a vital either/or quality about them, unlike more tolerant religious rules of the present day. These older rules paint a portrait of a holy and just God, one whose will cannot be dismissed and whose word cannot be ignored. On one occasion that illustrates the stringency of these rules, a bystander tried to save the ark of the covenant from a fall, but in so doing violated the rule of holiness and lost his life (2 Samuel 6:6–7).

In view here is a rule that preserves the special character of the most revered religious space at the time, the tabernacle. It was the one place on earth God would occupy, and it had to be treated with utmost reverence and care.

Only authorized personnel, the Levites, could handle and dismantle this special mobile God-space. On the human level, one reason for such severe rules was to dissuade ambitious men who might dream of controlling, through theft or cunning, the nation's access to God. Can you imagine what power (and wealth) such control would provide? But at risk to one's life, even the most ambitious would think better of exploiting the tabernacle.

On the divine level, God has always demanded the respect, allegiance, and obedience of all people everywhere. Though we rightly celebrate God's mercy and love today, the Bible is clear that God's judgment on sin will mean certain punishment and spiritual death for those who presume to invade God's holy space apart from cleansing faith in His sacrificial lamb, Jesus Christ. The same severity of the Old Testament rule of holiness is in force today, to be applied on the day of final judgment.

## NUMBERS 2:32

### Why all the fuss and bother, order and regimen, just for Israel's boring task of wandering in the desert?

The people of Israel were far less unified than Hollywood depictions of the Exodus lead us

This is the oasis of Marah (Bitter Waters). The Israelites rested here during their wandering in the desert.

to believe. Not all Israelites were convinced that Moses had proper authority. Tribes were often more loyal to each other than to the whole. Small and large rebellions tore at Israel's fragile sense of purpose. Frustration with their wilderness discomforts prompted many to resist the authority of leaders. With so much fragmentation in the ranks and so many corporals who wanted to be colonels, the imposing of rigorous order gave the Israelites a kind of military discipline that their survival on the long journey required. A more freewheeling, hang-loose, do-your-own-thing approach would have produced a people totally unfit for the challenge of battle for Canaan.

## NUMBERS 3:12–13

### Why does God claim only firstborn males for special ownership?

When God chooses to do anything, His choice involves saying yes to something and no to something else. Here, the choice seems arbitrary to our thinking. It could as well have been firstborn females, or last born, as far as we can judge.

The Bible is full of God's choices. God chose Israel as a "firstborn" (Exodus 4:22). Then God spared the firstborn of Israel in the tenth plague (Exodus 13:2). Then God claimed special ownership of all firstborn males. In the New Testament, God's choice is called *divine election*. Theologians have named it predestination, and the arguments pro and con question the fairness of an all-powerful being choosing some and not others for special blessing, with no appeal from His choice.

Yet God chooses, from the start of history until the end. In every case, these choices remind us that: (1) God is sovereign and His will supreme and nonnegotiable; (2) God is love, and His choices are grounded in His character and lead to His promise of eternal

salvation; (3) God is not a passive bystander but involved, active, and shepherdlike.

In the case of firstborn males, the choice puts a symbolic imprint on every family. No parent can claim exclusive, omnipotent control over a family. In even the most intimate human relationships, God has a prior claim. Even Jesus' parents observed the claim by presenting their firstborn son at the temple. The intimacy of His claim reminds us of God's intensely personal love for His people. Here is a God whose chief point of interest is the person. How unlike all other gods, figments of human creativity that purport to enjoy vast temples and collected riches. God's choice of the firstborn male is itself a guide to our own most important choice—that of believing in the firstborn Son of God, Jesus.

## NUMBERS 4:15, 20

### Why does touching or seeing the sacred utensils invoke the death penalty?

In the Old Testament, ceremonial objects were vested with the power and presence of God Himself, creating situations in which the objects, representative of ultimate power, were to be treated as ultimately precious, even holy. Just as a person would never consider looking directly into the face of God (Exodus 3:6), so viewing or handling the objects vested with God's presence is likewise forbidden. God is holy and not to be trifled with.

But wouldn't a lesser penalty be a bit fairer? The Old Testament world was much more of a life-and-death world than our own. Today we mitigate criminal sentences based on the context of the crime and the mind-set of the criminal, but in ancient times, capital sentences were carried out with much less concern over the individual's loss.

With respect to sacred objects, a breach of law there violated the most important boundary in all the world. A person who imposed himself wrongly into divine space or presence preempted a privilege completely beyond his station in life. Only the Sovereign Lord had the right to admit people into His presence. Moreover, a trespasser placed all of his associates in grave peril, since punishment for violations of sovereign law often fell on the entire group. The trespasser's death sentence was the first and strongest gesture to rectify an offense against divine prerogative; it saved the group from divine wrath through the pain of policing its own members.

## NUMBERS 5:1, 4

### Why segregate and punish people who need medical care?

In Old Testament times, medical care took second priority to the keeping of ceremonial law. In this case, the interest of the law was in a broad category of ritual impurity called

"uncleanness." Uncleanness in the presence of the Lord was to be avoided at all costs. The modern rights of "life, liberty, and the pursuit of happiness," which many governments today consider inviolable, were far down a list topped by ceremonial purification in several forms. Again, the main concern was to reflect God's holiness.

In this text the form concerned sexual purification. A woman's menstrual cycle, linked to childbearing and thus to Eve's judgment, was a token of the impure, and thus had to be dealt with. Corpses were also considered unclean, as were diseases of the skin, often labeled leprosy. One can see in these religious rituals the beginnings of concern over public health, long before modern science defined the physical basis of disease. In the absence of effective medical procedures and faced with the requirements of ritual law, the people treated these sufferers with relative kindness. Even today, when treatment of disease is impossible, we quarantine the ill so that healthy people may conduct business as usual.

## NUMBERS 5:14–15

### Why could an innocent wife suffer merely for her husband's jealousy?

What seems at first to be an outrageously sexist law turned out to work well in a culture that was decidedly patriarchal yet still had protection for certain rights of women and children. In this case, an unscrupulous husband would be sorely embarrassed by bringing false charges against his wife. Consider all the facts. The husband had to engage the services of a respected third party, a priest. The woman underwent a ceremony so fraught with danger (if she was lying) that only the innocent would reasonably take such a risk. The woman who successfully passed the test would be a living witness to her husband's malicious self-centeredness.

Leprosy was a very contagious skin disease. People with leprosy were quarantined to keep others safe.

One could well conclude that a woman guilty of sexual indiscretion would come to judgment long before this procedure would be complete, and the public and priestly nature of the procedure itself would retard any husband's quick temper.

As with all human law, this law carried the possibility of miscarriage of justice. Juries and judges today may decide wrongly, but the Old Testament divorce court had the added dimension of divine judgment and sentence. No reasonable person would tamper with that system on mere whimsy, nor would a priest permit a husband to engage the system if there existed any doubt about the man's motive.

## NUMBERS 5:21–24

### What is the sickness that punishes adulterous women?

The woman guilty of sexual misconduct was to lose her capacity for childbearing. This was a fearsome penalty indeed, for women in the ancient Near East established their sense of personal value and esteem on one activity only—bearing and raising children. Education, business, military status, community leadership—none of these were open to women; motherhood was everything.

With so much at stake, a woman had every motivation to resist the overtures of a scheming male suitor. Why should the burden of propriety fall on the female? A woman's sexual sensibilities would be entirely protective, a man's more frequently adventurous. But without the cooperative partner, a man obviously could not make his conquest. It was better for all to remain passionately monogamous and for the more emotionally stable woman to protect the integrity of marriage and family.

## NUMBERS 5:31

### Why did men guilty of adultery go scot-free?

This law does not turn a blind eye toward male culpability, but only addresses the difficult problem of due process when a man suspects his wife of sexual impropriety. It is better to engage a public process than to let a jealous man have his vicious way on the theory that a woman is mere property. Far from belittling women, the process recorded here protects them, effectively barricading them from physical abuse. Women in many parts of the developing world today would embrace such protection, and in the First World, the battered wife speaks powerfully to the need for communal constraints on the anger that lashes and destroys. In the light of most urban experience today, Old Testament procedure appears enlightened and effective.

## NUMBERS 9:13

### How is a person "cut off" from his people?

By banishment, which in the ancient world was the social equivalent of execution (also an option). Today, our identity and sense of self are radically individualistic. We believe that each individual has rights that a just society will distribute equally; that is, without respect to differences of race, age, gender, or matters of conscience such as religious preference. These ideas find their origin in Europe's emergence from feudalism and in the democratic revolutions of the eighteenth century.

But the ancient world held quite a different and more communal view of society. From the very beginning God made covenants with His people, not contracts with individuals. The idea of group accountability for violations of that covenant is evident throughout the Old Testament. Achan sinned, and his family bore the penalty with him (Joshua 7:24). David sinned, and thousands of people died of the plague (2 Samuel 24:15). Likewise, God's promises were group-oriented, emerging from the covenant God established with His people.

What happened, then, when an individual refused to accept the terms of the covenant, refused to identify with the people, refused to worship God, refused to follow God's plan and purpose? Could such a person continue to live among the people? No, the people could not endure such entrenched stubbornness. To tolerate the dissenter would be tantamount to agreeing with the possibility that his refusal was appropriate and reasonable. The person who refused the covenant must be cut off and could no longer live among the covenant people. In banishment, the dissenter acknowledged that he had no claim on the identity of his native group, and since no other identity was available, he had none at all. His sense of self had vanished.

## NUMBERS 10:33

### How did God "dwell" in the ark and in the temple?

Neither the ark of the covenant nor the temple of Solomon housed God in a literal, confining sense. God is both infinite and omnipresent. As the martyr Stephen declared, "The Most High doesn't live in temples made by human hands" (Acts 7:48; see also Acts 17:24).

The ark (as it rested within the Holy of Holies inside the temple) served as a place where the leaders of Israel could meet with God, primarily to bring offerings that would atone for the nation's sin. God's presence did indeed fill the temple, much as He now fills believers with His Spirit. For this reason, under the new covenant, Christians are called the "temple of God."

## NUMBERS 13:23

### Why is the metaphor or image of a vineyard/fruitful vine so commonly used in the Bible?

Ancient Israel was an agrarian society. This explains why agricultural imagery figures prominently in the scripture's prophetic and didactic discourses. Illustrating truth using these kinds of homiletic devices communicated on a broader common level.

Canaan was noted for its many vineyards even before the Israelites took possession of the land. Vineyards required constant care, cultivation, and protection (Proverbs 24:30–34). A fruitful vineyard was evidence of

A man and woman pick grapes in a vineyard.

blessing, and hard labor there produced the wine used in joyful celebrations. Few situations were more disappointing to a farmer than an unfruitful vineyard. Thus it was appropriate for God to compare His people to a vine. Israel required a tremendous deal of divine oversight. Her lapses in faithfulness broke God's heart. During periods of fruitfulness, the nation also brought great joy to God.

## NUMBERS 14:6

### What is accomplished by ripping apart one's clothing?

If you feel passionately that your friends, your church, or your children are making a huge mistake, how do you express it? With simple calm, hands folded in your lap? Probably not. Each culture has its way of putting an exclamation point behind a speech. We might wave our hands, heighten our tone of voice, point a finger. Old Testament people added a dimension we no longer use—tearing one's clothes.

Clothes protect the body and ensure personal privacy. Surrendering the covering of clothes makes a person utterly and desperately transparent. "Here I am, all of me. You can take no more than this, unless you take my life," the speaker is saying. We talk about "putting it all on the line." As Martin Luther said before the church court, "Here I stand; I can do no other." Caleb and other biblical characters took their stand by tearing their garments to underscore their seriousness and to persuade their listeners.

## NUMBERS 14:18

### What is achieved by God's punishing children for their parents' sins?

God's judgments in the Old Testament seem harsh in comparison to judgments we make today. For example, a criminal today goes to jail, but courts never order jail time for the children of criminals. Moses' statement must be read in context. Full of love, God's first impulse is not harsh and vengeful, but caring and forgiving. Yet the weight of God's judgment on sin ripples through time, affecting lives in the next generation and the next. Nothing remains the same when God

acts. No social safety net can harness the impact of His judgment or protect the nearby innocent from bearing some of the weight. Anyone intending to disobey the commands of almighty God does well to consider the impact, then and now, personal and familial, immediate and long-range.

## NUMBERS 15:22

### If misbehavior is unintentional, why is it punished?

All sin is an offense against a holy God, and all debts for sin must be paid. In this case, the debt is distributed to the community as a whole. No family carries a proportion greater than any other family's, since no individual guilt can be applied. It is a fair and equitable way of covering for offenses that come along in the normal course of life, offenses that could not be anticipated, avoided, or not even known in advance. It was the community's insurance policy against a debt it might not even be aware of—the kind of thing we do today in confessing our general sinfulness over the confession of particular sins.

## NUMBERS 15:32–36

### Why was gathering wood on the Sabbath a capital crime?

The Sabbath was a once-weekly rest from normal business to worship and honor God. Those who sought to gain commercial advantage during this respite were not only upsetting the community's economy, they were also offending God. Everyone knew the Sabbath requirements, so no one in the nation could plead ignorance of this all-important rule.

A man who broke the Sabbath is being stoned.

The question remains, however. Would God be willing to obliterate all of His works? The account of the Flood bears witness to the severity of God's judgment. Only a few faithful were spared. Clearly God has within His character a righteous anger that intends with holy will to purify His creation. To our great relief, Jesus is God's answer to that process, for in Jesus all sin is answered and through faith in Jesus all risk of judgment is removed. The gospel is the promise of life when the sentence was death.

By Jesus' day, Sabbath rules had grown into an elaborate system that had forgotten God's prior concern for the poor, helpless, and hurting. Absolutely no effort could be expended on the Sabbath, regardless of the need. Jesus opened Himself to prosecution with His recovery of God's intentions for the Sabbath. The ancient wood-gatherer, however, could make no appeal to higher principles such as helping a person or animal in distress when weeklong laziness or greed was the obvious reason for his Sabbath work.

## NUMBERS 16:45

### Would God really annihilate His chosen people?

One cannot take lightly the announced intention of God to destroy life as payment for rebellion and betrayal. God is sovereign, all-powerful, and answers to no higher moral standard than Himself. His judgments are final, good, and effective. Moses reacts to this announcement by interceding once more for a spiritually wayward people, with the result that God's judgment is mitigated by mercy.

## NUMBERS 18:10

### Why were males selected to eat holy food?

What may sound to modern ears discriminatory was at the time a simple command that all members of the Levitical priesthood partake of the gifts reserved for it. Only males served in the temple, thus only males are mentioned here. Both sons and daughters, however, are recipients of gifts in the next verse, and we may safely infer that the wives of Levites were not left to starve. The distribution of goods was equal among the families.

## NUMBERS 22:18

### Why did the pagan priest Balaam call God "my God"?

Something happened to Balaam that changed his life. God spoke to him. When God speaks to us, when His Word touches us, when His Spirit moves us, the mind's pagan shuffle becomes the heart's holy dance. Balaam received a gift completely undeserved. Through no credit of his own, he met truth, and it was good. Balaam's confession—"my God"—was the most sincere phrase he had ever spoken. Even then, however, he needed the threat of an angel to steer him toward obedience (Numbers 22:34). Some people are twice blessed.

Balaam doesn't see the angel at first, but the donkey does. God gets Balaam's attention by causing the donkey to speak.

## NUMBERS 22:28

### Why does God use such an odd device as a talking donkey to deliver His message?

The story illustrates how hard-of-hearing, spiritually, we can be. Balaam apparently needed words from both a donkey and an angel before he understood God's purpose. Such phenomena are rare in the history of God's relationship to people, but the problem is hardly less profound now than it was then. We should note that Balaam was an international consultant on matters of religious knowledge, but he was less perceptive than his donkey toward God's action in his own vicinity.

The story points to the persistence of God, the mercy of God, and the involvement of God in human affairs. Its odd devices are for ears that barely hear.

## NUMBERS 23:19

### If God does not change His mind, why is He often described as doing just that in response to Israel's behavior?

God's mind is fixed with respect to the elements of His character and the terms of His covenant with His people. God is love—that does not change. God is good, true, and communicative. God blesses and leads His people to a promised land of freedom, peace, and fulfillment.

But God's immediate intentions and attitudes are frequently described as "changing" in response to His people's response to Him. Everywhere the terms of the covenant are clear: obedience brings blessing and disobedience forecasts loss. Because God is the source of all blessing, He may increase it, withhold it, or withdraw it altogether. God may punish as well as postpone punishment. God may send rain or drought. Even today God urges that all people come to faith in Jesus. His intentions are at all times good. But the warning of judgment is real.

## NUMBERS 25:6–9

### Is God offended when people from different nations marry and establish families?

The offense in this case was not transnational marriage but pagan worship. The lure of sexual gratification had compromised worship of the true God, and a plague had been sent as a wake-up call to the people. But the plague did not work. Only through the violent act of the priest Phinehas did Israel realize its mistake, abandon the practice of taking foreign wives, focus worship on God alone, and recover its direction.

Cross-cultural marriage was practiced in the Old Testament at times with God's blessing (for example, Moses married Zipporah, Boaz married Ruth), and it becomes a nonissue in the New Testament. Faithful monogamous marriage is God's way, but more important still is faithful worship.

## NUMBERS 27:12–14

### Why should long-ago problems keep Moses from finishing his journey?

Why didn't Moses get parole for good behavior? Even hardened criminals today, if they mind their manners, may be granted reprieve, let loose, set free. Following his mistake, Moses' behavior was exemplary. Couldn't he get a break?

The answer has to do with God's will, pure and simple. God issued Moses' penalty, and it was done. Justice was served; mercy was plentiful. God's will does not operate under the terms of parole boards or criminal courts, nor is God beholden to answer to modern definitions of justice. God is just. Justice is not an abstraction by which we measure God's behavior; rather, God established justice by His own deeds and declarations.

Didn't Moses deserve a break? He got one: life, leadership, mission, and a peaceful passage to God's presence.

## NUMBERS 30:1–2

### Should we make a "vow" before God today?

The vows in this case were intended to maintain proper sexual relations and guarantee family stability. Such vows are still entirely proper and are made every day in marriage ceremonies around the world. The bigger question is whether irrevocable commitments should be made to God, given our human penchant toward inconsistency and moral fatigue. Such commitments today, especially those involving a high degree of self-discipline (celibacy and poverty, for example) are made with escape clauses that recognize life's unpredictability.

Nonetheless, it is a mistake to enter a vow with any secret doubt as to one's willingness to keep it. Moses reminded the people that vows made to the Lord are inviolable. Vows made to other people are known to the Lord, who holds every person responsible for the words of his or her mouth (Matthew 12:36–37).

# NUMBERS 31:17

## Why were innocent women and children killed in battle against the Midianites?

The sentence of death in this case was not against age and gender, but against disloyalty and betrayal of the true God. Groups that had participated in baiting Israel toward religious diversity (Israel's paramount stumbling block) received the capital sentence, while groups that had not (prepubescent females in this case) were spared.

Modern just-war theory requires that violence be restricted to combatants, that harm be directed against military targets (not civilian populations), and that the least possible damage be inflicted to achieve legitimate military objective. These ideas have firm grounding in biblical principles of justice and fairness, though some Christians believe even just-war theory is wrong since it sanctions killing. War, justice, and morality had different configurations in ancient times. The notion of human rights was dimly perceived through the general fog of international distrust and pagan worship. (Imagine your regard for human life if you believed that all gods were wicked, cruel, and jealous.) Gradually, the loving character of the true God came to be seen and understood through the psalms, prophets, and later the preaching of the gospel.

During battles, not only were warriors killed, but so were women and children.

# DEUTERONOMY

*God sometimes speaks not once, but twice. In this Bible book, you'll discover some things already expressed, some things brand-new, and some things that raise a few other questions.*

## THE BOOK OF DEUTERONOMY

### What does *Deuteronomy* mean, and why was the book written?

The book of Deuteronomy was written by Moses. The word means "a copy of the law" or "a second giving of the law." The law was first given by Moses to the Israelites soon after their deliverance from slavery in Egypt. This second telling of the law was written at the end of Moses' life, forty years after the Exodus, and recounts all that God has done for the chosen people.

As Moses prepared to die, he said, "Take to heart all the words of warning I have given you today. Pass them on as a command to your children so they will obey every word of these instructions. These instructions are not empty words—they are your life! By obeying them you will enjoy a long life in the land you will occupy when you cross the Jordan River" (Deuteronomy 32:46–47). This book of law contains truth that guides relationships with God and neighbor. Moses hoped that the people of Israel would remember all God had done for them and pass these truths on to the next generation.

## DEUTERONOMY 3:26–27

### Isn't God a bit severe to punish Moses for one mistake, especially if, as Moses says, God was angry with him because of the people of Israel?

The incident is described in Numbers 20. The people of Israel were again complaining to Moses because they lacked water. Over and over Israel had seen God provide manna from heaven, but they continued to complain. Moses and Aaron consulted with God. The Lord told Moses, "You and Aaron must take the staff and assemble the entire community. As the people watch, command the rock over there to pour out its water." Instead, when Moses gathered the people, he raised his staff in anger and struck the rock twice. Water gushed out, and the people were satisfied, but Moses and Aaron were reprimanded, "Because you did not trust me enough to demonstrate my holiness to the people of Israel, you will not lead them into the land I am giving them!" (Numbers 20:12).

It is hard for us to imagine anyone who works his whole life at a job with one goal in mind just to be disqualified by one mistake—in Moses' case, one very human error. But the Old Testament is clear that God's holy character is more important than any-thing else, even human life. A clear view of God's holiness would lead us to ask: Who can negotiate a mistake with the most holy God? Who can sit at the bargaining table to ask for concessions on human error? Who dare suggest that a little rebellion is no great blemish in God's world? The holiness of God does not allow for any blemish. This makes God's plan of salvation and forgiveness through Christ all the more remarkable.

## DEUTERONOMY 5:9

### What's fair about punishment that extends to the third and fourth generation? Isn't each person responsible to God for his or her own actions?

The Bible teaches that each person stands before God for personal sin. Eternal life is not denied to any person because of an-other person's actions (John 3:16; Romans 6:23; 1 John 2:17). Yet the consequences of personal sin are felt by succeeding genera-tions in at least two ways.

First, if parents hate God and do not speak the truth of God to their children, the children may also hate God. The counter-part, of course, is that families who love God and obey His commands will enjoy God's blessings for "a thousand generations" (Deuteronomy 5:10).

Second, while God forgives sin, the consequences of sin are not necessarily re-moved. Recall David's adultery with Bath-sheba (2 Samuel 12:13–23). David con-fessed his sin and the Lord forgave, but the child died.

This principle of generational conse-quence is clearly seen where the abusive sin of a supposed caregiver leads a child to a life of bitterness, anger, and confusion. If these consequences are not corrected, the victim of abuse often becomes the abuser of another generation. Except for the grace of God, we

would all be locked in patterns of sin. But God provides a pattern-breaker. We are not trapped by the past. Our failures (even our parents' mistakes) are correctable. Our lives can be freed from sin's consequences. How? By accepting the new hope of God's message, committing life to Him, and reestablishing the bonds that lead to joy. It's a matter of deciding to whom you will listen.

## DEUTERONOMY 16:21

### What is an Asherah pole?

Asherah (also called Ashtoreth) was a Ca-naanite goddess of fertility, love, and war. King Solomon followed the worship of Ash-toreth in 1 Kings 11:5. Apparently an Asherah pole was a symbol used in the worship of this fertility goddess.

Fertility idols found in Judah.
Asherah was a Canaanite fertility goddess.

## DEUTERONOMY 22:28-29

**Old Testament law requires a man who rapes a virgin to marry her. Why force the victim of such a terrible crime to marry the perpetrator?**

Ancient Israelites attached a severe social stigma to rape. A young woman victim was "ruined"—she became an outcast with no means of financial support and no prospects for a family of her own. So the law imposed on the perpetrator the responsibility of care for the victim—providing her a home and family—at considerable cost to him. Such an arrangement also reduced the need of the victim's family to seek forcible revenge, thus sparing the culture much violence.

## DEUTERONOMY 26

**How do the concepts of first fruits and tithes relate to us today?**

Offering the first produce of a harvest (first fruits) acknowledged that crops were given by the Lord. God provides our needs, and the offering was a response of worship. Giving a tenth of one's overall produce was a big "thank you" for God's care throughout the year. These tithes also provided for the needs of the Levites (who led in worship) and the destitute (the alien, fatherless, and widow), who required care from the common purse. These gifts reminded the Israelites about community responsibility.

Today, tithing is still an important statement about God's ownership. Gladly giving to the Lord is one way we praise and worship God for provision and care. The New Testament does not require a percentage of income but advances the concept of a cheerful giver (2 Corinthians 9:7) who plans to give (1 Corinthians 16:1–2) and provides for the needs of the community (Acts 4:32–34; 2 Corinthians 9:11).

## DEUTERONOMY 28

**When Moses gave his final words of blessing and reminded the people of God's covenant, why did he include such a long list of curses?**

We make choices every day of our lives. Ultimately, in these choices, we either obey God or reject God. Each choice leads to consequences. If we are obedient, the outcome is benefit and blessing; if not, punishment. Moses wanted the Israelites (and us) to be very aware of the importance of choices.

Choosing the good is not always easy, since short-term gain often makes sin an attractive option. And some choices (consumer choices, for example) seem not related to God's will—potentially a subtle form of idolatry since they establish clothes or cars or other physical things as our own exclusive property. Moses reminds us that God is ever present, and our lives are to shine for His glory in every way.

# JOSHUA

*After wandering forty years in the wilderness, the people were ready to enter the promised land under Joshua's able leadership. But the new situation they faced raised new questions and challenges.*

## JOSHUA 1:1–5

### Why is Israel called the "promised land"?

Because of God's great promise to Abraham (Genesis 12:1–3). God challenged Abraham to leave his homeland and extended family and to follow divine guidance. God promised to bring Abraham to a new land and to make his offspring a great nation. When Abram packed his bags, he had a wife, no children, and God's promises. He didn't know what the future held, but he trusted God with his destination, allowing God to choose a homeland for his family. So Israel (Abraham's primary line of descendants) is as much a promised nation as the land it claims is the promised land.

God shows Moses the beautiful land He
had promised to give His people.

## JOSHUA 1:7

**How do Bible promises, such as Joshua received, "You will be successful in everything you do," apply to people today?**

The promise in this verse does not allow for just any definition of "success." Daily meditation on God's Word will shift our definition of success away from power and wealth to service in Jesus' name, from status to disciple-making, from control to friendship and even sacrifice of self for others. Success as a child of God will be much different than success in worldly terms. The ultimate measure of success for a Christian will be to hear Jesus say, "Well done" (Luke 19:11–27). The next time you hear someone tout his or her success in terms of property owned, degrees earned, goods or services sold, or retirement secured, ask yourself whether that measure of success stands up to biblical scrutiny.

## JOSHUA 1:8

**What is meditating on God's Word?**

The discipline of meditation involves first having God's Word, then reading it, studying it, memorizing it, considering its meaning for you, and acting on it. Here Joshua focuses on the final steps of this sequence.

Pagan meditation invites people to empty their minds through repetition of phrases without content. In sharp contrast, God wants us to do our finest mental work—to listen intently to His Word for us—by examining words and phrases from scripture, looking for patterns, principles, and applications that address our life needs. Biblical meditation includes prayer. We can pray as the psalmist did, "I have hidden your word in my heart, that I might not sin against you" (Psalm 119:11). This kind of meditation immerses us

in God's Word so that it informs and motivates us through all the troubles and opportunities life presents.

## JOSHUA 2

**Why did God allow Israel to honor a deal with the lying prostitute Rahab—and how did she get away with it?**

The spies' arrangement with Rahab was honored because she sided with God and His people (Hebrews 11:31). She risked everything based on her limited understanding of God. Yes, she lied to protect the spies. She apparently saw no other way. But her later behavior proved she was growing in her understanding of the true God. Israel's deal was also honored because the two spies gave their word, binding Joshua and the people to special treatment for Rahab and her family. Rahab is one of only five women listed among the ancestors of Jesus Christ (Matthew 1:5).

## JOSHUA 5:13–15

**Who was the "commander of the LORD's army" who met Joshua outside Jericho?**

Shortly before he led the people of Israel in victory over the fortress city of Jericho, Joshua had an unexpected visitor who was holding a sword. "Friend or foe?" Joshua asked. The response probably made him think twice. "Neither," the stranger replied. "I am commander of the Lord's army," clarifying who was in charge of the operation to take the promised land.

This stranger was a high-ranking angel, commanding God's forces at work at Jericho. As such he was a special representative of God, and the place where the interview occurred was holy ground. The angel commanded him to remove his sandals, and Joshua quickly acknowledged his servanthood. Worship preceded battlefield victories.

## JOSHUA 6:20; 10:12–14

### Can we still believe in miracles like the walls of Jericho tumbling down? What about the sun standing still?

Questions like this may be curiosities about how an event occurred or expressions of doubt about God's ability to do the impossible. The God who raised Jesus Christ from the dead and created the universe would not have any trouble causing walls to crumble or the sun to stand still. If God did not raise Jesus from the dead, it doesn't matter what other miracles may have occurred.

Regarding the means, we may speculate

Joshua's men take Jericho as the walls come tumbling down.

that God used a localized earthquake or that the walls simply collapsed at God's command. Astronomically speaking, it would be more technically correct to say that the sun stood still because the earth slowed or in some way God prolonged the day.

Can we still believe in miracles? The real question is, will we believe in the God who can do such miracles?

## JOSHUA 6:15–21

### Why did God sometimes order the people of Israel to destroy entire cities, along with the people in them?

God punishes sin in both individuals and nations. The kind of punishment depends on God's purposes. In Exodus 7–11, for instance, God used ten different forms of punishment to correct the Egyptian people and to set Israel free. Plagues, national disasters, and the death of firstborn sons all made it clear that God meant business. The cities of Sodom and Gomorrah were in such poor moral condition that not even ten righteous people could be found in them (Genesis 18:32). God destroyed them with a fiery disaster.

The people of Jericho, along with the other city-states of Canaan, had a long-standing date with judgment. The land was filled with pagan, immoral, and cruel practices. Meanwhile, the people of Israel were undergoing extensive training and discipline first as slaves in Egypt, then as wandering pilgrims in the desert. God wanted to ensure their purity as His people. God's use of violent means of judgment may be difficult for us to understand or accept. The Old Testament, however, reports that God used this approach consistently. Nations such as Israel served to administer God's punishment on other nations, and also received similar punishment from God when they rebelled against His laws. More than anything, the harsh and shocking measures taken by God ought to alert us to the seriousness of sin. The comfort and ease of our own surroundings should never cloud our awareness of the utter destructiveness of sin.

# JOSHUA 7

## Why were God's judgments on sin so swift and harsh, as with Achan?

Not only were God's judgments swift and harsh, they also were comprehensive. Families were held responsible for the sins of a family member. Achan disobeyed God's order that none of the riches of Jericho were to be kept by the Israelites when the city was destroyed (Joshua 6:18). Achan took a bar of gold, some silver, and a costly robe and hid them under his tent. Meanwhile, the people became over-confident as a result of the crushing defeat of Jericho. They assumed that tiny Ai could be defeated even without supernatural help. The humiliation they suffered quickly revealed that something was desperately wrong. They turned to God for an answer.

When God judges, neither uncertainty nor lack of proof cloud His decisions. The Judge has witnessed everything. God sees perfectly what no human witness could ever see—intent, motives, circumstances, all the factors. No excuse or possible alternative explanation will confuse the issue. God judges without a shadow of doubt. Before the great victory at Jericho, the people were warned that the consequences for disobedience would harm the nation. Achan and his family became the center of a painful but necessary lesson.

God keeps His word. God's promises are dependable, and His warnings are unwavering. So many of what we call "little sins" are actually large acts of disrespect toward a holy and all-knowing God. Rather than attempting to hold God responsible for His judgments, we ought to be humbled by His infinite patience with us. His mercy often withholds the punishments we deserve, and His grace often pours out benefits that we do not deserve.

# JOSHUA 24:14–15

## How do godly leaders balance responsibilities for their families with leadership duties?

Joshua understood that his role in leading the people of Israel had boundaries. Leadership did not relieve him of personal responsibilities before God. When he prepared to relinquish his title, he reminded the people that they still had to decide whom they would serve. Then he expressed a greater priority in his own life by declaring, "As for me and my family, we will serve the LORD" (Joshua 24:15). Joshua challenged the people to make a choice, but he could not make the choice for them. When it came to his own home, Joshua understood his responsibilities. He spoke for himself and his family. No matter how large the stage of your leadership duties, don't neglect your relationship with God and your spiritual responsibilities for your family.

# JUDGES

*After Joshua's death, the people of Israel did pretty much whatever they wanted. God sent judges to help, but moral chaos and indifference reigned.*

## JUDGES 2:11

### Who is Baal?

Baal was one of the main gods in the land of Canaan. God had instructed the Israelites to stamp out everything in the land that had anything to do with idolatry and false gods. However, the Israelites ended up joining the Canaanites in their worship of Baal. One interesting note is that the word *Baal* has an additional meaning in Hebrew; it means "husband." You could say that, by their worship of Baal, the Israelites "married" a foreign god.

One of many figures of the Canaanite god Baal.

## JUDGES 2:22

### Why test Israel when the outcome of such a test is almost certain failure?

God wanted perfect obedience from Israel; He wanted a holy nation. And yet He had to give them the freedom to obey or not obey. After all, if God compelled Israel to be obedient and holy, if they had no choice in the matter, such obedience and holiness really wouldn't be worth that much. In fact, it would probably end up like the obedience that a robot might display.

Our faith is also tested by having to live in a sinful world and having to deal with our own sinful natures. Like Israel, we will fail sometimes. However, we are offered forgiveness through Jesus Christ.

## JUDGES 3:5-6

### Why was intermarriage so closely linked to idolatry in Israel's chart of sins?

Marriage in Israel involved a person's whole family, society, and way of life, including, of course, the partners' values and particular gods. Say that you, young Josiah Ben Smith living in 1240 B.C., were set on marrying young Sally the Canaanite. It would be a safe guess that you would end up with a lot of pagan Canaanite ideas and idols in your household. Anything that replaced the worship of the true God was idolatry. Better to remain single than to lose the worship of God.

## JUDGES 3:20-23

### How does murder serve God's will and win God's approval?

Ehud killed the king of Moab, Eglon, by plunging a sword into his stomach. However, Eglon's death was a result of God's punishment for oppressing the people of Israel for eighteen years. It is not a question of murder serving God's will. Rather, God used Ehud to carry out His judgment upon an unrighteous man. God allows people to die, to be killed, to suffer, as a result of sin in the world. There is a balanced dynamic between sin, consequences, and judgment that is as natural as the law of gravity.

## JUDGES 5:24-27

### Why celebrate a murder in a song?

Song was a powerful form of mass communication for those times. It was a fast and easy way of communicating to a big audience. So why not use it as another version of the five o'clock news? The incident that was celebrated here was about when Jael killed the sleeping

Sisera by pounding a tent peg through his skull (Judges 4:21–22). Sisera had been the commander of an enemy Canaanite army that had oppressed the people of Israel for twenty years. It is perhaps not correct to call this murder. Rather, what Jael did must be looked at in the larger context of God punishing sin and rescuing His people. With that in mind, the song is instead a celebration of God's deliverance.

## JUDGES 6:12, 27

### If Gideon was such a mighty hero, why is his first act of leadership so riddled with fear?

Gideon was a mighty hero. At the same time, however, he was just a normal man. Being a hero doesn't mean having to possess perfect virtue and absolute courage. Rather, like Gideon, we become heroes when we allow God to use us. It doesn't matter if we trip and stumble along the way. Our own flawed natures reflect the fact that God is merciful and patient enough to use such normal people like us, just as He used Gideon. It is in such a relationship between God and a willing but flawed servant that great things can happen.

## JUDGES 7:13-14

### Can God put thoughts into peoples' heads?

God can and does put thoughts into peoples' heads. Sometimes it is in the form of a dream, as in the seventh chapter of Judges. Other times, it can be a hunch, or a premonition, or what we call a nagging conscience. Still other times, God will put direct words into our heads.

If we accept the fact that God made everything in the universe, from the biggest red giant star to the tiniest hair on our head, it isn't such a big thing for Him to whisper inside our minds.

Gideon prays to God for guidance as he prepares for battle.

## JUDGES 8:28

### What made Gideon such an outstanding leader and national hero?

Two reasons explain why Gideon was an outstanding leader and national hero. To begin with, God chose him. God looked around and decided that He would use Gideon. The second reason was that Gideon simply was willing to be used by God. It was not a case of Gideon being taller, smarter, or stronger than everyone else. Rather, it was that God chose him and that Gideon responded. Heroes are really just normal people who are willing to step out from the crowd and answer God's call.

## Why would a brutal and willful warrior choose assisted suicide just as victory seemed secure?

Abimelech had his servant kill him because he was dying anyway. Right in the middle of the battle, when Abimelech was fighting next to the city walls, a woman dropped a stone on him from the top of the wall and cracked his skull open. Even though Abimelech's army was about to win, his pride took first place. He couldn't face the humiliation of having been done in by a woman, having to face his victorious men with the shame of what had happened to him. Abimelech took the easy way out and had his servant run him through with a sword.

## Why was a bees' nest in a carcass such a secret?

Samson killed a lion and left the carcass on the ground. One day walking along, he saw that a hive of bees had set up residence in the carcass and were producing honey. Samson ate the honey and then gave some to his parents. However, he did not tell them where he got the honey. According to Jewish law, anything that had come in contact with a carcass was unclean. So this honey was unclean. Samson's parents were God-fearing people and would surely have refused the honey had they known the source.

Samson kills the lion and leaves the carcass on the ground.

# RUTH

*Few stories of loss and love are as famous as this one. Yet some of the arrangements connected with this romance and the meaning they hold for us raise a few questions.*

## RUTH 3:7–11

### Was Ruth, with Naomi's advice and consent, "coming on" to Boaz?

Yes, in a manner appropriate to the culture. Boaz was punctilious concerning tradition and propriety. He lived by a code of honor, respect for the law, and belief in the true God. He was also wealthy and at least in his middle years (see the reference to a "younger man"). Ruth was a Moabite woman, a poor widow, and probably attractive. Coached by her mother-in-law, Naomi, Ruth more or less asked Boaz to the dance. He accepted, and the rest is Old Testament history. They gave birth to Obed, the grandfather of King David.

This romance carries no hint of seductive adventure or clandestine meetings. Two people mutually attracted, meeting family obligations, get married and raise children. The woman made the first move. There is nothing terribly unusual about that.

## RUTH 3:12

### What is a "family redeemer"?

Often called a kinsman-redeemer, this person was responsible for protecting members of the extended family—a big brother, so to speak. If a woman's husband died, a relative—the family redeemer—was obligated to take over the husband's duties and care for his wife and children. He would "redeem," or buy back, any property in order to provide for them. Boaz was not the first relative in line. So he secured the permission of the first man in that line, with public witnesses, and then filled the role, encouraged to do so by Ruth's own expression of interest in becoming his wife.

# RUTH 4:11-12

## Why was childbearing and fathering so important in Old Testament days?

In the ancient world, ensuring a family line was absolutely necessary for security and survival. What else could a person leave behind? Books and writings? Probably not. Money? Yes, the family property might insure prosperity for a generation or two. Sons and daughters? Definitely. Without heirs, why accumulate an estate?

Descendants, especially sons, were all important. They perpetuated the family's name. They carried on the family's story to another generation at a time when memory was a matter of the mind, not a computer chip.

# 1 SAMUEL

*Why would people follow a loser like Saul, or question a winner like David, or join a revolutionary like Absalom? The first of the Bible's official books of history raises a number of questions such as these.*

## 1 SAMUEL 1

### Where did the practice of dedicating children come from?

Parents in the Bible, such as Hannah, dedicated children to God to acknowledge God's part in giving them children. They were remembering that their children belonged to God. This practice had particular importance when the first son was born.

In many societies, firstborn sons have special privileges, including the right to most of the family's estate. The birth of the family's first son brought special honor to the mother—she had provided her husband with a future to the family name. Certainly Jewish families felt blessed by firstborn sons.

The Bible gives firstborn sons an important teaching role. Each of the patriarchs (Abraham, Isaac, and Jacob) were affected by the handling of firstborns. The death sentence passed on the firstborns of Egypt as the final plague before the Exodus made it clear that the very future of that nation was in God's hands (Exodus 11:1–12:30). At that same time, God told Moses, "Dedicate to me all the firstborn sons of Israel and every firsborn male animal. They are mine" (Exodus 13:1).

Although other nations practiced child sacrifice, God's people were instructed to "redeem" their firstborn sons by offering a substitute sacrifice (Exodus 13:12–16). In Hannah's case (1 Samuel 1:11), dedication of a child involved leaving the recently weaned Samuel with the priest Eli to be raised as a servant of God. In most cases, Old Testament parents recognized God's ownership by dedicating their children through an animal sacrifice.

A modern form of child dedication is practiced in some churches as a means of committing and entrusting that child to God's sovereign care.

## 1 SAMUEL 1–2

### Should childless couples attempting to get pregnant pray for God's help?

Infertile couples face difficult temptations today, such as whether to consider their condition as punishment from God; to resent

God for the seeming unfairness; to lose hope. These temptations were very real to some of the Bible's most respected women. Sarah, Rebekah, Rachel, Hannah, and Elizabeth all struggled with infertility. Each eventually bore children. In none of these cases does the Bible indicate that infertility was a form of punishment. Rather, God received glory from the eventual pregnancies.

God's blessing on these ancient women of faith cannot mean that God intends for every woman to bear children; but, rather, it shows that God is able to display His divine character and carry out His plans even through difficult human experience. Couples today have every reason to follow the biblical example of prayer and faith shown by these women. Today we can also consult the best medical help available—another of God's providential mercies to childless couples trying for offspring.

## 1 SAMUEL 6

### If the ark of the covenant was so special, why were the Philistines allowed to have it?

On its own, the ark was little more than an interesting piece of furniture. But the ark held the Ten Commandments and symbolized God's presence. Any attempt to see power in the ark itself (as in the popular *Indiana Jones* films) is tantamount to idolatry. The people of Israel made this mistake frequently. They assumed that possession of such a powerful instrument as the ark gave them some control over God Himself, since God was obligated to guarantee the success of anyone (or any group of people) possessing it.

But the ark was not the covenant. It was only a conduit, not the reality. God had promised blessing to the people and demanded compliance with certain essentials of worship and conduct, of which the ark was a tangible reminder and symbol. The people's disobedience brought punishment, including the capture of their most treasured reminder of God's

promise. God allowed the ark to be taken in order to get Israel's attention. It was a stunning wake-up call for Israel to clarify its relation-

The Levites carry the ark of the covenant that contains the tablets of the Ten Commandments.

ship to God. When covenant promises and duties were reaffirmed, the ark came home. In the meantime, however, the fate of the ark was never out of God's control.

## 1 SAMUEL 8:6–9

### Did the kings help or hurt Israel as a nation?

In demanding a king, Israel became like every other nation of the world. Instead of asking God for relief from counterfeit spiritual leaders, they cried, "Give us a king!" They rejected God's rule in favor of human leadership.

Moses had written about the danger of a human monarchy (Deuteronomy 17:14–20). He warned future kings against large stables, horse-trading with Egypt, collecting many wives, and accumulating wealth. The lives of

Israel's kings appear to be an effort to do exactly what God had warned against.

# 1 SAMUEL 13–15

## How could a leader who has everything at the start—like Saul, Israel's first king—fail so miserably?

Blessed with height and good looks, Saul was chosen as Israel's first king. He quickly showed that his insecurities were no match for the job. Had he remained faithful to God, those traits could have been amended. Unfortunately, he did not.

Saul's honeymoon as king was short-lived. Unwilling to depend on God, his political instincts were weak and he never learned to correct them. Saul's decisions were controlled by fear, jealousy, anger, and impatience. Fear of Goliath drove him to send the boy David out to fight in his own place. Jealousy of David led to repeated attempts to kill the man who would take his place. Anger with his fiercely loyal son Jonathan hurt their relationship. Impatience caused him to act without waiting for God's guidance. Insecurity over the future led him to a disastrous consultation with spiritualists. For all his potential as a leader, Saul marched headlong into tragic failure, an example of a leader who started with widespread public support and God's blessing but never hit his stride. Saul based his reign on the talents and gifts of someone not adequate to the job—himself—and never reached for God's help or hand.

# 1 SAMUEL 15:22

## What's the meaning of Samuel's proverb, "Obedience is better than sacrifice"?

Samuel understood that sacrifices aren't always sacrificial. He confronted Saul with the sin of going through the motions of sacrifice to avoid doing what God commanded. Saul was like the spoiled child who was ordered to leave the cookies in the jar. Instead, he cleaned out the jar but left one cookie behind, saying, "Well, I didn't take them all!" He thought the "surrender" of some of the spoils of victory made up for his blatant disregard for God's instructions. Samuel made it clear to Saul that God reads people's intentions just as clearly as their actions. An external sacrifice to God will not cover up willful acts of disobedience.

# 1 SAMUEL 16

## What made David one of history's outstanding leaders?

God declared that His choice for a new king would be "a man after his own heart" (1 Samuel 13:14). Not that David was perfect, but his attitudes and inclinations were in the right direction—toward praise and faith in God as an almighty, all-caring sovereign. One glance at David's life can't miss the glaring mistakes he made, but David never tried to blame others or make excuses for his sins. He took some terrible detours along the way, but his life was consistently directed toward God. He did not resist or resent God's painful corrections. David sinned blatantly, but he confessed openly and trusted boldly. He did not pester God to make him rich or famous; he simply and persistently pursued God as his highest love. David's psalms do not glorify himself; he was convinced of God's beauty and grace as the source of whatever success and happiness he enjoyed.

## 1 SAMUEL 17:40

### Why five stones for David's battle with Goliath?

Several explanations help us understand David's minimal but adequate preparations for history's most famous confrontation: (1) a successful first shot may have drawn out the Philistine warriors, and David wanted ammunition until his own reserves arrived; (2) Goliath's armor bearer might require military follow-through; or (3) David was preparing for prolonged fighting, dodging the heavily armed giant while peppering him with shot.

We don't know David's thoughts as he marched out of Israel's trenches, but his preparedness was more in the faith he carried in his heart than the stones in his pouch. Facing powerful adversaries requires a big heart more than a big weapon. Nonetheless, David was not presuming a magical first shot would end the contest. Who knows? Perhaps David was as surprised as anyone that one shot was all he needed.

## 1 SAMUEL 20

### How did Jonathan manage to honor his father, King Saul, and still warn his friend David of Saul's murderous plot?

Jonathan was caught between two intense loyalties. His father, the king, wanted to kill the popular warrior David, Jonathan's best friend. Would Jonathan betray his father to save his friend?

When David first told Jonathan about Saul's plan, Jonathan was doubtful. For Saul to move on David's life was so foolish, so counterproductive and futile, that Jonathan perhaps thought the plan was only a rumor. Yet he could not doubt the honesty and passion in David's words, "Kill me yourself if I have sinned against your father" (1 Samuel 20:8). Knowing David's innocence, Jonathan agreed to warn David if the incredible turned out to be true.

Saul's bitterly angry response to Jonathan's defense of David confirmed the worst suspicions. When Jonathan could not stop Saul's march toward evil, he could warn the intended victim, thus averting a tragedy.

David defeats Goliath by knocking him unconscious with a stone and then cutting off his head.

David plays his harp for King Saul.

## 1 SAMUEL 24

### Why didn't David kill Saul when the opportunity arose?

Even with self-defense as a perfect alibi, David refused to eliminate his chief adversary at the time. David's restraint indicates that there is more than one kind of Goliath in life and that duty to God requires different responses.

Killing Saul would have been a quick way to the throne of Israel, already promised to David by Samuel's anointing. But Saul had been chosen, too. Though a failed king, Saul was still the office holder, and God still the one who had put Saul on the top seat. Getting rid of Saul was rightly God's business, not David's. David's restraint shows that he fully trusted God's timing in his life and would not work a situation to his advantage to accelerate God's plan.

Today we are often confronted with failed authority figures—people in church office or other positions whose judgment is spoiled by deceit and blinded by prejudice. Living under this authority may seem ridiculous, but sometimes it is also necessary. Removing a failed spiritual leader is God's business. The palace coup that displaces an old "has-been" leader with an ambitious "righteous" leader is only trading one set of problems for another.

# 2 SAMUEL

*David's rise to power established a strong and prosperous Israel. Though David let his eyes wander and his sons started to squabble, God was still in control.*

## 2 SAMUEL 12:1–11

### When should Christians "call to account" someone in authority?

When a person falls into sinful activity and appears to be unaware, it does not matter what the person's title may be or how much worldly power that person may possess. God is not intimidated by titles or human achievements, and God's standards do not change for powerful people. The military or political leader who begins to believe that he is above the law of God has taken the first step toward ultimate defeat.

In the prophet Nathan's case, the risk involved in confronting David was reduced by their mutual confidence and friendship. Nathan's mission was not easy, but at least these were not two strangers trying to figure out if ulterior political motives could lie behind the spiritual admonition. And Nathan's confrontation of David was also conducted in such a way that David actually confronted himself. Nathan cleverly led David to recognize the moral standards that he himself had violated. When confronting another Christian about a sinful habit, try appealing to the person's own understanding of Christian responsibility as a first tactic toward repentance and renewal.

## 2 SAMUEL 22:2

### How can God be like a rock?

Rocks are inert, lifeless, and speechless. Rocks cannot respond to human sympathy, cannot shape themselves into anything useful, and eventually erode into gravel. Is this what God is like?

Obviously, any metaphor from nature can never be completely descriptive of the sovereign God. In this case, David's life seemed to be crumbling around him, his kingdom was in shambles, his army was confused, and his priests were divided. Indeed, his own family was against him. In the face of this chaos, perhaps the stability and weightiness of rocks was exactly the picture that David needed to assure himself of God's unchanging, stable love.

Build a fortress out of rock and it will last a long time. Carve a message on rock and many rains won't wash away its words. God's love endured through the storms and upheavals that David felt, and in that sense, comparing God to a rock seemed like just the assurance he needed. Praise God for the imagination to find spiritual meaning in the humblest of God's creative works.

# 1 KINGS

*Tucked into this royal roll call are stories of God's grace to sinful people, just like us. And these same people raise some questions that parallel ours today.*

## THE BOOKS OF 1–2 KINGS

### What's the point of reading about all these ancient kings?

First and 2 Kings trace the history of Israel during the four hundred years from the death of King David to the destruction of Jerusalem.

Each king is judged on whether he was obedient to God or did evil in His sight. Many lessons follow from these stories. We learn what motivates people to reject God. We observe sin's consequences. The primary message is that Israel's tragic descent from David's golden reign to exile and captivity was the result of unfaithfulness. If only those people had known— if only they could have seen! And what about us?

A king is being attended to by his servants. The stories of the kings of Israel demonstrate obedience to God or failing to listen to Him.

## 1 KINGS 1:6

### Despite all his courage in battle, was David a wimp as a father?

Just because someone is good at one thing does not necessarily mean that he or she will be good at another. Just because David was a courageous and skilled warrior does not automatically mean that he did well as a father. If such a correlation were true, then we should expect to read impressive stories of all the families and children of our own military forces.

Rather, David seemed to be a failure as a father. Maybe in part it was because he spent so much time away from home fighting his wars. The son he had fathered so badly, Adonijah, was very handsome. The Bible hints, in the first chapter of 1 Kings, that David was indulgent of his son because of this very fact. Overlooking a son's faults just because he is handsome is definitely not the sign of a good father.

## 1 KINGS 2:3, 5, 9

**In the same breath that David urged Solomon to walk in the ways of the Lord, he plotted the assassination of his opponents, assigning the deeds to Solomon. Was that right?**

God raised up kings so that they, among other functions, would carry out His mercy and judgment among the people that they ruled. David did no wrong when he instructed Solomon to punish old enemies who had wronged him. Solomon needed to do away with God's enemies to secure the throne.

But note that while urging Solomon to clean out his enemies, David also instructed Solomon to show kindness to people who had helped him long ago. The image of the king carrying out retribution and at the same time showing kindness is a reflection of God Himself, who visits judgment on those who have done wrong and mercy upon those who have lived righteously.

## 1 KINGS 2:24, 32, 44

**As Solomon eliminated his opposition, he attributed the killings to the Lord. Was Solomon avoiding responsibility, deflecting guilt, or rightly naming the Lord as the ultimate executioner?**

The Lord is the ultimate executioner, regardless of whether or not Solomon was just in punishing those who were condemned. In saying that the Lord was repaying those being punished, however, Solomon was simply indicating and affirming the particularities of his own position as king. That is, the king was a tool of judgment in the hand of the Lord.

Correspondingly, if Solomon was unjust in his executions, if innocent blood was on his hands, then it would be irrelevant if he actually was avoiding responsibility or deflecting guilt. Whatever Solomon's intent was, the Lord still was the ultimate executioner, and if the king had erred in his judgment, then he himself would receive his own punishment from the Lord.

## 1 KINGS 3:1–3

**Why did Solomon compromise religious purity from the very beginning of his reign?**

Solomon certainly was not perfect. Despite his impressive pedigree and the fact that he loved the Lord, he had his own particular sins. In this case, Solomon sacrificed and burned incense at the high places. This behavior was in direct opposition to the word of the Lord.

Solomon made a significant mistake at the very beginning of his reign. He went and made a treaty with Pharaoh, the king of Egypt. That might not have been too bad by itself; however, Solomon then married Pharaoh's daughter and brought her home to Jerusalem. Marrying outside of Israel was something that God had specifically commanded the Israelites not to do. Foreign wives brought their foreign gods with them, compromising the worship of the Lord. It was probably due to the influence of his wife, the Egyptian princess, that Solomon was soon hiking up to the high places and making sacrifices there.

## 1 KINGS 3:15

**Does God direct our lives through dreams today?**

God does not usually direct our lives through dreams; however, if He were to choose to do so, He could. Directing us through dreams is only one of several ways that God can bring direction to our lives.

God chose to speak with Solomon through a dream, offering him whatever he desired. The fact that it was a dream was not special of itself. God could have done just as well if He had written on a palace wall, opened the mouth of a donkey and had the beast speak, or sent an angel.

Most people dream frequently. Just because you have a dream does not necessarily mean that God is speaking to you. Some dreams might just mean that you should not eat certain foods right before you go to bed. But, then again. . .

## 1 KINGS 10:1

### Who was the queen of Sheba?

Sheba was a land that roughly corresponds to modern-day Ethiopia in northeastern Africa. The queen of Sheba heard of Solomon's great wisdom and decided to journey to Israel to see for herself. Apparently, the queen was impressed with Solomon's wisdom. She had many difficult questions to ask, but Solomon answered them all through his great wisdom.

Legend says that Solomon and the queen of Sheba had a son together. Legend also says that this son took the ark of the covenant from Jerusalem and brought it back to the land of Sheba. In modern-day Ethiopia, one can still hear it told that the ark is hidden in an ancient monastery out in the wilderness.

## 1 KINGS 11:1

### If the wisest man of all time was a committed polygamist, why don't modern societies organize marriage that way?

Just because someone is extremely wise does not mean that the person has a monopoly on wisdom. All people have a sin that trips them up. Solomon's was women. His seven hundred wives and three hundred concubines do not indicate wisdom on his part.

When Adam was lonely, God brought Eve to be his wife. God did not bring several women. One was enough. The first marriage, that of Adam and Eve, was

The queen of Sheba arrives in Israel to hear the wisdom of King Solomon.

created by God. We would be wise to follow their example rather than that of the wisest man who ever lived.

## 1 KINGS 14:12–13; 15:29–30

### Why should children of evil men be punished for crimes they did not commit?

Children are a physical extension of their parents. This was especially true during Old Testament times. The family was viewed as a cohesive whole, each person responsible for and part of the others. Children are also sometimes a moral extension of their parents. In Old Testament times, evil parents influenced their children, and their sin bore consequences in their children's lives.

In the case of 1 Kings 14, Abijah, the son of Jeroboam, was actually a good prince. His father, Jeroboam, was an evil man, but somehow the father's evil had not corrupted the son. Abijah died because God wanted to give him an honorable death—the only honorable death in the family. Later, when God brought judgment on the house of Jeroboam, everyone died miserably and shamefully.

## 1 KINGS 17:22–23

### Why can't Christians today duplicate the miracles performed by Old Testament prophets like Elijah?

Christians today don't raise people from the dead, multiply food, or call down fire from heaven as various people in the Bible did. In those days it was a less unusual occurrence to see the supernatural in everyday life. People expected and assumed the existence of the supernatural. They had faith in the supernatural, the existence of God, of gods and demons, of strange powers and wonders. Therefore, when God need someone through whom He could work, someone like Elijah, someone whom He could use to demonstrate His power, He didn't have to look very far.

These days, many people don't believe in the supernatural and are skeptical of things that are not verifiable through science. Many no longer have faith in God's intervention. Such thinking has also affected the church. Even though Christians have grown up reading about miracles and wonders in the Bible, and even though they acknowledge that such events actually happened, they do not expect to see these things in our modern life. Many have closed the door on that part of God.

## 1 KINGS 18:38

### How could fire destroy something saturated with water?

When Elijah called down fire from heaven, fire came down and burned up his offering and the wood the offering was on. The fire also burned up the stones that the wood was stacked on. To make the event even more emphatic, Elijah had soaked the entire altar with water. The fire burned up the water as well. Fire burning water can be startling; however, what is even more startling is the fact that the fire consumed the stones. You usually do not see this happening in nature.

Of course that is the whole point of the story: this wasn't any old fire—this fire was supernatural and sent from God. If the fire had taken the shape of violins and had played the "Hallelujah Chorus" while burning up Elijah's offering, the event would not have been any more startling. The stuff of creation is at God's command to do with what He wills. Remember, He is not a tame God.

# 2 KINGS

*If you're looking for examples of moral failure, here they are in this second history of the kings. But a bright spot shines through: Elijah's mantel was passed on to Elisha.*

## 2 KINGS 2

### Whatever became of Elijah?

Elijah was a faithful prophet who had condemned evil Ahab, king of Israel. God rewarded Elijah's faithfulness by telling him when he would be taken from earth and then by sending the whirlwind-chariot, sparing Elijah the pain of a normal death experience.

This incident bears similarity to Enoch's experience in Genesis 5:21–24. Enoch enjoyed a close relationship with God throughout his life. Then suddenly he disappeared when God took him. Like Enoch, Elijah was a faithful servant whom God swept into heaven by divine means.

Elijah is taken up to heaven in a chariot of fire.

## 2 KINGS 17:21

**God promised David that his dynasty and kingdom would continue for all time (2 Samuel 7:16), but later the Lord "tore Israel away from the kingdom of David" (2 Kings 17:21). What happened to the promise?**

At this point in Israel's history, God was tearing the northern kingdom, Israel's ten tribes, away from Judah. Despite all that God had done for Israel, including repeated warnings through His prophets, Israel would not listen. They were stubborn and refused to believe (2 Kings 17:14). So God rejected the descendants of Israel. Leading Judah (the southern kingdom) at this time was King Hezekiah, a descendant of David. When Judah was taken captive, a remnant of Jews remained faithful to the Lord.

But God's promise was not forgotten. Jesus, in the family line of David (Matthew 1:17), fulfills the promise to David by inaugurating a new kingdom that will last forever, a new chosen people who believe in Jesus Christ as Lord and carry His name before all the nations of the earth. Notice the shift from a political kingdom under David to a spiritual kingdom under Jesus Christ. Jesus leads a new Israel, the church (1 Peter 2:9–10).

## 2 KINGS 18, 20

**King Hezekiah seems so wise in dealing with Sennacherib from Assyria yet so foolish in dealing with envoys from Babylon. How can one person be so smart and yet so dumb?**

At the beginning of his reign, Hezekiah was strong in faith. Confronted by enemies, he went into the temple of the Lord and prayed. The Lord honored his faith and sent an angel to destroy the Assyrian military encampment. When Hezekiah became ill, he prayed and was healed. Hezekiah repeatedly trusted in the Lord, and God delivered him.

Yet when the king of Babylon appealed to Hezekiah's sense of importance with letters and gifts, Hezekiah took the bait, showing off his palace and wealth. Confronted by the prophet Isaiah, Hezekiah seemed unaware that his pride was showing—a warning to all of how quickly we can be inflated with arrogance and self-congratulation.

## 2 KINGS 21

**If Hezekiah was such a good king, how did his son Manasseh become such an evil king?**

Throughout the Old Testament we see the sons of godly parents reject the Lord. Something goes wrong, though we often do not have enough information to make a specific judgment. Such is the case with Hezekiah, father of the bitterly evil Manasseh. Chances are, kings paid very little attention to child rearing in those days; it may have been that Manasseh hardly knew his father, which in itself might tell much.

Clearly, God holds parents responsible for raising children in the fear and knowledge of the Lord. As kings ignored their family duties, offspring like Manasseh wrecked whatever their faithful fathers might have achieved. Likewise, the sons of Samuel, once appointed to replace their father, turned to greed instead of faithful service (1 Samuel 8). (For some biblical insights on child rearing, see Deuteronomy 6:4–9; Proverbs 3:11–12; and Hebrews 12:5–11.)

# 1 CHRONICLES

*Let's admit it. This is not the first book most Christians read for morning devotions. But don't let the lists and numbers distract you. God has much to teach us in this history of how people should live.*

## 1 CHRONICLES 1–10

### Why does the Bible include so many genealogies?

"All Scripture is inspired by God and is useful," wrote the apostle Paul in 2 Timothy 3:16. Yet many Bible readers come to sections like this and say, "Skip it!" However, genealogies underline the importance of heritage. Ancestry matters. Records such as these gave the Jewish people a sense of belonging. Genealogies remind us that individuals matter to God, whose worldwide care is also for particular people like Joktan and Jabez (1 Chronicles 1:20; 4:9–10). Genealogies show that Jesus met the Old Testament requirements that the Messiah be a descendant of Abraham and David (see Matthew 1).

The many genealogies in scripture remind us of God's work in history. If God has been faithful throughout the ages, then the appeal to trust and obey Him makes good sense today.

## 1 CHRONICLES 10:14

### If Saul committed suicide (1 Samuel 31:4), how could it be said that the Lord killed Saul?

This question demonstrates the "harmonic tension" between the sovereignty of God and the free will of human beings. Saul had been rejected by God because of his defiance and disobedience (1 Samuel 15:22–23). God arranged for Saul's ultimate defeat in battle so that Saul would die and the kingdom pass into the hands of David. Saul took his own life (1 Samuel 31:3–4) just before the Philistines were about to kill him. Thus, God's will was done according to both divine sovereignty and human responsibility.

A depiction of Jerusalem in Bible times.

## 1 CHRONICLES 11:3-8

### Why are there so many names for Jerusalem—Jebus, Zion, City of David?

For the same reasons that many modern cities acquire different names (for example, Rome is "The Eternal City"; New York is "The Big Apple"; Hollywood is "Tinseltown"). The different names stem from different historical periods, specific attributes, or incidents. Jerusalem was called Jebus during the period of the judges (Joshua 15:8; Judges 19:10) because at that time it was controlled by the Jebusites. Zion was originally a rocky ridge near the Kidron Valley; in time the name became synonymous with the entire city. The moniker "City of David" became popular during and after the reign of King David.

## 1 CHRONICLES 13:1-14

### Why was Uzzah killed for merely trying to keep the ark from toppling over?

The text simply says that "the LORD's anger blazed out against Uzzah, and he struck him dead because he had laid his hand on the Ark" (1 Chronicles 13:10). Long before, God had given explicit, strict instructions about how the ark of the covenant was to be handled and by whom, and how it was to be moved (Numbers 4:5–15). Here, instead of carrying the ark on poles, the Levites were transporting the ark in an ox-drawn cart, similar to the way the Philistines had moved it (see 1 Samuel 6:1–8).

We cannot judge Uzzah's motives. Maybe they were pure; perhaps he had a secret and

The Levites carry the ark correctly by using poles, just as God instructed.

sinful desire to touch Israel's holiest object. Whatever the case, he and the others had disregarded the clear command of God and instituted their own plan. For this disobedience Uzzah paid with his life.

## 1 CHRONICLES 14:3

### Why did David ("a man after God's own heart") keep so many wives?

The Bible never explicitly condemns polygamy. Many Old Testament leaders accumulated wives in a manner similar to the pagan kings of the ancient Middle East without divine disapproval. A closer look, however, reveals that God originally defined marriage as "a man joined to his wife, and the two. . .united into one" (Genesis 2:24). In addition, God warned Israel of the dangers of its kings taking many wives (Deuteronomy 17:17). The stress caused by multiple marriages is seen in every biblical family in which polygamy occurred.

## 1 CHRONICLES 16:4

### Why did David appoint certain Levites as worship leaders?

Worship is merely ascribing worth or value to someone or something. Whatever we give our time, energy, effort, resources, emotion, attention, and affection to is what we value most. We are looking to that to give us life. In short, that is what we worship. By commanding and providing for the ongoing worship of God, David was declaring to the nation that the God of Israel, nothing else and no one else, deserved all their worship. He would be their focus. They would acknowledge Him above all else. They would trust Him.

# 1 CHRONICLES 19:4–5

## Why did King Hanun of the Ammonites cut off the beards and robes of David's ambassadors?

Hanun's advisers convinced him that David's men were spies who had not come in a spirit of goodwill. To send a message and perhaps consolidate power, the newly crowned Hanun ordered the Jewish ambassadors shaved and stripped. To be forcibly shaved and sent home half-naked was a gesture of utmost humiliation. Hanun's point was made.

# 1 CHRONICLES 21:1–7

## Why was David in trouble for taking a census?

This census had its origin in pride. David wanted to revel in the size of his army and boast of his military might. These desires were nothing less than satanic (Ezekiel 28:12–19). Unlike the census in Numbers, this head count was neither ordered nor sanctioned by God. God moved swiftly to discipline David because He wanted the king's (and the nation's) trust to be in Him and not in human power.

# 1 CHRONICLES 21:1–7

## Some numbers in 1 Chronicles do not agree with similar accounts in 2 Samuel (compare 1 Chronicles 21:1–7 and 2 Samuel 24:9). What can these differing numbers mean?

In 1 Chronicles, Joab reported the number of fighting men as 1.1 million in Israel and 470,000 in Judah (not including the tribes of Levi and Benjamin). In 2 Samuel the figures are cited as 800,000 Israelites and 500,000 men of Judah.

One theory is that the 1.1 million figure in 1 Chronicles represents the grand total of fighting men in all the tribes. If so, taking away the 470,000 men in Judah would leave 630,000 in Israel. The 800,000 Israelites mentioned in 2 Samuel might then represent an estimate of 170,000 Levites plus the already-counted 630,000. And the 500,000 men of Judah might include an estimated 30,000 Benjamites.

# 1 CHRONICLES 21:14

## Why did 70,000 people die for a sin David committed?

Our society, which glorifies individual autonomy and responsibility, recoils at the thought of innocent people being punished for wrongs committed by another. In ancient times, leaders of families, tribes, or nations served as representatives of their people. Both success and failure belonged to all. It is entirely possible that David had consulted his advisers beforehand and they had agreed to his plan, making the census a corporate decision.

This principle of "the innocent suffering for wrongs committed by another" is still true. Because God designed us to live in relationship (families, friends, neighbors), our actions always affect others, either positively or negatively. To borrow the body analogy used by Paul in 1 Corinthians 12, when one small part suffers, the whole body hurts.

# 2 CHRONICLES

*The story here is that disobedience bears consequences. We can learn from the hard experiences God's people before us have gone through.*

## 2 CHRONICLES 1:7

### Does God give open-ended promises today as He gave to Solomon?

To what degree can we count on God's help? Is God like a banker, helping the successful to become more so? The New Testament is filled with seemingly open-ended offers of divine assistance if not downright provision. In Matthew's Gospel, Jesus makes an offer to His disciples that makes Solomon's offer pale in comparison (Matthew 6:29–33).

Yet Solomon's offer was not completely open-ended. He knew not to expect God's help if he did not also obey God's law. Solomon clearly knew that the covenant under which he would prosper carried significant responsibility (2 Chronicles 6:16). This was no free ride. Solomon was obliged to live in a manner honoring God if God was to continue to bless his reign.

Likewise, God's promises today are not free rides. While we cannot earn God's favor, we are responsible to live in faith and obedience to God. Good works will not increase God's generosity to us, but obedience responds to God's love in gratitude.

## 2 CHRONICLES 2:11

### Could a pagan king like Hiram of Tyre also be a secret believer?

Hiram's reply to Solomon could have been just a politically astute way of honoring Solomon's curious beliefs. After all, a huge business deal was hanging in the balance, so why not humor the ambitious new king? Or, Hiram may have been reflecting the common pagan assumption that multiple deities had their own national favorites—Israel's God was good for Israel; other gods were good in their own territories.

Two coins from the seaport city of Tyre.

Joseph rules Egypt and feeds the people during the seven years of famine.

Or, Hiram could have been exploring the first overtures of conversion. For him, the evidence concerning Israel's God may have been convincing. Perhaps he was a serious inquirer, and his business deal with Solomon would give occasion for more serious discussion of spiritual truth. Perhaps Hiram was saying, "God, I respect you and admire your work, and I don't think I'm included in your covenant, being an outsider. Nonetheless, I'd like to believe."

We cannot know what Hiram really meant. Nor can you guess the condition of your neighbor's spiritual life or the readiness of people around you to believe. But if you care about people, you'll use openings such as Hiram provided to witness to the truth of God's salvation through Christ.

## 2 CHRONICLES 6:26

### Are droughts and famines the result of sin?

Surely they are, in the sense of ultimate cause. But not necessarily, in the sense of proximate cause. It appears that God used these events as judgments at times.

The Bible describes a "fall" of humanity into sin, which affected all of creation—human life, ecology, language, everything. In a sinless world, weather patterns might still be unpredictable, but food supply would not be cut off as a result of dry spells. The Fall and the collective effects of sin introduced the possibility of ecological and meteorological disaster, as much as any other kind of problem.

But no one should take sin's influence as an excuse for doing nothing scientifically to fix the proximate causes of famine or drought. Where soil depletion creates dust bowls, strong action can replenish soil fertility. Our task is to fight sin's influence on several fronts—by prayer first, then the use of spiritual gifts, then the gifts of human reason and practical acumen, nurturing the environment, and taking dominion of creation, as God originally instructed (Genesis 1:28).

## 2 CHRONICLES 6:32

**Why was it necessary for Solomon to ask God to listen to prayers of foreign people, as if God must be convinced to lend an ear?**

Perhaps it was Solomon who needed convincing, and his prayer was God's way of leading him to the big picture: God's love extends far beyond Israel's borders.

Prayer often asks God to do what God is already predisposed to do. "Forgive our sins" we pray, but God has promised already to do that. "Lead us not into temptation" we ask, but since when does God lead us into temptation? "Give us daily bread," we entreat when promises of God's provision are everywhere in the Bible. Repeating in prayer those needs that God promises to meet makes prayer less a vehicle of adjusting the world and more a reminder of God's generosity and love. And that's all right.

Solomon's prayer on behalf of outsiders indicated Israel's own foreign policy: People of all backgrounds were welcome there. That kind of hospitality was an indication that divine wisdom was flowing through the new king at this stage in his reign. God was sovereign over all the world, and all people could find refuge in His care.

## 2 CHRONICLES 10:16–19

### Is civil rebellion ever justified?

The Bible is not definitive on this point, so each person, church, and movement must come to peace with its position. Certainly the Bible includes several stories of resistance to government, even armed resistance. Sometimes, as in this passage, no moral judgment is attached to the report of resistance. Warfare is constant throughout the Old Testament, including warfare ordained by God.

The New Testament contains admonition to submit to civil authority (Romans 13:1), to render to government its due (Matthew 22:21), and to make an effort to be peaceable (1 Thessalonians 5:13). The triumphant mood of Old Testament violence gives way to the submissive posture of New Testament suffering (Matthew 5:9). Whereas in the Old Testament a nation was to be built, in the New Testament the very idea of national citizenship seems secondary compared to citizenship in the kingdom of God.

In view of these changes, is civil rebellion a Christian option today? It may be, under conditions of limited and controlled violence (or passive resistance, without violence) directed toward relieving oppression, when all reasonable negotiation has failed. In the above instance of the stoning of Adoniram, we know too little about the context. By New Testament standards, some other plan would certainly find greater sanction.

## 2 CHRONICLES 12:1

### Why do strong rulers tend to abandon God?

The impulse to rule is one of the most formidable of human emotions and has certainly been responsible for considerable suffering.

When unchecked by true devotion to God, it employs power to achieve its ambition and leaves destruction in its wake.

There is a kind of devotion to God that also can feed the impulse to rule without modifying its passion. That devotion comes to believe so completely in the rightness of rule, that God is counted as an ally and nothing thereafter can stop the surge or qualify its extent.

Strong rulers tend to abandon God because they do not want to submit to God in the first place—they only want to use God as a means to their own achievements. Once in power, God and every other inconvenience is dumped as the petty ruler blissfully cherishes the myth of his or her own invulnerability.

The key to strong, enduring, and righteous rule is strong faith in and submission to God, whose righteousness alone is worth serving. No earthly rule can last forever, but rule without God is worthless, corrupt, and undeserving of loyalty.

## 2 CHRONICLES 13:17

### How could ancient Israel sustain 500,000 war casualties in a day?

The battle of Gettysburg, the bloodiest three days in U.S. war history, saw about 100,000 men fall. The entire Vietnam war involved about 55,000 U.S. casualties. A half-million dead and injured in one day is a staggering sum, almost more violence than we can conceive an army enduring.

Bible scholars have long contested the high numbers reported through the Chronicles, arguing that units of thousands may have been counted but with fewer actually present. With respect to the half-million figure, counting so many dead probably would have surpassed the capability of a field army anyhow, so we must rest with estimates and not be too insistent that the half-million number reflects a head count, man by man.

Ancient warfare was usually hand-to-hand combat with many casualties.

## 2 CHRONICLES 15:1

### How did the Spirit of God "come upon" ancient leaders?

The mechanics are unclear, as always, but the result was a special sense of divine help and presence that enabled the leader to do God's will. In very few places in the Bible is the coming of the Holy Spirit described in any detail (see Acts 2), but the Spirit descends, fills, and empowers according to God's will and purpose. In this case, Azariah's filling enabled the delivery of a word from God to King Asa. The result was a strong stand by Asa against pagan worship in his kingdom.

## 2 CHRONICLES 16:12

### What's so important about seeking God's help with disease?

Healing the body is an art and a science. Beyond that, the Bible assures us of God's interest in health and healing (Luke 9:11), though in some cases an ailment is allowed to linger for reasons connected to spiritual growth. Asa's not seeking divine help with his foot disease is mystifying, but the note included here is a warning to others: Consultation with doctors is important, but God's role in healing cannot be dismissed as nonscientific or irrelevant.

While some religious sects have abandoned science and count only on divine intervention, many more have abandoned God and count only on science. Even medical practitioners, however, increasingly recognize the importance of prayer and faith, though few have the ability to explain it.

## 2 CHRONICLES 17–18

### Does God always set conditions for His blessing?

Yes, always, but not forever. The most well known of all announcements of God's blessing, John 3:16, holds within it a condition: "so that everyone who believes." Only in heaven itself, when the possibility of sin is past, will that blessing be unconditional. There, goodness will be pure and temptation absent, eliminating the need for conditional promises and introducing God's people to such wonders and blessings as the mind cannot imagine.

## 2 CHRONICLES 18:21–22

### Does God endorse deception?

Everywhere the portrait of God's character in the Bible is that of integrity, trustworthiness, and honesty. God hates lying (Proverbs 12:22). Lying is a human trait, not a divine one (Romans 3:4). Liars deserve condemnation (Revelation 21:8). God is totally opposed to lying and stands completely against it as a means of achieving His will. How then does God approve of lying in this instance?

If the description of the scene here is taken as a stenographer's record of the facts, then God has made an exception to His general prohibition on lying. If the description is rather an explanation aimed at achieving a result with Ahab himself, then the account is a prophet's depiction. God, portrayed as open to the use of lying, is given a "character" role in a story that does not reflect the real existence and character of God.

In any case, the endorsement God provides in this story is so exceptional that it cannot be taken as predictive of His normal operating procedure. God opposes lying, and God cannot oppose Himself.

## History remembers Ahab as an evil king. How can a person avoid that kind of legacy?

A good legacy comes from a life well lived in the service of God, filled with generosity and forgiveness, loyalty to friends, and honesty to all. Is this possible?

The first step to such a life is recognizing that God has a claim on us, that God's will is our duty, and that service, not wealth and honor, is our goal. Holding these values sincerely requires coming to God in faith and trusting Christ as Lord. Once forgiven of sin and strengthened by the Holy Spirit, a person can build a legacy based on virtue rather than on power and greed.

## Why does a good leader ignore the advice he has worked so hard to receive?

We live in a world of conflicting loyalties. Friends may want us to do something we know is not approved by God. A boss may want us to work through our normal worship time. Conflicts never cease.

Perhaps Jehoshaphat felt some kinship with his fellow monarch Ahab, hard as that may be to imagine. Perhaps Jehoshaphat pitied Ahab for the hard married life he had endured. Perhaps Ahab threatened to call Jehoshaphat "chicken." You can imagine reasons yourself why a sensible, sane, and moral course of action is exchanged for a questionable plan that no right-minded person would approve. Jehoshaphat's mistake is a lesson on paying more attention to the kind of friends you keep.

The evil King Ahab dies on the battlefield after a stray arrow wounds him.

# 2 Chronicles 20:21

## What sort of battle plan has a choir leading an army?

None that makes much military sense, if using traditional tactics is the key to victory. The genius of God's ways is that they are not our ways. Tactics that should fail do in fact succeed as God's way of showing His power in our weakness. At Jericho, the victory was preceded by priests blowing horns and circling the city seven times. Against the Philistines, David's single slingshot led to an amazing victory.

Yet, on second look, perhaps Jehoshaphat's plan was not without military cunning. As music stirs the soul, armies have learned to use music for motivation and bravery. The roll of drums or bugle blast can stir the soldier to selfless action. The Normandy invasion of World War II is associated with the first movement of Beethoven's Fifth Symphony. Why shouldn't Jehoshaphat's army hear the sound of many voices praising the God of protection and might? If you were an archer in the ranks that day, wouldn't you want a little music to calm your jitters, make you brave, and remind you of God's power?

# 2 Chronicles 21:4

## How could anyone be so cruel as to execute all his brothers?

Jehoram was the world's best-known fratricidal maniac. He waited until power was solidly in his palm, then wiped out all possible bloodline competitors. The crime carried little strategic advantage, and alternatives, such as appointing brothers to cabinet posts, might have been more effective in securing Jehoram's reputation and power.

The crime speaks to the decrepit condition of Jehoshaphat's family. He may have had some kingly qualities, but his fathering skills were at rock bottom. Only one of his seven sons survived, and that one was the killer of all the rest. Jehoshaphat may have learned to sing in battle (2 Chronicles 20:21), but he never learned to sing to his own kids at bedtime—and probably never taught them about the goodness of the Lord, the source of all joy and strength.

# 2 Chronicles 24:18

## Why would good leaders quickly and completely turn against God?

Judah's unnamed leaders here wasted no time rushing for popular approval by promoting multideity religion and abandoning worship of the true God. It's as if they read the polls, figured the masses wanted lots of religious choice, and wanted to be first in line for reelection.

Greed, lust for power, and prestige often cloud human judgment. When the promotion of self or career takes priority over God, bad things happen. These leaders let power go to their heads, failing to see how history would judge them, not to mention how God Himself would. Fortunately, one voice for God remained in that pack of rats. It was the prophet Zechariah, son of the man who raised Joash from childhood. By then Joash was so compromised that he agreed to Zechariah's public execution.

These leaders did not survive for along. Not a year passed before marauding Arameans attacked Judah and dispatched them all to the judgment they did not foresee. Imagine their fright when they discovered that polling data failed to account for the one opinion in all the universe that matters most. God will have His way.

## Why is the number seven so special?

The number seven is associated with completeness and perfection. God rested on the seventh day of creation (Genesis 2:2). Forgiveness extends to a function of seven (Matthew 18:21). All churches are represented by seven (Revelation 1:4).

Biblical numerologists attempt to locate hidden meanings in some numbers, as if God communicates to us in code. These attempts are misguided. God's message is open and transparent, ready for all to hear and follow. No need exists for secrecy in the communication of the gospel. The number seven, associated since ancient times with the lunar calendar, is no more or less holy than any other number. To give it special status (license plates, lucky dice, etc.) is to approach creating an idol.

## Do angels intervene in human affairs?

This story and several others tell us that angels may direct, alter, or guide the course of human events at God's command and pleasure. We cannot know how or when such intervention may occur. Indeed, we are warned that often it happens discreetly and without fanfare (Hebrews 13:2).

Is it possible for praying Christians to direct the activities and energies of angels, to enlist their aid? No. Angels respond only to God's voice and will. Otherwise, humans could conceivably aggravate rebellion in heaven, directing angels toward sinful human goals. Prayer should always be directed to God, not to angels.

Angels praise God in heaven and serve Him by helping His people on earth.

## 2 CHRONICLES 35:20–22

**Why did the Israelites settle so many issues by killing instead of negotiation and political compromise?**

The Egyptian king Neco appears to be a more peaceable ruler than the Israelite leader Josiah. Neco wanted passage, not a fight. Josiah chose to fight and lost his life. What makes a person choose violence over peace talks?

The Bible is not explicit about Josiah's reasons. But the Bible offers one reason why Josiah, and others like him, make bad choices: sin. In this case, sin was expressed in pride, a false sense of valor, and possibly some wrongly forged alliances. Josiah may have boxed himself into a corner, allowing few alternatives and forcing him into a showdown with the Egyptian army.

Such showdowns are never foreordained, however. Josiah could have chosen the less violent road, the path of honorable peace, the compromise that keeps core values intact while saving lives and reducing harm. Creative negotiation can often avert disaster without jeopardizing faith and fortune.

## 2 CHRONICLES 36:16

**Is there a sin for which no remedy exists?**

The remedy for all sin is God's forgiveness. It is the only remedy, and it is available to all. God is eager to forgive, and He does so at His own cost. We pay nothing but only believe.

Forgiveness, like all gifts, however, can be refused, spurned, or mocked. The Bible warns that those who mock God's gift will find the offer of forgiveness discontinued. What a tragic situation. People who are loved by God, offered life and hope, can end up without any hope at all because they repeatedly spurn the gift.

Yes, there is a sin for which no remedy exists: the sin that refuses to accept the only remedy for sin and thus loses God's generous gift forever.

# EZRA

*Leaders anywhere, anytime can benefit from this courageous priest and scribe. Ezra had what it takes to see the truth and motivate people to follow it.*

## EZRA 1:1

### Why did Cyrus allow the Jews to return to their homeland?

King Cyrus of Persia was basically positive and tolerant toward Israel's faith. He believed it was good for his kingdom to allow different groups some degree of independence, especially with respect to religious practice. Above and beyond Cyrus's religious tolerance, God moved his heart to allow the Jews to return to Jerusalem. God frequently "stirred the heart" of pagan kings to get a mission accomplished or an individual out of trouble.

## EZRA 1:5

### Why was it important for Ezra and his followers to restore the temple?

The temple represented the center of Israel's religious life, the glory of Israel, the symbol of all that made Israel special as the people of God. While the temple lay desolate, the people's sense of identity and unity was in disrepair. Until they attended to the house of God, things would not be right in the house of Israel.

## EZRA 9

### Why was Ezra so upset about mixed marriages?

Israel's greatest problem throughout its history was syncretism—the mixing of pagan religion with worship of the true God. God judged Israel severely for failing to keep worship clean and pure. And one of the easiest inroads to Israel's heart was through intermarriage with pagan peoples. Ezra knew this well, thus his vehement and emotional opposition to taking foreign spouses.

God's overriding concern was that the nation of Israel be distinct from surrounding nations. As Israel obeyed the Lord's commands, they witnessed to other nations of the glory of God above all other gods. So the injunction against intermarrying was to prevent the loss of witness to the truth, as with Solomon whose several foreign wives were said to turn his heart from God (1 Kings 11:1–13).

The prohibition against intermarriage was not absolute. Deuteronomy 21 contains regulations for marrying women taken captive in war. Examples of interracial marriage include Moses and a Midianite woman, Boaz and the Moabite Ruth. The key issue is faithfulness to Christ. Any marriage that jeopardizes faith is wrong.

Ezra, a priest and scribe, honors God and follows His will by teaching the people God's law and encouraging them to rebuild the temple.

# NEHEMIAH

*Building walls might seem like boring work, but when God's plan called for perseverance and hard labor, no one responded as well as this leader.*

## NEHEMIAH 1:4

### Why did Nehemiah weep at news of conditions in Jerusalem?

Nehemiah was probably born into slavery in Persia. Though he knew himself to be a Jew, the son of Hacaliah, his only knowledge of his family's homeland came from the scriptures, people's stories, and the occasional news brought by travelers. Jerusalem had been destroyed in 586 B.C., and most of the people had been displaced to Babylon. Within fifty years, a trickle of refugees began returning to the land. By 515 B.C. a small version of the temple had been rebuilt. The rest of the city and land remained in shambles.

Daniel had prophesied that the promised land would remain desolate for seventy years. Nehemiah knew this time was coming to an end. He was probably eager to hear what efforts were under way to rebuild the city and resettle the land. His weeping came as he realized how desperate the conditions were at home. He was also overwhelmed to think that God might have placed him in position to accomplish the task of revitalizing the land of Israel.

Leaders are often people of great passion, and passion may be displayed in several ways. Bible characters often weep in agony over conditions of people and places far away as God's vision for reconciliation begins to take shape in their minds and hearts.

## NEHEMIAH 1:4–11

### How did Nehemiah practice prayer?

Nehemiah is an example of a person who lived by prayer. He responded to difficulty with prayer. He planned in prayer. He prayed before he spoke. When he evaluated his work, he did so in prayer. When others attacked, mocked, or threatened him, Nehemiah prayed.

Nehemiah didn't become effective in prayer because he had only big matters to pray about. He prayed about everything and became very good at doing it. Nehemiah lived by the principle described by Paul centuries later in Philippians 4:6–7: "Don't worry about anything; instead, pray about everything. Tell God what you need, and thank him for all he has done. If you do this, you will experience God's peace, which is far more wonderful than the human mind can understand."

## NEHEMIAH 2:5

### Why would God arrange to destroy the temple (accomplished by Nebuchadnezzar in 586 B.C.) only to order its rebuilding later?

Jerusalem and the magnificent temple that crowned the city belonged to God, but God was not bound to them. The temple was not God. Centuries later, in Athens, another stunning temple city, the apostle Paul said, "Since he is Lord of heaven and earth, he doesn't live in man-made temples" (Acts 17:24). Nehemiah realized that the destruction of Jerusalem had not been an accident of history. God had warned the Israelites that forsaking Him would lead to suffering and humiliation. The warnings were specific, but they were ignored. God kept His word.

God was not done with His people or His plan, however. Even His promises to punish included a ray of hope. Just as God had rescued His people from slavery in Egypt, He promised to bring them back from exile in Persia.

God was willing to allow His temple to be destroyed and rebuilt, not because He was interested in building and cities but because He was after people's hearts. As long as the temple represented the people's devotion to God, things went well. When devotion to the temple became a substitute for obedience to God, life became difficult.

## NEHEMIAH 8

### Why was Ezra's reading of God's law so powerful?

The events that occurred at the Water Gate in Nehemiah's time can be described as a spiritual revival. The people knew that God had made it possible for them to rebuild the city. Now they were ready to hear what else God would say to them. They listened intently. When Ezra opened the scroll of God's law, they stood out of respect and anticipation over what they were about to hear.

Then the people responded personally, corporately, and immediately to God's Word. In the days that followed, they were quick to put into practice what had been read. The Water Gate revival was a time of significant obedient listening by God's people to God's message, a recovery of a vision and a hope.

The temple of God is destroyed by foreign armies.

# ESTHER

*This book has all the elements of a great story: a powerful king, a beautiful queen, and an archenemy. Would God's people survive?*

## THE BOOK OF ESTHER

### The book of Esther doesn't mention God, so why is it included in the Old Testament?

True, Esther doesn't mention the name of God, yet underlying the story are veiled references to God. Cousin Mordecai encourages Esther to go before King Xerxes saying, "Who can say but that you have been elevated to the palace for just such a time as this?" (Esther 4:14). He was implying that God might use Esther to deliver the Jews. Esther then asks Mordecai to gather the Jews and fast; she herself fasted for three days (Esther 4:3) showing her petition to God for assistance.

Scenes from the book of Esther.

While not mentioning God directly, Esther does illustrate God's amazing provision for and protection of His people. Sometimes actions speak louder than words. Esther demonstrates God's providence without articulating what would be obvious to the Jewish reader.

# JOB

*Renowned for his patience, Job was just a man who had to deal with much loss, anger, depression, and finally submission to God's will . . . as we all do at one time or another.*

## JOB 1:6–7

### Are Satan and God on speaking terms?

The Lord speaks; Satan speaks. They talk about Job as if they are negotiating over the evil initiatives that Satan proposes and the constraints that God imposes. Do cosmic conversations like this really happen?

The Bible often pictures a divine council discussing human events—how lives will unfold, how events will transpire. Using analogies to human experience, Bible authors describe these episodes to explain how a good all-powerful God, tolerates and then redeems evil in the world. These are not newspaper reports, eyewitness accounts of divine summits; they are the best way to understand a vast spiritual warfare being conducted behind and through the events of world history and our personal histories. This warfare is between God, whose victory is certain, and Satan, who futilely yet persistently seeks to subvert God's plan.

God and Satan, pictured in discussion here, are not equals in a contest over the universe. Satan is as much a creature as we are, yet without hope and pathetically underequipped for the task to which he aspires. He can run but cannot hide. He rejects God's authority but cannot escape God's sovereignty. Here Satan needs permission to proceed. Once he wrecks Job's life, Satan disappears from the drama.

## JOB 1:12

### Why does God allow Satan to wreck a good man's life?

What God allowed in Job's life and what Satan attempted provide a laboratory for examining spiritual warfare, the battle of good over evil being waged behind the scenes throughout history. Job becomes a prototype of every person who seeks to understand justice and of every victim of injustice. Satan wanted to demonstrate the purely pragmatic basis of religious yearning: People will believe when life is sweet but rebel when things go sour. God granted permission for the experiment to proceed within certain bounds.

Satan's experiment backfired. Job did not curse God, though he agonized over the "why" questions. Job was not destroyed—he prospered in the end. Faith is not fraudulent, but strong and sturdy. And the universe is not malicious, but just and merciful, since God's character, not Satan's malice, defines the moral life of human experience.

Did Job grow in faith? Painfully and slowly, yes. Did Job discover more about the meaning of personal trust in God? Through coming to terms with his own finitude and culpability, yes. Are these life lessons vitally important for every person? Yes, indeed.

Fortunately, not all of us endure the extent of Job's tragedies—but none of us is far from the taste of grief or guilt, either. Job emerges with a new understanding of God's care, and so can we. His life was wrecked only in the short term. God redeemed it in the end. Job lived this tragic story so that we could see more clearly the extent of God's care and protection.

## JOB 1:21

### How did Job endure his tragedies?

He had a pretty good life, all a person could want. Then he lost it all by such a string of tragic coincidences that someone could imagine a plot behind the trauma. Then Job got his life back, and more. While the end was happy, that's a tough roller-coaster ride for anyone.

Job may be the oldest book in the Bible, yet it deals with questions people wonder about every day: Why do bad things happen to good people? Why isn't life fair? Does God

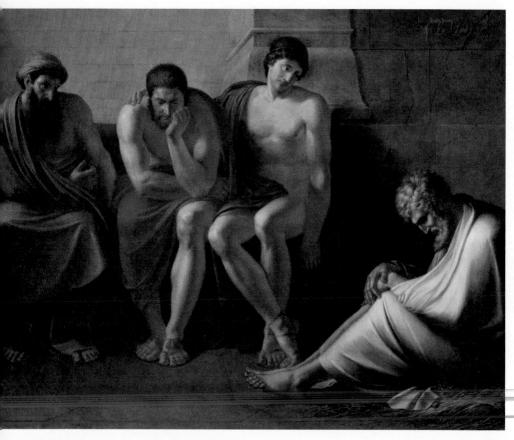

Job's friends gather around and share in his tragedy.

care? Some of these questions are answered in Job; some are not. One of the book's central lessons is that God does not owe His creatures an explanation. Yet we owe God trust even when we don't understand what is happening.

God had something better than "answers" for Job—a relationship grounded in the nature and character of God alone. God does not test us (James 1:13), and we are not to examine God (Deuteronomy 6:16). God doesn't reject questions; God rejects attitudes and motives that demand from Him, or suspect malice, or doubt His justice, or question His authority. God submits to no one's cross-examination; yet God reaches out to the needy and the miserable with tender mercies that Job profoundly experienced, mercies that carried him through the valleys and up to the mountaintops.

## Job 2:11

### What's the right way to help a friend through a tragedy?

Job's three friends helped at the start, but ultimately they failed in the difficult task of assisting someone through tragedy. Their first approach was to identify and share, as much as they could, in Job's grief. They cried with him, tore their clothing as a sign of sadness, and threw dust on their heads. They just sat with Job for a long time, no words needed or spoken. All this led Job to express his deepest feelings to them. This was good and helpful.

Then things changed. Job's deepest feelings were mixed with too many probing questions for the three friends, who wanted (and apparently had) an airtight view of God and moral goodness: All bad events are linked to human sin. To this group, Job's tragedy was linked to some hidden fault that Job needed to confess. The friends became accusatory. We can understand this. If Job

was not at fault, who was?

The friends could have admitted their own ignorance before Job's questions. They could have asked God, with Job, for more understanding. Instead, they forced Job's experience into their own grid, insisting that Job's life held the clue to his downfall. They had to assign guilt, and Job was the only candidate.

Personal responsibility must surely be a part of every person's approach to hard times, yet these friends would have been more effective by listening more sympathetically to Job's distress and sharing his immense confusion and pain, not by trying to impose their boxlike theologies onto his well-rounded questions. Sometimes listening is a greater gift than talking. And as a help in suffering, the lecture method is almost always a loser.

## Job 42:16

### What did Job gain from his ordeal?

Through his difficult experience, Job realized two facts about his questions concerning God: Some were based in ignorance, some in arrogance.

The questions themselves were not the problem. Job was not wrong to vent his grief in questions concerning justice and morality. But he (and we) act in ignorance when we persist with questions God has already answered, and we act in arrogance when we persist with questions that God has chosen not to answer—or not to answer to our satisfaction. Either track—ignorance or arrogance—demonstrates a profound misunderstanding of God and a confusion over the rights and roles of Creator and created. Job discovered that he could humbly ask God anything; he also learned that God is not obliged to put all the pieces of the puzzle in place.

Job also gained back his fortunes. He was

vindicated and restored, not as a payment for enduring Satan's test, but by grace pure and simple—God's choice for his life, joy in the sunshine after the rain.

And that is precisely the promise of God to every person on earth. No bargains, no payments for services rendered, no contracts for "doing well"—just the benefits of God's sovereign generosity freely given to all who trust in His magnanimity, shown to us in Christ primarily, and in answers to prayer and daily blessings as little reminders of the heavenly treasures waiting to be revealed.

# PSALMS

*Perhaps the most widely read book in the Bible, these songs and poems lead us to ask why someone so big (God) would care about things so small (us).*

## PSALM 1:2

### Should people today take time to meditate?

With so many message "inputs" competing for our attention, now is the best time in history to meditate on God's Word. No previous generation has ever been so media rich and meditation poor. Who can hear God through the roar of cellular phones, television comedies, Web sites, and special-effects motion pictures? Most people never think about God during the day, much less meditate on His Word.

Granted, meditating on God's Word means less time for sales and fewer billable hours. In a culture that trades time for money, meditation carries a cost. Can we afford it? People today who take time to meditate are choosing spiritual wealth as the first priority. Who can afford *not* to?

## PSALM 5:5

### Is God capable of hate as well as love?

Any description of God will necessarily use terms and ideas solidly anchored in human experience. Our own experience, after all, is our only reference point for knowing God. It should be no surprise, then, that most of the emotions people feel are attributed to God at some time: jealousy, fatigue, rapture, love, and even hate.

What kind of hate would God feel? Not the hate born of fear, as a soldier hates an enemy. Not the hate born of blind rage, as a jealous lover hates his competitor. Not the hate that seeks to conquer, as a tyrant hates people living just over the border. Not the hate of political intrigue, as an office-holder hates the other party.

God's hate is directed at evil. It is hate that burns at offense against God's own character, which is altogether holy and good. God's hate smokes when creation witnesses to a reality other than God, namely, a reality based on greed and anger. God's hate is directed toward purification, not annihilation. God's hate seeks recovery, not death.

Does God hate people? A careful distinction must be kept here. The Bible is clear that God wants all people to know His forgiveness and grace. But some will refuse, mocking God's character and rejecting His overture of mercy. When that refusal becomes entrenched, God promises judgment apart from the mercy of

Christ. When rebellion against God becomes the identifying mark of a person, that person must become the object of God's righteous hatred.

We can safely say that God has a steady hatred toward sin and a reluctant hatred toward committed sinners. In an odd way that reaches beyond human experience, God hates as a function of His love. That is, God's defining characteristic is love. Included in God's love is hatred for all that stands opposed to His character and violates His intentions.

gift and responsibility settled on humans, by God's design and will.

People, therefore, do not rule over creation as final authorities. Rather, people are stewards over God's creation. A good manager cares for the property of his employer and is compensated according to the growth of assets in his domain (Matthew 24:46). Whether your vocation is law, plumbing, education, forestry, or ministry, God is pleased when your circle of responsibility is well managed—that is, handled with integrity, virtue, and vision.

## PSALM 8:6

### In what sense are people rulers over creation?

At creation, God set humankind above all other species to rule and subdue the earth (Genesis 1:28). Conceivably, reason, intelligence, and self-consciousness could have been given to fish or birds, but, in fact, the

## PSALM 18:7–15

### Why does God seem so frightening?

The psalmist has an extremely high view of God's ability to respond mightily to the believer's plea for help. He uses poetic language to describe the indescribable—God's almighty power. God sounds frightening because He is. When God acts to help someone prevail over injustice,

God brings the animals to Adam and Adam names them. The odd shape red outlines are repairs to the actual tiles in the original mosaic.

the energy God expends will be much more frightening than the victim's adversary.

While God's omnipotent power is awesome, the believer can be assured that God acts on our behalf, not against us. The forcefulness of God's intervention may be like a hurricane, affecting everyone around, but the intention is always to rescue the faithful believer from sin and suffering.

## PSALM 23:3

### What is the practical value of God's promise to "renew my strength"?

Some Bible versions translate this phrase as "He restores my soul." The modern era has often been called the psychotherapeutic age. More people are seeing counselors than ever before; more counselors are in business than ever before. Something must be wrong with the soul. Indeed, there is. Causes are numerous, complicated, and controversial. But this much is certain: Many people are unhappy and don't know why. Their sense of self-worth is bruised by job loss; their sense of moral rightness shattered by divorce, bad decisions, or children who have rejected family values. People need help.

Perhaps, after food and shelter, renewing and restoring the soul is the most practical need we have. A restored soul

♦ does not take the blame for every problem in the world but does accept personal responsibility and intends, by forgiveness and reconciliation, to restore broken relationships.

♦ does not run itself into the ground with criticism but does cheerfully accept gifts and weaknesses as God's grant to live to His glory.

♦ does not dwell on failure—or believe failure to be inevitable—but does count on the promises of God as the one sure hope.

The practical result of restoring the soul is the difference between a defeated life and a life victorious in Christ, rich with potential, realistic about its purposes, and able to love even when it hurts.

## PSALM 25:13

### Does full-hearted devotion to God lead to prosperity?

Yes and no. If the prosperity you're after is colored green, comes in quantities of thousands and hundred thousands, and

A small terracotta jug and ancient coins. Many people think prosperity means to be wealthy, but to God it means something different.

carries portraits of American presidents, then no. Sorry. Devotion to God is not a guarantee of financial prosperity. Certainly, there are biblical principles of stewardship that, when followed, enhance financial security. But many Christians today (and in the past) are very poor yet nonetheless prosperous spiritually.

If the prosperity you seek centers on being happy, hopeful, capable of love, sure about life after death, and eager to try activities that present an element of risk and adventure, then answer the question in the affirmative. In faith, all people "prosper" when they live in relationship with God.

## PSALM 30:3

### Where is "the pit"?

"The pit" is called "Sheol" in some translations, and this psalm presupposes that actual places exist in the realm of the spirit. Not quite.

Just as heaven cannot really be reached by flying "up," so Sheol, the place of the dead, cannot really be reached by digging "down." Yet spatial terms are the only tools we have to describe where the spirits of the dead "go." So the Bible regularly describes Sheol, the place of the dead, as a downward hike toward the center of the earth, as if a huge underground grave existed for semicomatose spirits waiting

for something. The Bible also describes people ascending into heaven (Elijah in 2 Kings 2:11; Jesus in Acts 1:9).

We might more accurately say that Sheol is the Old Testament's "waiting area," where the souls of the dead rest (and in some passages, suffer the pain of judgment). Nowhere is Sheol described as a place to be eagerly anticipated, and how souls graduate from Sheol into some other happier place is not terribly clear.

In the New Testament, however, these questions are answered much more directly. The souls of those who trust in Jesus for salvation enjoy His presence in a place of joy and reunion (John 14:1–4). Souls who depart this life apart from the merits of Jesus' sacrifice on the cross must anticipate, at a minimum, the boredom of the Old Testament's picture of Sheol; and at worst, an eternal environment of suffering the penalty for their own sins (Matthew 13:42).

## PSALM 33:19

### Do Christians ever starve?

The psalm does not suppose to establish a fact, but to praise God for promises made and for daily care over even the most ordinary life needs. That God would care about our food needs would have been a radical idea in Old Testament times. Pagan gods cared, in the imagination of pagan worshipers, only about their own selfish reputation, never about those who gave them homage. Pagan deities were "me-centered," but the God of Israel actually provided for His people, again and again.

This is not to say, though, that in times of crisis, including famine,

Statues depicting a time of famine in Ireland.

only nonbelievers succumb. Christians feel hunger along with their neighbors and often perish in the same disasters that afflict their region. The pervasive influence of sin works against the intentions of God. It is the job of Christians to resist sin in all its forms, so churches are right to send food relief to hungry people worldwide. When one region shares its abundance with another, we witness to God's grace by overcoming, if only temporarily, the hurtful impact of sin.

## PSALM 34:6

### Will God eliminate all trouble from our lives?

Some Christians actually preach this idea, and many people become disillusioned when their experience turns painful. The only people who can claim to live trouble-free are those who redefine "trouble" into a word that describes absolutely nothing. Only with this kind of word play (theology run amok) can Christians claim that their life experience is trouble-free. The Bible's most mature believers (for example, Abraham, Moses, David, and Paul) endured considerable trouble. But they faced their trouble in the belief that God would certainly win in the end—a vindication of good over the pernicious influence of bad.

This is God's twofold promise: (1) In all our troubles, He gives us strength and grace; His love is present even in the worst situation; and (2) at the end of our lives (or at the end of history), He will indeed save all of His children from trouble—and take us to heaven for an eternity of happiness and joy.

Surely this psalm reminds us that people who are broken, at their wit's end, and at the brink of hopelessness can find in God a Helper who will never abandon or forget them—and always lead them through the crisis to victory.

## PSALM 34:10

### Will God give us anything we want?

To lack nothing (the promise of this psalm) is not the same thing as to have everything. And to imagine that God is ready to open His sack of goodies to put all our wants under our beds during the night is to live in a hopelessly imaginary world where the triune God of the Bible is remade into a giant version of Santa Claus.

Yes, some of the Bible's instructions about how to pray and how to share could lead a person to believe that anything, absolutely anything, is obtainable with sufficient faith. Want to be filthy rich? Pray in faith. Want to recover the fitness of a seventeen-year-old? Pray in faith. Want to have this, want to do that. . . ?

God's promises hold immense value, but not as people measure value. God's promise that we will "lack no good thing" cannot mean perfect bodily health and worldly wealth, those being typical human measures of happiness. To lack nothing rather refers to: (1) spiritual resources to meet life's difficulties, and (2) eventual heavenly resources to vindicate God's holy community in Christ. On the first count, God promises joy, peace, strength, and hope. Life will bring its hits, but God's resources are there to carry us through. On the second count, Christ has paid the penalty for all human sin, and God has gathered a very large "community of saints" that will celebrate forever Christ's victory. That promise of celebration is God's guarantee before the fact. In heaven we will lack nothing, for all will be provided.

## PSALM 38:4

### What is the point of feeling guilt?

Guilt is bad, many counselors and therapists tell us. Guilt is therapeutic, we learn from the counsel of the Bible. Which is right?

To feel guilt is to:

♦ *Admit need.* You have fallen short of expectations, and you're ashamed. You want to do better, but how? You want to enjoy the respect of people around you, but how to recover it?

♦ *Admit imperfection.* What a moment of insight to discover that you're not perfect. Something's wrong and needs to be fixed. Who's going to fix it?

♦ *Admit hope.* You're looking for something more, something lasting, something pure—happiness not mixed with greedy motives or self-centeredness. Where can you find it?

Guilt leads to God: our need for God, our hope in God. That makes guilt a very good thing. Don't run from guilt, or dismiss it, or regard it as a psychological complex amenable to therapy or drugs. Let guilt lead you straight to God, who always forgives, restores, and lightens the load. In Christ, guilt is forgotten, dismissed, washed, and drained. Guilt is a hunger for God, and God has a feast ready for you.

## PSALM 49:15

### Before Christ, how did people get to heaven?

People have always gotten to heaven by one way only—God's way—through the work of Jesus Christ, His Son. That is the gospel, God's Good News: God has made a way through an

God is on His throne, and His followers are worshiping Him and giving glory to His name.

intractable divide between human sinfulness and divine holiness. That way is Jesus.

In the Old Testament era, believers (more often called "God's people") saw the gospel only through the system of ritual and sacrifice that was a prelude to the one perfect sacrifice (Jesus' own life) for sin. To die in the community of the covenant was to be assured that God would somehow provide prosperity in the afterlife. That was David's hope in this psalm.

In the New Testament, the way to heaven is much clearer. Everywhere the Good News is given: "Believe on the Lord Jesus and you will be saved" (Acts 16:31). Old Testament believers anticipated Christ's death and resurrection, while people in the Christian era look back to it.

## PSALM 56:6–7

### Is praying for revenge okay?

Revenge as a common human feeling has a long history. Legal scholars, for example, believe that revenge is the basis for all jurisprudence. When Harry first stole a cow from Joe, Joe took two of Harry's goats. Then Harry grabbed three of Joe's turkeys. And Joe, seeing where this could lead, mustered the village elders. Thus the first court was born. We seem to have an intuitive sense of justice and fairness that wants all wrongs to be made right, especially wrongs done against us. Revenge is our impulse to fix injustice. In that sense, praying for revenge may be just another name for praying that God will hear our tort claims, judge wrongdoers for their unjust deeds, and levy a just sentence. Thus we will not need to seek revenge ourselves.

Revenge today, however, also carries the sense of "eye-for-an-eye" get-even politics. Revenge seems mean-spirited, primitive, and adversarial. Surely Christian forgiveness offers a more advanced option than retribution at the hand of a divine judge.

Praying for God's justice removes our need to seek revenge. When a grievous injustice has been done, prayer is the only course of action that will quiet the cycle of violence. Imagine how Tutsis and Hutus in Rwanda, for example, could ever repair their broken relationships apart from leaving revenge to God alone, whose mercy and justice are both limitless. Better to leave to God the task of righting wrongs than to live with neighbors always notching up the price of being made whole.

## PSALM 60:8

### Does God "put down" certain nations?

Yes, God decides to prosper some nations (Old Testament Israel most dramatically) at the expense of neighboring nations (three are mentioned in this psalm). As land is limited, when God gives land to Israel, it must come at someone's expense. In this case, Canaanite fiefdoms "lose." In that sense, some nations are put down.

The more difficult question is whether God puts down certain nations today. Some Christians teach that America was (and maybe still is) a blessed nation, while America's adversaries have been subject to God's judgment. Many First World Christians have imagined that their prosperity is a sign of God's favor, while the poverty of the Third World shows divine "put down." Such reasoning is treacherous, for it leads the wealthy to disdain the poor and gives wrongheaded theological support to racism and class prejudice.

Prayer today should include calling on God to restrain evil in certain lands, retard the influence of rulers bent on violence, and encourage the work of peace. In praying for such intervention, we may well be asking God to "put down" a nation, while leaving the means and extent of such restraint to divine wisdom.

## PSALM 63:4

### Why lift up your hands to worship God?

Outstretched arms are a common sign of welcome, joy, and peace. For Christian worshipers to raise hands while singing or praying is a gesture signifying God's greatness and the joy of worshiping a loving Savior.

Lifting arms upward, of course, does not make the hands any closer to God than the feet, since God is not located in an "up" direction. We commonly believe, however, that heaven (God's abode) is up, not down, so we may be excused when we temporarily adopt mythic directional notions and raise hands rather than lower them. Either gesture, if intended to honor God, would be appropriate for worship.

## PSALM 70:1, 5

### Is it all right to ask God to "speed it up"?

The request that God speed His intervention is not a complaint about slowness so much as a free expression of the writer's acute sense of need. Everywhere the Bible encourages believers to speak openly with God about feelings, moods, and attitudes. The God of the Bible is not like the jealous, hypersensitive pagan deities who must always be placated and stroked to win their assistance. The true God desires intimacy and integrity with His people, not showy displays that mask the truth about human need and hurt.

Nonetheless, divine and human timing rarely coincide. People who feel intense need seek resolution to their crisis sooner rather than later. Prayer itself is a signal that a need persists, and each hour and day before deliverance makes pain more acute. God's promise is always to hear and answer, though not always when and where a given prayer might stipulate.

## PSALM 71:9–18

### Why ask God to remain faithful, as if God needed reminding?

The same question might be raised about any prayer on any subject. Why articulate requests to a God we confess to be omniscient? Isn't that like telling a math wizard that two plus two equals four?

In fact, prayer often recites the virtues of God in a way that serves our own memory and faith. We may passionately ask God to care for us, knowing full well that every promise in the Bible says He will. Such a prayer constitutes a reminder to us, since we cannot imagine in any real sense that we are informing God about matters unknown to Him. That we should pray is a clear biblical mandate. Intimate communication with God is the believer's privilege. Impossible by human skill alone, each prayer is a miracle.

## PSALM 78:34

### Does God kill people?

Death is one form of punishment by which God signals that violation of His holy commands carries a fearsome penalty. Death entered human experience after the Fall (Genesis 2–3), and occurred thereafter as a judgment for specific sin (Joshua 7:10–12). God, the giver of life, may also take life when purposes higher than human longevity are served.

Pagan deities were believed to hold powers of inflicting early death, so it is important to differentiate between God's judgment and pagan imagination. God is neither vicious nor fickle in life-and-death judgments. God is not merely trying His powers over human life, but moving history toward holy purpose. God does not regard death casually, as if expired people were no more significant than modern video-game villains. God may punish through death to express His holy and loving nature—which puts the issue of divine judgment in a completely different context than pagan retribution.

Finally, God's judgment on Achan and others is a preview of a much more fearsome and terrible judgment referred to in Revelation 20:11–15. This "second death" is to be avoided at all costs, for the Bible offers no remedy once this judgment is passed.

## PSALM 91:11

### Does everyone have a guardian angel?

The idea that a particular angel is assigned to each person or believer was popular during the medieval era but suffered under the theological housecleaning of the Reformation. Only one distant reference to the possibility occurs in Matthew 18:10.

Angels are God's servants to assist in achieving God's will, chiefly in communicating the gospel. Angels appear throughout the Bible to help people in trouble (Acts 5:19) and to assist the church (Acts 10:3).

Today we cannot know whether that close call averted was the result of angelic intervention, but we are reminded not to dismiss or disregard the work of angels (Hebrews 13:2). You may not have a particular angel assigned to your case, but a sovereign God knows your needs and meets them in His own way—sometimes, the Bible leads us to believe, through the work of angels.

## PSALM 102:10

### Why would God discard someone?

This psalm reports the writer's feelings, not the activity of God necessarily. In the middle of considerable trouble, the writer feels that God has abandoned him. After all, what other explanation could account for such distress? Surely trouble must have found a tear in the protective mantle of God's care. But if this psalm reports only feelings, still the question remains: Does God actually throw people out?

Only as a last resort (Revelation 19:20). At the final judgment, God will "discard" or banish from His presence every vestige of evil, everything not purified by Jesus' sacrifice on the cross. In eternity, holiness and sin cannot coexist. In the meantime, we may feel discarded, but the assurance of the Bible is that we are not. God is always ready to hear our prayers, even at the end of life, and He always welcomes the sinner who seeks to be forgiven. When you feel abandoned, pray and take comfort in the psalmist's rediscovery (verse 12) of God's presence and care.

Angels are God's servants and messengers.

# PROVERBS

*If this book does not raise questions for you, none will. In addition to those questions, however, look for plenty of wise answers.*

## PROVERBS 4:7

### What is wisdom?

Wisdom enables a person to live a life pleasing and honoring to the Lord. It includes knowledge but goes far beyond mere information. Wisdom is the ability to use knowledge to serve God—to blend heart, mind, and will in a unified life of devotion to God.

King Solomon, known for his wisdom, judges between the two mothers who claim one child as their own.

## PROVERBS 9:10

### What is meant by "fear of the LORD"?

While an element of literal fear is involved, this kind of fear refers more to a loving, reverential respect of God. The man or woman who "fears" the Lord will submit to God's will and care more about God's honor than self-esteem or wealth.

## PROVERBS 31:10

### Should women today cultivate the traditional kinds of behaviors honored in the Proverbs?

The Bible is sometimes accused of supporting a patriarchal culture and a husband-dominated home. Nothing could be further from the spirit and tone of these proverbs. Here, women lead in smart financial decisions, in style and fashion, and in that elusive but nonetheless universally celebrated quality of sexual attractiveness. This ideal wife cares about her family, has a variety of specialized skills to put to the service of people around her, and is not captured by false images of beauty her culture puts forward as the norm. Beauty, in fact, goes much deeper than cosmetics and body shape, this proverb notes well.

Does the woman celebrated here possess those strong inner qualities of wisdom, discernment, care, loyalty, and courage? Is the woman portrayed as a person living to the height and depth of her being? Yes, emphatically. Is the woman described here caught in a time warp of traditionalism, tied to her chores, prancing to the drumbeat of men, second class, and like a Barbie doll? Not a chance. God's advice to men and women is consistent over time: Cultivate the virtues that reflect the love and care God has for all people, and you will find peace, contentment, and passion. That's a message for every decade and era.

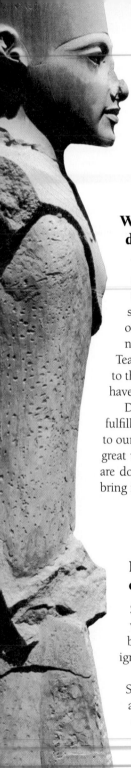

# ECCLESIASTES

*When you really think about it, much of life doesn't make sense. In this very honest Bible book, the author, widely believed to be Solomon, bares his soul and finally finds answers in God alone.*

## ECCLESIASTES 1:1–11

### Why should a man who has everything feel so depressed and despondent?

The Teacher in Ecclesiastes has everything, yet he still manages to feel depressed and despondent. The reasons he gives for his depression are the apparent meaninglessness of life and the fact that man cannot find satisfaction or contentment. Each new day is just a repetition of all the other days that have gone before. In fact, there is nothing that is actually new, nothing that is fresh. In a restless and weary turn of phrase, the Teacher coins the well-used quote: "History merely repeats itself." According to the Teacher's reasoning, there is no worth to be found in doing things that have already been done and seen and experienced by other people.

Depression is an easy pit to fall into. Absolutely nothing in life will bring fulfillment if we do not realize and understand that only God brings validity to our lives. We can achieve the highest statesmanship, amass fortunes, create great works of art, or spend our lives in humanitarian causes. If these things are done in the absence of God as Lord in our lives, however, they will not bring fulfillment; instead, they will only bring emptiness.

## ECCLESIASTES 1:18

### If knowledge brings grief, why should anyone be educated?

Solomon, the Teacher, remarks that the increase of knowledge and wisdom only brings greater grief and sorrow. This state of affairs naturally begs the question: Why be educated? Why not live out your life in happy ignorance?

Knowledge and wisdom are gifts from the Lord, however. Even Solomon himself advises that wisdom and understanding (knowledge) are to be greatly sought after. Specifically, he instructs the reader to "cry out for insight and understanding. Search for them as you would for lost money or hidden treasure" (Proverbs 2:3–4).

The Teacher goes on to say that wisdom and knowledge will allow you to understand the fear of the Lord and to gain knowledge of Him. If a side effect of being able to understand the fear of the Lord is greater sorrow, that side effect—sorrow—cannot be so harmful.

# ECCLESIASTES 2:8

## Why would the wisest of all men actually employ his wisdom for sexual adventure and variety?

Solomon employed his wisdom in a cold, calculating sort of way when he experimented with sexual adventures and variety. He was curious as to whether or not he could find any particle of meaning or happiness in living a life of foolishness. That foolishness, among other things, included wholesale sexual immorality. Solomon declares, in reference to his sexual license, that he "had everything a man could desire!" Yet even in that pleasurable indulgence, he found that it was all a chasing after meaninglessness; he was only trying to grasp the wind.

It is interesting to note that the wisest of all men still had a foolish streak in him. Solomon knew what the writings of Moses had to say about sex. He already knew what was right and wrong. But even in all of his wisdom, he still had to go out and learn the hard way.

# ECCLESIASTES 2:22–23

## Why should we work if hard work provides so few rewards?

Solomon investigated hard work as a possible way of supplying meaning to life. He

Noah's sons work hard at building the ark. They built it at God's command and according to God's instructions even though they didn't understand why.

realized, however, that if he worked, at the end of his life he would have to leave all the fruit of his labors to people who had not worked. He concluded that this would be foolish and extremely unfair. Besides, he goes on to say, work only brings a person pain and difficulty sleeping at night—particularly if the person has been loading camels all day and has only a lumpy mattress to go home to in the evening. Solomon realized that there was some satisfaction to be found in work. This satisfaction comes straight from the hand of God. People should enjoy the reward of their labor because such fruits are a gift from God (Ecclesiastes 3:13).

## ECCLESIASTES 3:1–11

### Against so many biblical commands, how can Solomon advise that there is a time to kill, to tear down, and to hate?

Solomon's list of times and "seasons" must be viewed within the larger context of life and history. He is not necessarily saying, "Hey, it's twelve o'clock, time to kill—so go out and bump someone off." Rather, Solomon insists that human life takes place within a larger framework of events that repeat down through history: laughter, tears, killing, healing, destruction, building, death, birth. We should not be surprised or think it strange if such things happen to us. Such has happened before to countless people and will happen again to countless more—the seasons and rhythms of life, joyous and sad.

## ECCLESIASTES 3:11

### In what way is eternity planted in our hearts?

God has planted eternity in our hearts as a longing after heaven, a longing after Him. In fact, the restlessness and discontent that Solomon complains of in the first chapter of Ecclesiastes is actually a demonstration of this condition.

When we long for something that we cannot see, when we cannot put into words that which tears at our hearts, when we are homesick within our own homes, these are all evidences of the eternity that God has planted within our hearts.

## ECCLESIASTES 5:8

### Should Christians be complacent in the face of government corruption?

Government corruption is an unavoidable condition. The concept of government necessitates larger and larger groups of sinful people making rules and carrying them out. Such an arrangement always leads to corruption; the larger the group of sinners, the more sin is devised and enacted.

Such habits of state do not mean that Christians should blithely ignore injustice. On the contrary, God calls His people to defend the oppressed, the poor, the strangers. Particularly when the practice of government directly opposes the laws of God, Christians should speak up for righteousness, take a stand, and make a difference.

# SONG OF SONGS

*The only book of the Bible that calls itself a song, this is about love, passion, and sexual tenderness. Everybody dreams about it, but few people find it. Search on.*

## SONG OF SONGS 1:1–4

### Is erotic love okay?

One theme rings throughout this unique Bible book: Falling head over heels in love is fantastic! The pleasure of sexual intercourse is celebrated here in language that leaves no doubt. This book has been interpreted by some as an allegory, devaluing the erotic element in favor of a more vertical meaning (God's love for Israel, for example). But the plain language of the book is devoted powerfully to celebrating God's gift of love to a man and woman. So, let's face it—if you're going to meet and fall in love, do it this way.

Other important statements in the Bible put this love song in its proper context, faithful monogamous marriage. The Song of Songs is not a license to promiscuous pleasures but an invitation to the romance of two people becoming "united into one" in a life of devotion and tender affection (Genesis 2:24). Solomon himself got in trouble when he institutionalized promiscuous pleasure in his royal harem (1 Kings 11:3–4). Oddly, he missed the point of this book that bears his name. Here's a vision of romance that feels the magnet of sexual attraction, enjoys each moment, and is utterly fulfilled in its pleasure. Take this book as an example of what Christian marriage should be.

Erotic love is beautifully experienced within the context of marriage.

## Should people be talking about these kinds of things in public?

Perhaps not in public-public, because that makes a market out of intimacy and tends to turn true love into pornography. Too much public talk makes sex more the activity of animals and less the activity of gifted human beings living before a God of love. The most intimate of all human encounters should be protected from too much public exposure, lest intimacy be lost and the dynamic of love itself be prostituted.

But in many Christian circles, the opposite problem is the norm. There is not enough discussion about sex as a gift from God. How futile! Christians who think that silence will suppress the topic are kidding themselves. From the start of sexual feelings in puberty, to the quieting of sexual drives in older age, the topic should be given a lot of talk in the family and in the church. We need to understand this remarkable part of our being, and our understanding needs to be informed by God's Word and repaired (because often it is broken) by God's saving love.

# ISAIAH

*The most prolific of all the prophets, Isaiah recorded his intensely personal experiences with God—the result of a deep inner faith and a searching intellect.*

## ISAIAH 1:11–14

### Why did God say He was sick of the sacrifices offered by the Israelites?

The people of Israel were outwardly religious but inwardly rebellious. Rather than obeying God from their hearts and faithfully keeping His covenant, they modified their religious practices to suit their own desires. The result was an eclectic, idolatrous hodgepodge in which the Holy One of Israel (the prophet's favorite name for God) was barely acknowledged. God's strong indictment, delivered through the prophet, read: "They honor me with their lips, but their hearts are far away! And their worship of me amounts to nothing more than human laws learned by rote" (Isaiah 29:13). For these reasons, God told the Israelites to stop their useless, hypocritical behavior.

## ISAIAH 2:3

### What is the "mountain of the LORD"?

This is a general metaphor for Jerusalem, also called the "city of David" and Zion. Geographically, Jerusalem is perched on a rocky plateau about twenty-five hundred feet above sea level (thirty-eight hundred feet above the Dead Sea). The roads leading into the city are inclined, which explains why pilgrims sang and spoke of going "up" to Jerusalem.

More specifically, the mountain of the Lord is a reference to the temples (of Solomon, of Herod, and some believe, the future millennial temple) located on an elevated site across the Kidron Valley from the Mount of Olives, where the Muslim Dome of the Rock now stands. The ancient Jews who heard this phrase no doubt thought of God's rule and protection, as mountains symbolized strength, stability, security.

Isaiah weeps over Jerusalem because the people there would not repent of their sins and return to God.

## ISAIAH 5:5

### Why were the people of Israel (and Judah) so indifferent to the sobering words of prophets like Isaiah?

Human nature being what it is tends to turn a deaf ear to bad news. People resent being asked to make changes in their lives. Just ask any politician who ever campaigned on an austere "Let's all sacrifice" theme!

In the spiritual realm, whether from pride, disbelief, or fear, people recoil from the unpleasant idea that they will one day have to account for their lives. This is clearly seen in passages such as Isaiah 30:10–12. The people told the prophets, "Don't tell us what is right. Tell us nice things. Tell us lies. Forget all this gloom. Get off your narrow path. Stop telling us about your 'Holy One of Israel.'"

Judah wandered from God for the same reasons Israel did, and for the same reasons religious people do so today. They got careless with God's commands and failed to pass them on to their children (Deuteronomy 4:9). They took a lax view toward sin and sinners (Exodus 34:12–15), succumbing to a kind of national peer pressure. Often they became enamored with their prosperity and forgot the source of their earthly blessings (Deuteronomy 8:11–18). When the worship of Yahweh became burdensome, unpleasant, or unexciting, they sought or created new gods more to their liking (Exodus 32:1; Deuteronomy 11:16; 29:18; 1 Chronicles 5:25).

When people tire of listening to God, spiritual decay sets in. It can be nearly imperceptible, except to those who are vigilant.

# ISAIAH 6:1

## How can Isaiah say he saw the Lord, when many scriptures declare that no one has ever seen God?

Isaiah 6 records the prophet's vision of God, "I saw the Lord." Yet Exodus 33:20; John 1:18; and 1 John 4:12 state that no one has ever seen God.

One answer holds that God the Father and God the Spirit are invisible, but God the Son is visible. In this line of thinking, Isaiah saw the preincarnate Christ exalted in heaven. Another answer claims that Isaiah merely saw the reflected glory of God and not God in His pure essence, similar to when Moses confronted the burning bush in the wilderness. God was there, the fire was visible from a distance, but God's identity and person were only represented, not physically apparent.

# ISAIAH 7:14

## What was a "virgin"?

Scholars have debated the interpretation of Isaiah 7:14 for centuries. Three primary views tend to dominate the discussion. One view holds that the prophecy "the virgin will conceive" refers to a young, unmarried woman of marriageable age (the literal meaning of the Hebrew word translated "virgin"), who actually lived and married in the time of Isaiah and then gave birth to a son. Thus, this was not a "virgin birth" but a normal instance of marriage and childbirth. In this view it is required that King Ahaz knew such a woman, would have recognized these events, and would then have been comforted by what they signified: the certain destruction of the ominous northern alliance between Israel and Aram.

A second view sees this prophecy as exclusively messianic; that is, it refers solely to Mary, the mother of Jesus, and the birth of the Messiah (see Matthew 1:21–23).

A third position sees a dual fulfillment in this prophecy—that it was directed primarily to Ahaz but also had secondary and ultimate fulfillment in the birth of Christ some seven hundred years later.

# ISAIAH 8–9

## Why do Isaiah's prophecies (and those of almost all the other prophets) vacillate so wildly between declarations of doom and pronouncements of hope?

Prophetic literature is often hard to read because there is no set structure. The writers do not follow a discernible pattern. One minute they are speaking to a foreign Gentile nation about imminent doom. The next moment they are relating Israel's glorious future. Essentially, the prophets spoke different messages because they often addressed different audiences. Isaiah's prophecies were directed to those living in his own time (chapters 1–36), as well as to his countrymen (not yet living) who would one day be exiled in a foreign land (chapters 40–66). Thus, he warned the former group of impending destruction. To the latter group he spoke of future restoration and peace. The content of the message depended upon the need and destiny of the particular audience.

That is the twofold message of the prophets in a nutshell. God would punish His people for their refusal to keep the covenant, but He also pledged to restore His people and give them a future.

## Why did Isaiah slip out of chronological order in the events surrounding King Hezekiah?

Most Bible scholars agree that King Hezekiah's illness (Isaiah 38) and his foolish reception of the Babylonian dignitaries (Isaiah 39) took place before the Assyrian invasion (reported in Isaiah 36–37). The probable reason that Isaiah did not put these events in chronological order is that he intended this historical material to serve as a bridge between the two major sections of his book. By describing Sennacherib's invasion in chapters 36–37, Isaiah was able to conclude the first part of his book where the antagonist was the Assyrian empire. Then, by mentioning the Babylonians in chapters 37–38, Isaiah was able to introduce the nation that would serve as the primary enemy of Judah for the remainder of the book.

## What can we say for sure about the so-called "new heavens and a new earth"?

Here God says, "Look! I am creating new heavens and a new earth—so wonderful that no one will even think about the old ones anymore." The same phrase appears again in Isaiah 66:22–23; 2 Peter 3:13; and Revelation 21:1 (referred to there as "new heaven," singular), yet few details are known. All that can be said with certainty is that God's re-created cosmos will be marked by the sure rule of God and that the inhabitants of this eternal state will experience safety, peace, prosperity, and joy. It is with good reason that the final two chapters of the Bible have been a great source of comfort to so many saints down through the ages!

A montage of the planets in our solar system.

# JEREMIAH

*Do you ever feel like screaming out the truth? This prophet put his screams into a book, one of the most powerful statements ever written about God's awesome power and our responsibility to obey Him.*

## JEREMIAH 1:5

### How can God know anyone before he or she is born?

God knows us before we are even fertilized eggs in our mothers' wombs. You see, God is the one who creates each person, knows and understands each person's individuality, and examines the entire path that each life is going to take. It is important to realize this. This is why we can know that each person born is already known, chosen, and cherished by God. Therefore, whether a child is conceived by apparent accident, as a result of violence, or within the love of a family, that child was first known by God.

## JEREMIAH 2:20, 33; 3:1–3

### Repeatedly, Israel is compared to a prostitute. What is the reason for this?

When God chose Israel to be His holy nation, He intended them to be solely devoted to Him. Israel was like a beloved bride who had saved herself for her one man. Throughout Israel's history in the Old Testament, however, the nation was constantly breaking its commitment with God and making alliances with other nations and with other gods. Because of this flirting with and loving other gods besides the Lord, Jeremiah compares Israel to a prostitute.

## JEREMIAH 4:4

### How is it possible to "change" or "circumcise" the heart?

Circumcision was a physical sign of the covenant, of entering into an agreement with the Lord. The physical act of circumcision, however, didn't always guarantee that the person actually was in covenant with the Lord. It could quickly become a case of merely going through the motions.

Cleansing and circumcising the heart, on the other hand, means that you are entering into a covenantal agreement with the

Lord where you really live, down among the true motives and desires of your private self. Circumcising the heart means that you are allowing the Lord to be Lord of your whole being, Lord of your life, of your desires, will, and thoughts. Cleansing your heart means confessing and turning from sin. Physical circumcision can be easily done in a day and then forgotten. Circumcision of the heart, however, can only be done through God's Spirit and goes much deeper.

## JEREMIAH 7:23–26; 13:1–11

### Why do people regularly fail to listen to God?

People seem to have a monopoly on being stubborn and determined that their way is the right way. You can see it in the way a toddler is set on touching the hot stove. Nothing is going to stop that child. Parents can reason with the child, explaining their own

teetering toward that stove, "all systems go" to learn the hard way.

We follow the same routine with God. Regardless of His goodness and faithfulness in the past, our memories short circuit and we scramble for the hot stove as soon as we get a chance. We all have a fallen, sinful nature that makes us prone to rebel against God.

## JEREMIAH 9:12–15

### Are malnourishment and dehydration really spiritual problems at the core?

God used all manner of instruments when He judged His people for their sin. Because the people had forsaken God's law, he promised to make them eat "bitterness and give them poison to drink." Whether or not this was meant to be figurative or literal, it remains true that the people's spiritual condition led to their suffering and God's judgment.

We cannot say that all hunger and famine

An illustration of the years of famine during Joseph's time in Egypt.

experiences with a hot stove or discussing the physics of heat transfer through solid objects. Why, they can even give the child a swat or two on the behind if he or she gets too close to the stove. The child's determination and stubbornness, however, will send him or her

are caused by someone's sin. But it does seem that most things in life have one kind of spiritual implication or another. Sometimes we suffer because of our own spiritual rebellion toward God. Other times we suffer because of evil in other people's lives. We might receive the backlash from someone else's "spiritual problem" and sin, whether that means dying of famine because of greedy government or getting hit by a random bullet in inner-city crime.

## JEREMIAH 14:11–12

### Does God become so angry as to refuse to listen to prayers?

God always listens to prayers. That does not mean, however, that He is always going to answer them or necessarily be pleased that the person is praying. In Jeremiah 14, God had already made up His mind that He was going to punish Israel for their sins. He told Jeremiah not even to bother praying for the people. Furthermore, He told Jeremiah that He wasn't going to listen to the cries of the people.

In that situation, it wasn't a case of God not listening to the peoples' prayers for mercy and deliverance. Rather, the prayers were irrelevant because the people were sinning greatly and only began praying when judgment fell on them. As far as God was concerned, they might as well have saved their breath.

## JEREMIAH 15:1–4

### Would God really punish people, with no chance for an appeal?

God is a God of mercy and of judgment. Sin always has consequences; every sinful action will have a corresponding judgment of some sort. However, God is always willing to show mercy to His people, regardless of their sin. Even though God repeatedly chastised and punished the nation of Israel for their sins, bringing down various foreign invaders upon them and having them carted off to Babylon as slaves, He always offered them mercy within the very depths of their judgment.

We must also remember that God is slow

Christ on His throne. Christ pleads our case to God for redemption, but one day He will judge those who refuse to believe in Him.

to wrath. While people are engaged in their sin, God always offers chances for mercy and repentance before He reaches the point where He will bring judgment.

## JEREMIAH 17:1–4

### Is poverty, at the core, ever a spiritual problem?

People suffer in poverty and lack basic resources for many different reasons. In this passage, God says that His people would lose their treasure and wealth because of their rebellion and idolatry. Poverty sometimes can be the result of an individual's bad choices and sin. Poverty can be the result of a nation's collective sin. Poverty can also be inflicted on a person by the sin and selfishness of another person or group of people.

Being poor, though, is not always bad. God can use poverty as one way to refine a person's character. After all, He is more concerned with someone's heart being spiritually rich than with someone's bank account. Poverty can also be something chosen voluntarily. For example, monks and nuns will often make vows of poverty so that they can concentrate on such things as prayer, caring for other people, and church ministry.

## JEREMIAH 33:2–3

### Is ignorance, at its core, a spiritual problem?

Wisdom, the opposite of ignorance, is a gift from God. It is a gift that He gladly gives to those who ask for it in all earnestness and faith (James 1:5). Real wisdom and knowledge are spiritual in nature, having little to do with the inborn cunning of our common sense or the learned themes of education. "Fear of the LORD is the beginning of knowledge," Solomon said (Proverbs 1:7). Therefore, the absence of wisdom—ignorance—is definitely a spiritual problem. Ignorance means we do not know the things and ways of God, and that we are unfamiliar with His person and the intent of His will. All these traits of ignorance are spiritual problems and indicate a shallower life than the life of the person who possesses wisdom.

# LAMENTATIONS

*"I just feel like crying!" Jeremiah lamented as he saw God's judgment. But then he saw some sunshine through the clouds.*

## LAMENTATIONS 2:19

### Why does an all-powerful God allow children to suffer?

Of all the horrible things that happen in the world, the suffering and death of children may be the hardest to understand. Surely God would not allow those who are so clearly helpless to be hurt.

The question often focuses on the innocence of children. To argue that children shouldn't suffer because they are sinless—innocent—indicates a naive view of human nature. Sin is part and parcel of human nature. Sin affects every person and every human institution, and pain is its result. Only God can eradicate suffering. God has promised to do this at the end of history when His kingdom is established. If God *can* do it, why doesn't He do it now? We may never know this side of heaven.

Pushing responsibility for innocent suffering onto God sidesteps one of the core lessons of life: taking personal responsibility. No one lives as an isolated individual; decisions and actions always affect someone else. Innocent people suffer when someone chooses to boost his or her empire, take a foolish risk, or appease an evil appetite. Children suffer because God created a world where decisions really matter.

Will suffering be vindicated? Will moral justice ever be reached in human experience? Will the suffering of an innocent child ever be addressed in some court of appeal where restitution is possible? These questions are staggering. Yet God promises just this: in the kingdom to come, tears will be wiped away in the beauty of God's holiness, the comfort of His love, and the community of His people.

God knows the suffering people experience and has done something about it: He sent Jesus Christ the Messiah to redeem the world. Trust in God's holy Son, and know that suffering is only for a while.

## LAMENTATIONS 2:20

### Is it okay to complain to God in prayer?

For many people, expressing anger in prayer is the first time they actually get personal with God. Until that moment they may have ignored God completely. While anger can't be the sole basis for a relationship with God, it can be a start. People who complain to God are expressing some kind of connection with Him. The relationship may be in shambles, but at least communication is open.

The complaints, questions, and laments that make up much of Jeremiah's conversation with God are transparent and honest. Lamentations is comprised of five deeply moving meditations on the effects of sin in the life of a city, Jerusalem. The book is filled with the same questions we raise today in moments of sorrow and personal grief. Jeremiah sees flashes of hope and concludes that the only way to understand his pain is to let God be God. He also expresses feelings of despair that come when people recognize their sinfulness in God's sight.

God accepted those expressions and ultimately would redeem them, turning weeping into laughter and sorrow into joy. That's the promise of the gospel. God will make all things new and pure, including our tattered hearts and disrupted dreams. God is faithful (Jeremiah 3:22–23).

תפלת משה נגד מלחמת עמלק

God tells us we can come to Him in prayer in all circumstances.

# EZEKIEL

*Some of the most fascinating scenes in all of the Bible occur in this book. But what do they mean, and how should we apply them today?*

## EZEKIEL 1:15

### What do these "wheels" tell us about God?

People have always found it difficult to describe the essence of God. Ezekiel's vision of a wheel within a wheel was one part of an elaborate vision that represented the awesome glory of the Lord. Just as the wheels were able to move anywhere, so God's presence is everywhere and in control of all things.

Ezekiel, a prophet who was taken captive at the fall of Jerusalem in 597 B.C., was given many prophetic visions to give him courage as well as to reveal coming events. It was common for a prophet, at the start of his ministry, to have an encounter in which God revealed His glory and issued a special call. Isaiah saw the Lord lifted up in the temple at the start of his ministry (Isaiah 6:1–8), and Jeremiah related a conversation with the Lord during which the Lord touched his mouth (Jeremiah 1).

## EZEKIEL 2:1

### What does "son of man" mean?

The prophet Ezekiel is addressed as "son of man," a title used for him over ninety times throughout the book of Ezekiel. The title shows the contrast between Ezekiel, a man, and the almighty Lord. This name would portray Ezekiel's human limits and weaknesses in contrast to the glory and greatness of God.

The term "son of man" is used twice in Daniel (7:13 and 8:17), the only other references in the Old Testament. Daniel 7:13–14 describes the "son of man" as one "coming with the clouds of heaven" who is "given authority, honor, and royal power over all the nations of the world." This is often taken to refer to the expected Messiah. Jesus refers to Himself as the "Son of Man" in Mark 2:10, and elsewhere points to His identification with humanity as well as His deity.

## EZEKIEL 2:3–5

### Why would Ezekiel—or anybody—speak truth to stubborn people who refuse to listen?

God's call on Ezekiel's life and the task given him was based on who God was and God's hatred of sin. Ezekiel experienced God firsthand, taking in His Word (he ate the scroll given him by God) so completely that it was a part of him.

God's call to repentance and offer of forgiveness (which is the gospel, the story of God's love for us) is not motivated by audience reaction, but only by God's love and desire for relationship. Likewise, Ezekiel's call and ministry were not based on how people would respond, but on knowing the heart of God.

When we know God and His truth, we are responsible to tell others God's Good News no matter what they think, how they joke, what gossip they spread, or what derision they may initially show. God's message is for all people, and many people are troublesome. Let the Word itself be your strength.

## EZEKIEL 10:1

### What are cherubim?

*Cherubim* is plural for the Hebrew word *cherub*, or *angel*. In the Old Testament, cherubim were heavenly beings who served God. In the Garden of Eden, angels guarded the tree of life (Genesis 3:24). Two cherubim made of gold decorated the top of the ark of the covenant, symbolizing a covering of atonement (Exodus 25:18–22). Given that

The Virgin Mary with baby Jesus and the cherubim singing in the backround.

God cannot be contained or represented, these two angels with outstretched wings provided a location where God's presence was enthroned (1 Samuel 4:4; 2 Samuel 6:2). In Ezekiel 10 the cherubim take flight with the throne of God above them and move out of the temple, representing the presence of God leaving the temple.

## EZEKIEL 24:16

### Why was Ezekiel told not to grieve the death of his wife?

Ezekiel loved his wife, but God told him not to grieve publicly when she died. This was to be a living message to the people concerning their abandonment of God. Yes, grief would come to them, the grief of captivity. They would suffer at the hands of Babylonian conquerors, and their homes, lands, and precious temple would be destroyed. Would they be as mute as Ezekiel, or in grief repent of sin and return to the worship of God?

Ezekiel's personal sacrifice must have affected him deeply. Yet obedience to God puts unusual demands on leaders. No

Christian is called to be a stoic, accepting any and all pain without tears; sometimes, however, for special purposes, Christians are called to endure unusual difficulty for the sake of the mission. Ezekiel knew his assignment, and while others could not understand his façade, he did. It was God's call—God's way for Ezekiel to send a message the people would not hear through any other channel.

## EZEKIEL 37:1

### "Dem bones, dem bones, dem dry bones," the song goes. What message lies hidden in the dry bones?

The dry bones symbolized that the nation of Israel was dead and gone, scattered among the nations because the people had grown cold—made their hearts dead—to God. Only God could breathe life into them. Ezekiel speaks to the hope that the scattered exiles of Israel would hear God's word, would respond, and would again find identity as a people committed to God.

Ezekiel and the valley of the dry bones, symbolizing the nation of Israel as dead and gone. Just as the bones in Ezekiel's dream come back to life, God will bring the nation back to life,

# DANIEL

*Many Christians work in secular businesses. Daniel serves as an example of faith under scrutiny and faith above politics.*

## DANIEL 1:8–12

### Why did Daniel make such a big deal over his diet?

Though Daniel was a slave, his conscience was free. While his foreign captors planned to remake his life, his heart belonged to God. Daniel would not subvert an empire with arms, but he could maintain the practice of a faith his captors could not understand.

Daniel chose to make his witness known in areas of personal discipline: diet and prayer. As a young Jew, Daniel knew that God's law forbade certain foods and that preparation of food was also part of that law. Daniel's bold experiment with diet was his first way of saying to the bloated egos of the Babylonians, "My God lives!" Daniel and his friends stayed healthy, demonstrating a spiritual purpose much stronger than Babylonian political muscle.

## DANIEL 2–12

### Are some of Daniel's visions of the future still pending?

The most fascinating of Daniel's several prophecies involves Nebuchadnezzar's "forgotten" dream. In the dream, a statue cast in five layers of material represents the Babylonian empire and the four world empires to follow. The rock that crushes them all represents the kingdom of Jesus Christ, which overcomes all secular authority and vindicates the rule of God.

The fulfillment of this vision is not yet complete. Christ's kingdom is established through the witness of the church, but universal recognition is still to come. One day, all people will know the awesome power of God. In our lives today, we can know that power through faith in Jesus Christ.

## DANIEL 2:1

### Why did God use dreams and visions to communicate with so many people in the Bible?

Dreams and visions that carry God's message fall into three categories: (1) personal warnings and direction from God (such as the angelic dream assuring Joseph that Mary was pregnant by supernatural means—Matthew 1:20); (2) prophetic dreams and visions for immediate action (Pharaoh's dream about years of plenty and famine—Genesis 41); (3) prophetic dreams and visions regarding the course of history (the visions in Daniel 7; John's visions in Revelation).

The more God's written Word became a reality, the less God used dreams and visions as a communication tool. When God did use dreams, the situation was often critical, and failure to heed the dream or vision had dire consequences. People today who claim that God still uses dreams are seldom willing to put their lives on the line as a guarantee of the truth of the dream or vision, a clear requirement of scripture (Deuteronomy 13:5). Others who claim that God "retired" dreams when scripture was complete appear to claim that God is unable to communicate this way any longer. Either option is fraught with difficulty.

Since God would never contradict His Word, any dream messages God might

Guidance today does not depend on dreams; neither should dreams be ruled out as a way to better comprehend God's glory. In Nebuchadnezzar's case, we can only suppose that a king so remote from God's people would not likely listen to prophetic preaching. In mercy, God had a message for this lost monarch, and He chose a dream as the best vehicle for getting that message across.

## DANIEL 3:12

### Why didn't Shadrach, Meshach, and Abednego bow down to the golden statue?

People salute a passing flag, stand at attention for a presidential motorcade, and put hand over heart for the national anthem. Why not bow to the king's phony idol—just

Shadrach, Meshach, and Abednego are thrown into the fiery furnace for refusing to bow down to the golden statue, but God protects them from harm.

use today must cohere with the Bible's clear teaching and should always be confirmed through the counsel of mature Christians to prevent private aspiration from becoming confused with God's will.

another symbol of national identity? These men knew this image wasn't God, so what difference would it make?

Fear is a fertile field that yields a huge harvest of excuses. Daniel's friends could have used several excuses: (1) Pretend by bowing, but don't actually worship. (2) Go ahead and worship this time, then ask God to forgive later—God understands this kind of pressure. (3) If bowing this time is wrong, why would God put us in this position? (4) The king has been good to us, so let's cooperate. (5) If we show the people a little goodwill, maybe they will listen when we tell them about God. (6) Bowing down might not be the best choice, but think of all the worse things our ancestors did, even in God's own temple in Jerusalem! (7) If we lose our positions, the king will appoint pagans in our place and we won't be able to help our people anymore.

Some of these potential excuses mask compromise better than others, but each is a form of betrayal. Shadrach, Meshach, and Abednego valued their relationship with God more than they valued their lives. To show respect for national symbols was one thing; to worship an idol—even if no one believed in the idol's divinity—was quite another. The three young Jews drew the line at homage. Theirs belonged to God alone.

## DANIEL 3:19

### Does trusting God mean nothing bad will happen to us?

Trust in God is not a bargain we offer in exchange for freedom from pain, persecution, or threat of natural disaster. Trusting God means we don't waver when things are not turning out the way we planned. Daniel's friends told the king they expected to be rescued from the flames because they believed God was able to do it (Daniel 3:17). But they also told the king that even death, if God chose, would still accomplish their rescue (verse 18). Trusting God means we have a reason to hope even when it seems like everything bad may happen to us.

## DANIEL 3:25

### Who was the fourth person in King Nebuchadnezzar's furnace?

Perhaps this was an early visit by Christ Himself or maybe an angelic companion God sent to protect the three faithful men. Whatever his identity, the fourth person's appearance was different. The king described him as someone who "looks like a divine being." When the king called Shadrach, Meshach, and Abednego to step out of the furnace, he failed to invite the fourth person. Apparently, Nebuchadnezzar wasn't ready for a face-to-face encounter with whoever he was.

## DANIEL 4:31–32

### Why did King Nebuchadnezzar lose his mental health?

Nothing humbles like utter humiliation. Even though Nebuchadnezzar was impressed with God's power in the furnace incident, he did not come to terms with his own standing before God. His pride and position caused him to accept the worship of others as if he were a god. Though God sent him a dream to warn against idolatry, Nebuchadnezzar didn't take the warning to heart. What would get this guy's attention? Behaving like a dumb beast finally clinched the issue: If Nebuchadnezzar had no greater ears for God than a grass-chewing cow, let him act like one.

## DANIEL 6:10

### Why did Daniel ignore the law criminalizing prayer?

Daniel realized that the law against prayer was really against him. Babylon had captured his homeland but not his soul. To compromise by yielding to a statute forbidding prayer would be to deny the very basis of his life, to deny God's mercy and care for him.

Daniel's opponents thought they had him in a no-win situation. If he stopped praying out of fear, he was ruined—they would win. If he continued to pray, he was gone—they would win. Failing to understand Daniel's integrity, they were also blind to the ways of a God who delights to confound the "perfect plans" of cunning enemies of faith.

Daniel neither flaunted his prayer life nor privatized it in response to the law. Rather, he just did his thing as usual, accepted his punishment in the light of God's power and mercy, and waited for God's deliverance. Facing hungry lions is pretty scary, but the worse fright was in the hearts of his enemies when Daniel's God turned the tide—a lesson on who rightly to fear and who to obey when a showdown occurs. Daniel could not deny God or hide his identity as a believer.

Daniel prays and trusts God to save him from the lions.

## DANIEL 6:16

### How did Daniel survive the lions' den?

Daniel's survival was not the result of a force field set up by his strength of will or by compatriots feeding the lions just before he was locked among them. Daniel survived the lions because *God* protected him. Daniel's friends survived the furnace because *God* protected them. In both cases, those threatened with death did not presume God's intention to keep them alive; instead, they trusted in God's deliverance, whatever the outcome. Daniel lived by God's divine purpose—the only reason worth living.

At the same time, uncounted thousands of persecuted Christians have lost their lives; the "lions" (in many forms) have had their fill. God does not keep faithful Christians alive in every case. Some of the most convincing statements of genuine faith have been made by martyrs who calmly gave up their lives for Christ in complete confidence that God's promised deliverance was just beyond this life.

# HOSEA

*Few families could exist for long under these conditions. Discover how God's grace shines through in this worst-case marriage encounter.*

## HOSEA 1

### Is the story of Gomer and Hosea real history or an allegory?

Why would a holy God order His servant to marry a prostitute? The unlikelihood of such an order has led some to interpret Hosea as an allegorical picture of the relationship between God and Israel. However, the first three chapters of Hosea are presented as straightforward historical narrative. Nothing in the text points to anything less than a literal understanding of these events.

## HOSEA 1:2

### Why would God tell a spiritual leader to marry a woman who would cause him heartache and embarrassment?

God often required prophets to carry out what we would consider highly unusual object lessons. Jeremiah wore a ruined loincloth around his waist (Jeremiah 13). Isaiah paraded about stripped of clothing (Isaiah 20). Ezekiel lay on his left side for more than a year and on his right side more than a month (Ezekiel 4), shaved his head with a sword (Ezekiel 5), and was forbidden to mourn when his wife died (Ezekiel 24). These strange actions were primarily intended to get the attention of the hardheaded, hard-hearted people of God, to illustrate certain divine truths, and to serve as unforgettable audiovisual lessons for a people who had long since stopped listening to regular sermons and scripture readings.

## HOSEA 1:2

### Was the prophet Hosea the real father of Gomer's three children?

Most Bible scholars believe that at least two of Gomer's three children were the product of relationships with other men. Other scholars, however, argue that a precise reading of the Hebrew text may simply mean that Hosea's children were born in the context of a marriage to an immoral woman, not necessarily as a result of Gomer's career as a prostitute. So there you have it—the paternity of Gomer's children cannot be determined with absolute certainty.

## HOSEA 1:4

### If God chose Jehu to destroy the house of Ahab (2 Kings 9:7), why was Jehu condemned by Hosea for the massacre of Ahab's house?

Yes, God commanded Jehu to destroy the house of Ahab, but Jehu seized his opportunity and went beyond God's command in his slaughter of innocent people. Jehu was more zealous for his own family's protection and his claim to the throne than for the righteous judgment of the Lord. Even Jehu's killing of Baal worshipers in Samaria showed less than a wholehearted commitment to the Lord. God desires more than behavioral conformity; He requires that a person's whole heart belong to Him.

## HOSEA 2:5, 7, 10, 12–13

### When God spoke to Hosea about Israel's various "lovers," to what did this term refer?

God was calling attention to Israel's passion for various false gods, specifically the god Baal (2:13). Instead of acknowledging the Lord as the provider of all her blessings, Israel took the very resources given by God and used them to praise and worship Baal (2:8)! Supposedly wed to God, Israel was guilty of spiritual adultery in chasing after other gods.

## HOSEA 4:11–15; 5:3–4; 9:1

### Why the frequent references to prostitutes and prostitution in the book of Hosea?

Israel was guilty of participating in various pagan worship practices. This included actual, physical prostitution at many Canaanite shrines left standing after the conquest of Canaan. The idea behind these degrading sexual rites was that the Canaanite fertility gods Baal and Asherah would favor the participants with healthy babies and crops.

But Israel was also guilty of spiritual prostitution, selling her soul and freely giving her worship to these false gods, even as she maintained the pretense of devotion to the God of Israel. Morally and spiritually, God's people had proven unfaithful.

## HOSEA 7:8

### What's the meaning of Hosea's reference to "half-baked cake"?

In times of trouble, Israel had a habit of turning to foreign nations for help and protection. Instead of relying on God, the nation would form alliances with world powers like Assyria or Egypt. The point of a "half-baked cake" was to say, in effect, that Israel's actions were futile and self-destructive. God was saying that Israel was like a flat-cake left unturned on a hot fire—burned on one side, uncooked on the other. Such a cake would be good for nothing and rightly discarded.

The olive groves in Israel, originally the territory of the tribes of Ephraim and Manasseh.

## HOSEA 13:1

### What is the connection between the terms *Ephraim, Jacob, Judah,* and *Israel*?

Ephraim was the largest, most powerful tribe of the northern kingdom; therefore, it sometimes represented the whole nation. The name Jacob (son of Isaac, father of the founders of the twelve tribes, and the one whose name was eventually changed by God to *Israel*) was also used occasionally as a substitute for the more common name Israel (Hosea 12:2). Judah, the larger of the two tribes that composed the southern kingdom (the other was Benjamin) became the most commonly used name for the southern kingdom.

## HOSEA 13:7–8; 14:5

### Does God have mood swings?

The book of Hosea is a love story. Via the tortured and tense relationship between the prophet Hosea and his wife Gomer, a prostitute, the reader is given a picture of the relationship between God and His people. Perhaps more than any other book in the Bible, Hosea reveals the fascinating, all-encompassing personality of God—He has a mind, a will, and real emotions. God is not an impersonal force or a mere cosmic presence. He really aches and hurts when His people turn away to chase after other gods. Like any jilted lover, God feels both rage and betrayal.

The book of Hosea reveals that sin is more than merely breaking some abstract law of God; rather, sin breaks the very heart of God. But even when His heart is wounded, God does not react impulsively. He is faithful to His promises.

# JOEL

*This book continues our search of the "minor prophets," a phrase that describes the length of the books, not their importance. For us, they raise questions about God's purposes for human life.*

## JOEL 1

### Are natural disasters like floods, locusts, drought, and earthquakes God's methods of punishment?

The Bible cites many occasions in which God used natural disasters as a means of punishment. The little book of Joel, for instance, begins with an impending plague of locusts that will devastate the nation. Along with the warning comes an invitation to repentance. The people are told that a genuine turning from sin may save them, but they cannot assume a reprieve from punishment. The disaster may still come, no matter what the people do.

The Bible never claims that every natural disaster is God's punishment. Sin will be punished, but the time, place, and manner are not as predictable as simple formulas that equate weather disturbances with divine anger.

## JOEL 2:12–13

### How does Joel's message to Israel apply to anything today?

The message of Joel was first given to a specific audience at one time in history. Although all of the message applied to them, it applied in different ways. The same process works today. Application refers to the way God's Word covers us, governs us, and becomes the basis for action.

God's Word covers us when we realize that we are the kind of people described in a passage. When we identify with scripture, the Holy Spirit applies scripture to us—the vivid truth of God's Word for us personally. The people of Joel's day were covered by God's words of warning and hope. We are covered by those same words. Coming dangers may not be swarms of locusts or invading armies, but they are just as dangerous if we face them with unrepentant hearts that refuse God's care.

God's Word governs us when we take its commands seriously and recognize its authority. God doesn't have to earn the right to give us direction; we should be eager for and attentive to God's direction. The people in Joel's day who benefited from the prophet's words were not those who took it as curious information. Rather, those who heard God speaking through His prophet and obeyed were blessed and forgiven.

God's Word is meant for action. Verses in scripture can often find an immediate place in our lives. Joel wrote, "That is why the LORD says, 'Turn to me now, while there is time! Give me your hearts. Come with fasting, weeping, and mourning. Don't tear your clothing in your grief; instead, tear your hearts'" (Joel 2:12–13). These words confronted the people of Joel's day with an immediate call to repentance. That same call reaches across the centuries to us. Our persistent tendency is to turn away from God. Instead, we should take every opportunity to learn from God's Word.

## What is repentance?

Repentance describes the process of sorrow and regret over sin that causes a person to turn away from sin and turn to God. Like most human experiences, repentance comes in true and false versions. True repentance affects the deep inner springs of the human heart; false repentance settles for a change in behavior unconnected to any internal transformation. In the Bible, people often would tear their clothes as a sign of repentance. This was an effective demonstration when it conveyed real emotion. Unfortunately, this action became just an act. People discovered the efficiency of tearing clothing without that bothersome inward struggle involved in repentance. To these people, Joel's words stung.

Other people should be able to observe the effects of true repentance, but the real audience for repentance is God. He's never fooled by a mere outward show, but seeks the deep, inner connection to our spirits that signals authentic recognition of His holiness and our wretchedness.

A portrait of the prophet Joel, who called the people of Judah to turn back to God.

# AMOS

*While the idea of God's love fills the Bible, no one can doubt God's concern for justice as well, especially not after reading the prophecy of Amos. But where is justice today?*

## AMOS 2:11-12

### What is a Nazirite?

The state of being a Nazirite is the result of a vow taken by someone who will thereafter be "separated" or "dedicated" to the Lord in a special way. Nazirites were not priests but were used by God as examples of holiness to the larger population. Among the Nazirites were Samson, Samuel, and John the Baptist. They led ascetic lives, denying themselves many physical comforts. The drinking of wine was also forbidden to them.

People who took the Nazirite vow were set apart for service to God. They did not cut their hair. Samson was a Nazirite.

# AMOS 4:1

## Who are the "fat cows"?

Also translated as "cows of Bashan," the literal cows in this area were some of the finest cattle in all of Canaan. Here, however, the reference is to upper-class women of Samaria who had become wealthy by exploiting the poor.

# AMOS 5:26

## What are Sakkuth and Kaiwan?

Sakkuth was apparently a place of idol worship the people of Israel had constructed. Kaiwan was a related term, perhaps referring to an idolatrous image. Both are references to the worship of heavenly bodies, possibly Saturn.

# OBADIAH

*This prophet wonders how neighbors should treat each other. Since Jesus said everyone is our neighbor, it's a good question to consider.*

## OBADIAH 11–12

### What does friendship require?

For one thing, standing by your friends in time of need. When a friend is in his darkest hour, go to that friend, demonstrate your friendship, do *something*. When the cost of friendship is highest, the strength of friendship is strongest.

In Obadiah, God judges the nation of Edom for abandoning its fellow nation Israel during an hour of need. When someone has a reasonable expectation of friendly help, God expects neighbors to act.

## OBADIAH 15

### If God will judge whole nations, what good is individual virtue and obedience?

Nations are judged for the course of action they follow as a collective whole, the choices that affect and are agreed to by the whole society. God judges nations for such choices in the here and now.

Each person, however, is judged as an individual. It is according to our actions, our obedience to God, our relationship with Him, that each of us is judged—and punished or rewarded. And this particular judgment has eternal consequences.

Because God calls us to virtue and obedience, fear of judgment should not be our only motivation for obeying Him. If we are in relationship with God, we should be happy to obey Him. John states that the Christian who loves God will obey His Word (1 John 2:5).

# JONAH

*We see this prophet as a fool, running from God, complaining
about his own success. But let's not ignore the lessons Jonah
provides. We don't want to repeat his experience!*

## JONAH 1:17

### How can a person survive seventy-two hours inside a fish?

The sheer unlikelihood of this event has caused many to interpret Jonah's
book as allegory or parable, not history as such. Indeed, no other account
exists of a human being surviving such an event. Did it really happen to
Jonah, and if so, how did he survive?

First, consider biblical time periods. "Three days and three nights" could
mean one full day and parts of two others. This was the case in Jesus' death
and resurrection, which Jonah's experience clearly foreshadowed (Matthew

After being swallowed by a huge fish, Jonah prays to God,
is released, and goes to preach in Nineveh.

12:40). Jonah's time of food and water deprivation could have been considerably shorter than seventy-two hours.

Second, consider the scientific possibilities. Remote, indeed, are the chances that a large surface-swimming fish without digestive enzymes picks up a human being and hours later dumps the living but limp body in shallows near his intended destination. Very remote.

Third, consider the miracle. God is saying something important about all of human history through the life of this minor prophet. The gospel will come through God's own Son, who will succumb, as it were, to an implausible end: death as a criminal. Yet there is life beyond. God's miracle in Jonah's experience is one of many miracles God has chosen to communicate with the creation He loves. The greatest of those miracles was the Incarnation—that is, the coming of God Himself in human form, Jesus Christ, whose resurrection gives hope beyond the certainty of death.

## JONAH 3:6

### What explains a pagan king's eager repentance?

The king of Nineveh repented, and we wonder why. The only explanation for the king's confession (and for your own) is that God fills the emptiness in the human heart so effectively that our normal and natural response (albeit with the help of God Himself) is to seek God's forgiveness and comfort. The stubborn person who resists and refuses God's overture—not the repentant sinner—should be the cause of bewilderment.

The conversion of this person reminds us that a king's wealth and power are nothing compared to finding peace with God. In the New Testament, finding peace with God is worth everything a person owns (Matthew 13:45–46); nothing compensates for the loss of relationship with God.

# MICAH

*Again and again the prophets of Israel called people to pay attention to God. "It's your life," they said. "Don't lose it by ignoring God."*

## MICAH 1:2

### Why should people listen to God against their personal wishes?

It appears that the news will be bad. A crime has been committed, and God will be the chief witness for the prosecution—who is also God. The accused, the people, must listen. But unlike a normal criminal trial, God never forces people to listen, and these people certainly had a choice. Why choose to hear bad news?

The answer lies in the character of the speaker. God announces no bad news, only the truth about our human condition and His own provision to repair the damage. Yes, this news is not good—people have sinned terribly. Consequences will surely follow, a worst-nightmare scenario of fear and pain. But even then, despite the sin and loss, God has a heart to redeem and save. That's why people must listen. Without God's hope, pain is just pain. But in God's plan, pain recedes into restoration and blessing.

## MICAH 6:8

### Is the Old Testament always worried about ceremonial purity and ritual?

Much of the Old Testament rehearses very specialized ways of honoring God, but at the essence and core, the message is this: God wants your heart.

If your spiritual life is merely ritual, you're sleepwalking. God wants your heart. If you are the world's foremost ceremonial purist, you're as good as a musical composition that relies on the monotonous sound of a clanging symbol, as Paul puts it in 1 Corinthians 13. Micah says the

In a special ceremony, Samuel anoints David to be the king of Israel.

same thing in different words: The loving God, who redeems you from eternal separation and sin, wants your heart. Love God and follow His path all your days. That's the timeless message of the Bible.

# NAHUM

*If you have any questions about how God feels about arrogant nations, this book has some answers.*

## NAHUM 2

### What's so important about the prediction of Nineveh's downfall?

At the time of Nahum's prophecy, Assyria (of which Nineveh was the capital) was the most powerful empire on earth. For three hundred years the Assyrians had conquered all peoples in their path. Nineveh, the shining center of Assyrian culture, learning, and technology, was considered invincible with its high walls and state-of-the-art defenses. To predict its destruction was startling and unthinkable. Such a prediction posed the seemingly invincible power of worldly might against a seemingly invisible power of spiritual truth.

*How can invisible truth bring down an empire?* a secularist would wonder. *How can a mere empire stand against the power of almighty God?* a Christian would reply. Mere empires cannot get away with rebellion against God forever. Eventually, they meet real power.

# HABAKKUK

*If you have ever wondered if God was listening to your prayers, you'll find a soul mate here.*

## HABAKKUK 1:1

### Why does God make us wait for the answers to our prayers?

Habakkuk opens his short book with a question voiced many times by many people: *Who's listening to my prayers?* Several psalms echo the same sentiment (see Psalms 6 and 10).

We usually answer this common complaint by observing that human time and divine timelessness do not always match well. God is not limited by time. A delay to us is not a delay to God. This answer fails, however, because God the Creator established the circumstances of temporality and understands perfectly how time-bound people feel. God would no more insist that people disregard feelings about time than that they disregard the law of gravity. Both are absolute conditions of human experience.

The appropriate explanation to delayed answers to prayer is that God wills it so. God's will is not open to human review or judgment; neither is God obligated to pick up the phone, so to speak. God hears our prayers by His own generous will, and He answers likewise. God's wise answer may not correspond, either in substance or in timing, to our own choice in the matter. Neither is God likely to debate His will for us, as if His answer or timing needed justification.

The key to prayer is faithful communication with our Creator and Redeemer. Pray without ceasing, Paul urges (1 Thessalonians 5:17). In Habakkuk's case, prayer took the form of a complaint concerning God's willingness to listen. But the complaint itself demonstrates the prophet's underlying faith. There's no point in complaining in prayer unless you believe that God hears your prayers. Habakkuk believed this, and so should we—even when we are impatient for answers.

## HABAKKUK 2:14

### Was God's reputation tarnished when the Israelites were defeated and humiliated by other nations?

Perhaps in the eyes of political commentators of the time, Israel's God took a dip in the polls as the nation moved beyond its golden era and became a vassal state to passing empires. But God's holy reputation was strengthened here. It might have been truly tarnished—morally tarnished, its credibility questioned—had He allowed the Israelites to become invincible and proud and not judged them. Israel's national fortunes were linked indissolubly to the nation's allegiance to God. When fidelity to God's law waned, the nation suffered. Deep fissures in their loyalty to God resulted in national chaos and military loss. When other nations mocked God because of the moral perfidy of His people, God first judged His own people and eventually the mockers.

As much as God's reputation was tied to Israel, God's purpose in choosing a people was to reach the whole world. That same purpose prevails in the rise and fall of nations throughout history; however, Jesus introduces a new concept of God's kingdom, a spiritual kingdom geared not toward national prominence, but reconciliation with God.

Does the awesome fear of God really make a difference to the nations? Habakkuk said yes; and all the world's mockers will eventually echo the truth: The Lord is God, and there is no other.

# ZEPHANIAH

*Worship false gods? How foolish. But how many little gods do we pay attention to? How many times are we distracted from worship, diverted from prayer, and more given to greed than to kindness?*

## ZEPHANIAH 1:4

### Why was Baal worship considered so offensive?

All forms of idolatry were forbidden in Israel (Exodus 20:2–6; Leviticus 19:4), but Baal worship was especially popular among the people. Baal was one of the primary deities of the Canaanites. He was regarded as the god with the power to bestow or withhold fertility to both families and farms. Baal worship was always especially tempting for the Israelites (see Numbers 25:3; 1 Kings 18:18–19) because it featured ritualistic meals, sensual dancing, and male and female prostitution. This was in sharp (and alluring) contrast to the strict moral code of the Hebrews that required austerity and holiness in coming before Yahweh.

Another image of Baal depicts the god as a young bull. The people may have worshiped this kind of idol.

## ZEPHANIAH 1:5

### Who was Molech?

Molech was the chief god of the Ammonites (1 Kings 11:33), whom worshipers honored by sacrificing their own children (2 Kings 16:3; 21:6; Jeremiah 32:35). Jewish law (Leviticus 18:21; 20:1–5) and the prophets strictly forbade these kinds of heinous rituals. Zephaniah apparently regarded Molech worship as one of the most detestable forms of Semitic idolatry (see Jeremiah 7:29–34; Ezekiel 16:20–22; 23:37–39; Amos 5:26).

## ZEPHANIAH 1:7

### What will the "day of the LORD's judgment" be like?

According to Zephaniah, it will happen suddenly and will be unavoidable, global in scale, and catastrophic in nature. This coming day of judgment will involve both Israel and the Gentile nations (3:9–20).

The phrase, in its broadest sense, refers to the absolute and righteous reign of God over His creation. Hints of this day occur in history at various times when God powerfully intervenes to bring about judgment. The most important of those interventions is the first coming of Christ and His conquering of sin, Satan, and death by His own death and resurrection.

A more common view sees the day of the Lord (in its fullness) as future—an extended period of time beginning at the second coming of Christ and including all the events through God's re-creation of the heavens and earth (Isaiah 65:17–19; 66:22; 2 Peter 3:13; Revelation 21:1). The terrible judgments associated with the day of the Lord (Zephaniah 1:15–16) are described in Revelation 4–19.

# HAGGAI

*This prophet would not build the world's first skyscraper, but he would be satisfied with a temple. Not a bad place to build a life—the temple, our heart, God's home.*

## HAGGAI 2:3

### Why was rebuilding the temple so important to the Israelites?

The temple was the center of religious life in Israel since the time of David and Solomon. The ark of the covenant was placed there. The temple represented the presence of the Lord; there the Lord revealed His will to the people. It also was a mark of Israel's unity in the worship of the Lord.

The temple was destroyed and its contents carried to Babylon when Nebuchadnezzar defeated Judah and took its people into exile. Daniel records that the sacred objects of the temple of God were taken and placed in the treasure house of the god of Babylon. It was as if God had been defeated and taken captive. The temple's destruction was a graphic reminder of God's punishment for the people's rebellion and wickedness.

The rebuilding of the temple was a symbol for the exiles. It showed hope that God was still among them and affirmed their commitment to believe God's promise that the kingdom of David would be forever—that God would continue His covenant relationship by sending a new leader (the Messiah) to restore the nation.

The Western Wall of the temple in Jerusalem. The temple was the central place of worship for God's people.

# ZECHARIAH

*If we could reverse the videotape of our lives, what would we change? We cannot travel back in time, of course, but we can learn from the past.*

## ZECHARIAH 2:5

### How does God compare to a wall of fire?

Zechariah's prophecy was intended to inspire spiritual renewal among Jewish believers who had returned to Jerusalem and faced the rebuilding of the temple. Yet the prophecy greatly expanded that narrow vision. Instead of a temple where God would dwell, the promise is that God will dwell among them. Instead of stone walls for protection from aggression, the Lord will be a "wall of fire."

This accomplishes three purposes stones could never do: (1) It keeps enemies far away—there's no threatening approach with fire leaping into the sky. (2) It expands the city at will—a fire wall expands to accommodate more area or protect more people. In this case, people from many nations will join with those Jews protected by the Lord. (3) It consumes when it turns inward—the people must hear God's message and obey. The tone of the promise here is not to motivate through fear, however, but through faith in God's power to protect and provide. The future is full of possibilities. Be full of faith, the prophet urges.

## ZECHARIAH 7:11–14

### Does good listening determine the course of history?

All of God's dealings with the people of Israel boil down here to a willingness to *listen*, not merely to hear. The people heard God's word, but they failed to listen with intent to obey. In that sense, they did not hear God at all. The words of the prophets, priests, and patriarchs were, in sum, ignored and neglected. God then determined not to listen to the people, and with communication cut off, the people had no protection, no identity, and no purpose. They scattered. Isolated from their source of strength and national calling, they floundered in captivity. Listening was their most important task now.

## ZECHARIAH 8:5

### What are city streets for?

City streets serve the function of communication and commerce. Without streets, goods cannot be delivered and people cannot conduct business. But there's another function, perhaps even more telling.

The Lord says that when He revisits the city of His people, there will be children playing in the streets. This is a symbol of the gladness, hope, and security that God provides to those who trust Him. When play takes priority over commerce, then

- ♦ the people must be satisfied, their needs met, their cupboards full;

- ♦ evil must be gone or at least suppressed, as the most vulnerable are now occupying the very places where evil would otherwise prey;

- ♦ the gladness of recreation replaces the strain of work.

Only on holidays do children play on city streets. The picture here is of God's holiday to all believers in an eternal home, blessed abundantly and ever safe from harm.

## ZECHARIAH 8:16-17

### Is lying sometimes an effective strategy?

Anyone can imagine a situation in which a small fib or even a great lie seems like just the right thing. Yet this prophecy from Zechariah utterly scorches such efforts, insisting that truth be the keynote of every piece of business we conduct.

Lying is the normal way to gain advantage over someone else. In God's kingdom, however, no one needs undue advantage. All good things come from God, and we need not twist or change the truth to enhance our position.

Lying is the way people protect themselves. When we sense an attack, especially from a stronger opponent, deception becomes a survival tactic. (The insect world is rich with examples of deception for survival.) But in God's kingdom, protection is guaranteed.

As God eliminates the need to lie, God's people have every reason to speak the truth. And here the command to do so is linked to the heart of God: God hates lying. That's reason enough to make truth the keynote.

An ancient road in Israel.

# MALACHI

*This final Old Testament author is concerned about our overall relationship to the most important Father of all, God. Here, God asks the questions.*

## MALACHI 1:4

### Is it possible for God to hate a people forever?

It is possible if a people rebel against God and abuse His law. The Edomites had a long history of "hands-off" anything associated with God's people or true worship. Edomites had grown stubborn, intransigent, and self-willed, never relaxing their guard against the truth. The hate God expresses to such people is not a general hatred of people, for that would contradict God's character. The hate is against their willful rebellion. As God will never relax His holiness, compromise with sin, or negotiate with evil, so the hatred of God against sin stands as long as sin is a people's purpose and priority. The Edomites knew what they were about, and it was wrong. God's mercy, though not explicit in this passage, is everlasting and always welcomes repentant sinners into God's family.

## MALACHI 1:8

### Why would God care about the condition of animals brought for sacrifice?

Gifts express the nature of a relationship. Love is generous; indifference is stingy. Love wants the best for the other; indifference retains the best for oneself. Love establishes bonds through gift-giving; indifference seeks no bonds—its gifts satisfy social expectations only.

Is God careless about the nature of gifts we bring to Him in worship? We had better hope not! Actually, God's supreme gift, Jesus, settles the question completely. He gave His only Son for us. We should offer nothing less than pure devotion, gratitude, and love to God—small reflections indeed of the benefits we have received.

Only perfect animals could be sacrificed to God because they foreshadowed the perfect Lamb of God who would be the final sacrifice for sin.

## MALACHI 2:14–16

### Why are husbands singled out as the party responsible for keeping a marriage strong?

For good reasons, some of which are associated with the universal male tendency toward sexual conquest. In general, the heart of a man will roam, while the heart of a woman seeks a home. Male sexual energy persists past female menopause, causing men to seek younger partners—or at least to be vulnerable to the temptation of doing so. The male by nature has no long-term investment in pregnancy; he may inseminate regularly with no time lost for childbirth. How are these biological appetites to be curbed, directed, focused?

♦ By developing and nurturing the partnership to which a man commits himself during the height of his (and his wife's) sexual passion. Sex is an engine, but it's not the whole train.

♦ By understanding family as a gift from God, a holy union in which children are nurtured in faith and older age is met with grace and companionship.

♦ By using sexual fancy as opportunity for relishing the intimacy enjoyed with one's wife, year by year, through happiness and turmoil, until death stakes its claim.

Surely women enjoy sexual fantasies, too, and some are attracted to multiple partners. But the greater incentive is wired into the male mind and body, where marital breakdown more often begins.

## MALACHI 3:13–15

### What makes us attribute happiness to people of wealth, power, and arrogance?

We falsely believe that such people control their own destiny in ways the poor, disenfranchised, and humble do not. In fact, arrogant people are caught in the same mistake, failing to realize that God is always in control and that God's heart is always directed toward the poor in spirit, "those who realize their need for him" (Matthew 5:3).

By human measurement, freedom requires a degree of wealth and power, probably arrogance, too. But true freedom, the only kind that counts, is found in a relationship with God that recognizes the frailty and poverty of human life and depends entirely on God for strength and provision. This freedom gives work its meaning (service), the soul its energy (generosity), and the spirit its true measure (poor made rich in God). Banking on money, status, and ego is a bluff that cannot win.

## MALACHI 3:16

### What is the "scroll of remembrance"?

In ancient Israel, very few people had access to written records. Only a few people could read or write, and most records were kept by memory. The very act of writing something in a book made the information important indeed. It would last forever, or so it seemed.

Ancient rulers memorialized their deeds by keeping written records, which were cheaper than pyramids and able to store more data than stone monuments. These histories would tell the story of heroic actions, farsighted decisions, and the demise of vicious enemies. Thus the king's place in history was secure.

For the Lord to write a history, even a ledger, of people who feared Him was to bestow high honor. "Imagine that God would care to remember me by name," they must have said. Though God needs no written record to jog His memory, the symbolic importance of the "scroll of remembrance" would be widely understood.

## MALACHI 4:1

### When will the "day" come when evil is punished and good is revealed?

Every human being has a moral sense that yearns for justice and compassion in a world in which good is never pure, evil is mixed with economy, and resources are never sufficient to satisfy everyone. Someone is going hungry, someone is getting hurt, and who really cares? This is our constant problem.

The Bible looks toward a day when moral clarity replaces cloudiness. Evildoers will get their due and goodness will be plentiful. While Malachi could see only one distant point of fulfillment, we can see two from our place in history. The first was the Incarnation, God becoming man. In the presence of God, evil shows its despicable horror, and goodness is washed clean of rust and dirt. Good and bad take on distinct hues in the light of God's glory. The second is the consummation, the return of Christ at the end of history. God has promised judgment on evil and the victory of good, which all creation awaits. It's coming. Dimly visible, firmly promised, and definitely coming.

## MALACHI 4:6

### How is family love linked to God's blessing?

In families children learn how valuable they are. Most of that early affection is delivered by mothers, but fathers are just as important. Many fathers, however, are not natural caregivers; they must work at it. Some fathers may be more vulnerable to broken relationships with children and spouse, and less likely to patiently work things out. Perhaps that's why Malachi cites reconciliation between fathers and children as the surest sign that peace, love, and joy have overcome hurt and greed as dominant world forces.

God wills that families live in love and mutual support. That takes much work now. When it succeeds, however, the world is given a preview of good times to come. Fathers who love their children bear witness that God overcomes nature's stubborn resistance. The blessing of God, as manifested in loving families, previews an amazing life of peace and joy—and love—to come in His eternal kingdom.

A picture of the Last Judgment of God. Christ will return from heaven just as He promised.

# MATTHEW

*Here's a businessman (and not a popular one, at that) who gave his life to Jesus and found it changed forever. How could such a miracle happen? What questions about Jesus does Matthew answer?*

## MATTHEW 1:25

### How can a virgin give birth?

Physically, it is not possible. While certain organic species are able to procreate without cross-gender mating, humans have never done so apart from the miraculous conception here. It is not possible to formulate any scientific explanation for the fertilization and pregnancy process described in this passage. Nor are we given any information on the nature of God's role in this birth, other than attributing Mary's pregnancy to divine intervention.

A further question developed in the history of the church concerning Mary's perpetual virginity. The Roman Catholic Church adopted this teaching, which led to the near deification of Mary. We note that Mary had decided to marry before the announcement of her special birth (she was the "blessed virgin" surely, but also the "blessed fiancée"), and that Matthew 1:25 clearly points to sexual union between Joseph and Mary after Jesus' birth.

## MATTHEW 2:2

### What was the star the wise men followed to Bethlehem?

The best astronomical estimate is that the star seen by the wise men (perhaps astrologers from several different places) was the conjunction of Saturn, Jupiter, and Mars in 6 B.C. However, this situates the star two years prior to the best estimate of the year of Jesus' birth. Such a conjunction would have produced a remarkably bright light in the night sky. Another possibility, of course, is that God created a special light to signal Jesus' birth.

The three wise men from eastern lands saw the star in the sky and followed it to Bethlehem.

# Matthew 2:15

## Matthew quotes a verse from Hosea 11:1. What is the connection?

In Israel's early history, God's relationship with the nation was compared to a father relating to his son (see Exodus 4:22–23). God gently led His "children" out of Egyptian bondage, down to Sinai, and eventually into the promised land.

In the New Testament, Matthew invested new meaning into the historical event of the Exodus and Hosea's description of it as he recorded the flight of the young Christ child to Egypt. In essence, Matthew was closely identifying the Messiah with the nation's escape from Egypt. Just as Israel had done, the Messiah (God's Son) went to Egypt to avoid danger and emerged to fulfill God's plan. Israel's circumstances foreshadowed the life of Christ; Christ's life fulfilled the words of the prophet.

# Matthew 2:16

## Why did the people of Bethlehem not protect their boys from Herod's soldiers?

Surely this was one of the most brutal massacres of the Bible, if not in raw numbers, in terms of its victims. Only the most corrupted form of evil could lead a state to summarily execute innocent children. Why did the people not resist?

Perhaps because resistance was impossible. The Roman governor could do all within his power to keep a region under rule. Likely no political appeal was available to the Bethlehemites. Certainly they could not withstand the power of Rome's military superiority. Perhaps resistance would have increased the pain, with additional deaths as Herod's way of suppressing dissent. Losing the infants was terrible enough—it

would have been even worse exposing other children and adults to the slaughter.

Altogether, this incident explains the hatred of most Jewish people toward Rome. Though the Jewish leadership, who shared in Rome's privileges, was willing to work with the occupying nation, the average person was eager to find a political solution, longing for a Messiah to deliver them from Rome's grasp.

# Matthew 3:11

## What is baptism "with fire"?

Matthew and Luke include the phrase in their reports of John the Baptist's announcement concerning the baptism that Jesus will bring. Mark and John do not report it. What did John the Baptist mean?

Some believe the phrase "with fire" works like an adjective. In this view, Jesus will baptize with the "fiery Holy Spirit," an image that previews the arrival of the Spirit at Pentecost. Another view sees in John's distinction a baptism of grace (the Holy Spirit) and a baptism of judgment (fire). Note that Matthew's surrounding verses, 10 and 12, speak of fire in terms of judgment. All that Jesus did and said divides humanity between those two baptisms. Life cannot remain the same—there is no middle ground. With Jesus, one either accepts the word of reconciliation or continues in rebellion and finally into judgment. The conjunction *and* in verse 11 ("and with fire") does not join two elements of one baptism, but notes the two different types of baptism that Jesus brings.

# Matthew 4:10

## Is worship the antidote for temptation?

In all three temptations, Jesus counters with an appeal to His own accountability to God the Father. The final temptation, to gain all the nations, pits two extremes against each other and shows clearly that the life of reverence and worship, the "fear of the Lord" as the Old Testament puts it, is always the priority that sets the rest of the agenda. What good is ownership of the world apart from the reverent relationship with God that gives life its meaning? Satan's offer is hollow. Jesus understands that fully.

The antidote for temptation is the priority of God in our lives—putting Him first in our hearts. Our primary expression of God's priority is through worship. Jesus advises that worship precedes ownership and, in the case of this temptation, forecloses the hollow offer. The person tempted to sin would do well to worship first. The sequence, of course, robs the sin of its appeal. Without any sizzle, sin shows its true taste and texture. What looked like steak is really chalk dust. Who needs it?

## MATTHEW 4:23

### What was the "Good News about the Kingdom" that Jesus preached?

The full answer to this question requires that we start in Genesis and end in Revelation; that is, that we review the entire Bible and all of God's dealing with creation. The Good News

Jesus preaches the Sermon on the Mount.

about the kingdom is simply that God loves His creation and wills to save it, not destroy it. God's will was being accomplished before Jesus' immediate listeners, and is being done before all who hear Jesus' message today. This is the meaning of everything in the Bible from the beginning to the end: God has come, through His Son Jesus Christ, to seek and to save the lost.

## MATTHEW 5:4

### Why would Jesus claim that mourners were basically happy, or "blessed"?

Those who truly mourn (over sin, over death, over all manner of evil in the world) are the only people who can also experience true happiness, or joy, in the comfort of the Lord. The secular view of happiness requires that our senses be stimulated with experiences of gratifying pleasure. The Christian view of happiness requires that our spirits be assured that God loves us and will redeem us from a world of evil, greed, stupidity, and, finally, death. How can we embrace God's consolation if we do not feel deeply our need and mourn our condition?

Mourning is not moping, though. The Christian mourner is not to be long-faced and sluggish. The mourner may weep, laugh, hug, or go off alone to pray, but he or she does not wear an ashen face broadcasting perpetual sadness. The reason is clear: Christian mourning has been overcome now in part and overcome completely in God's future.

## MATTHEW 5:17–18

### What role do Old Testament laws and decrees play in moral decision-making today?

Matthew makes it clear that Jesus did not come to destroy Old Testament law but to fulfill it. Yet today we don't follow all of the decrees found in the Old Testament, such as the dietary and sanitary laws.

Old Testament law revealed the character of God and the requirements for a relationship with God. Paul writes in Romans that the law is holy, good, and shows us our sin. Yet no one can satisfy the requirements of the law.

Surely anyone coming into the presence of God needs to be blameless before the law. By the law's standards, therefore, people are forever excluded from their Creator. God provided a way to satisfy the law: Jesus Christ. All who are in Jesus Christ can enter the presence of God because sin is conquered and forgiven in the death and resurrection of God's own Son.

Of all the Old Testament laws, the Ten Commandments are the most relevant today. The first four commandments instruct us on God's holiness and the last six on human relationships. These requirements are affirmed by Jesus in the New Testament (Matthew 5–7) and have always guided Christian conduct.

Moses presenting the tablets of God's law.

passé, but its time of usefulness will come to an end when history closes and the heavenly kingdom in all its fullness begins. Then, law will be passé for sin will have ceased.

## MATTHEW 5:18

### Are Old Testament rules, commandments, and laws still in force?

In older translations, Jesus utters here His first emphatic, "Amen, I say unto you." That underlines the importance of the teaching here that God's law is fully operative and normative until. . .until when? In one view, until Jesus is raised from the dead and forgiveness of sin through faith in Jesus provides the new basis for salvation. In another view, the law is normative until the heavens and earth pass away, a point in time after which Jesus' Word will be eternally normative (Matthew 24).

Historically, the latter view has enjoyed wider acceptance. The law of God is not

## MATTHEW 5:22

### Are negative words directed at another person the moral equivalent of murder?

Murder is the last irrevocable act in a drama of several scenes, all of which relate to one person despising another. The root of the problem is hate; the final expression is murder. God's law is not concerned solely with eliminating the final act, but with eliminating the root problem. To hate someone is glaringly disobedient to God's law. Killing people is a heinous expression of hatred. The demeaning words we speak unveil attitudes of hatred that God condemns. Judgment is not only for those who manage to keep their hatred to socially acceptable levels but also for those who harbor hatred, for those whose hatred festers and spoils their heart. The kind of relationships God intends are impossible in an atmosphere of harbored hate. No group can truly praise God and still nurture hatred toward others, including its enemies.

## MATTHEW 5:29

### Wouldn't the world's people be totally blind if they followed Jesus' orders on sexual sin?

Literal obedience to this statement would eliminate many people's sight pretty quickly. While the solution cannot be literal here, it is nonetheless drastic and painful. In Jesus' clinic for sexual sin, the doctor's recommendation is always surgery *now*—no waiting period, no half measures, no consideration of side effects. Don't even wait for the anesthetist to arrive. This cancer must be thrown out without delay. Better to limp into heaven, so to speak, bearing the scars of surgery, than to leap into hell scratchless and manicured.

This kind of drastic action always carries personal pain. An adulterous affair may generate genuinely tender feelings, perhaps truer and more affirming than either party knows in his or her marriage. Jesus' solution: End the affair immediately and decisively; cast it away like throwing out an eye—with all the hurt and finality that such an act will involve.

An inclination toward same-sex love is such a culturally sensitive question today that any action advised by the culture is clouded in twice the normal murk—with no one wishing to offend any "lifestyle choice." Jesus' solution: Don't wait, don't fiddle with half-measures—the entire hand must go; the eye must go.

Whatever sexual attachments may seem vital to life today—"I cannot live without him/her"—if they present a break in one's obedience to God, they must be thrown out, whatever the personal price. Such decisive dealing with sin is God's severe mercy. Jesus has already promised that those who mourn will be comforted, and those who are pure of heart will see God (Matthew 5:4, 8).

## MATTHEW 5:48

### How can anyone be perfect?

Is that what the verse requires—utter perfection? The word often translated "perfect" refers to the maturing disciple who is reaching for the goal; the person who understands the requirements of goodness and grasps for that high standard; the person full-hearted toward others, brimming with mercy and wisdom.

Being perfect here is not a matter of scrupulous conformity to rules, as legalists might insist. It is not a matter of error-free intelligence concerning the will of God, as rationalists might insist. It is not a matter of theological precision, as if God could be perfectly understood. To be mature and merciful, reaching for the goal and growing in the faith, eager for life with God and steady in life with other people—to be living the whole of Matthew 5—that's what we can and ought to be.

## MATTHEW 6:8

### If God already knows what we need, why pray?

While the logic of this question may seem secure, it fails on theological grounds. If God did not know our situation, if He needed our prayers for His information, would God be God? If prayer is like a press briefing, bringing God up-to-date on our needs, then we had better get and keep God's limited attention fast. But all these thoughts fade away in light of the biblical portrait of God as omniscient (all-knowing).

Prayer is conversation. Since God already knows, we can simply talk over our troubles without ranking and describing them. We can

Prayer is conversation with God. He invites us to talk to Him anytime, anywhere.

more the clothing on His back (Mark 15:24).

Jesus meant what He said and practiced what He preached when He encouraged listeners to store up treasures in heaven and not on earth. While Jesus restored many people to physical health (Mark 1:34), He left others unhealed. His chief concern was spiritual healing and announcing the kingdom of God (Mark 2:17). Modern believers motivated by the prospect of earthly wealth and physical wellness do well to realize that money tends to diminish faith and that all people eventually surrender to the body's deterioration.

tell God our feelings about those troubles (yes, He knows those feelings, too). In the telling, we foster the relationship that God has initiated in Jesus Christ and that we need with our heavenly Father.

When you need to talk over your most personal troubles, do you seek a stranger or a friend? Likely, it's your best friend—the one who already knows you. The fact that God already knows us isn't a reason not to pray; it's the best reason to pray.

## MATTHEW 6:19–21

### Does believing in Jesus give us "health and wealth"?

Jesus' parents were poor (as evidenced by their offering on the occasion of His dedication at the temple, Luke 2:24). Jesus Himself never acquired worldly possessions. He did not have a house (Luke 9:58). He depended upon the support of others (Luke 8:3). He once even had to send Peter to catch a fish in order to pay His taxes (Matthew 17:27). When Jesus died, the Roman soldiers divided His possessions, which amounted to nothing

## MATTHEW 6:22–23

### How is the optic system related to spiritual health?

The term "eye" used here may be understood to represent one's life goals. The meaning of the metaphor is that the direction of one's life, the goals toward which one strives, ought to be fully God-fixed and obediently unidirectional. Looking toward one's riches, passions, or reputation is to be distracted from God's purposes. As the optic nerve feeds the mind, so the Christian should feed on ambitions of joyful obedience and service and generosity toward others. A certain carelessness can exist about having lesser goals that reach only to the edge of the horizon. The gospel enables us to see further, through the mist, toward heaven.

## MATTHEW 7:1-2

### How can a person make good moral choices without also judging someone?

To obey this command in the strictest sense would disallow even the judgment of whether to have jelly or marmalade on your morning toast. Everywhere the Bible urges the use of sound moral judgment throughout life, so something else must be at stake here.

First, the judgment to be avoided is the judgment of condemnation, not the judgment of discernment. We are not to presume to take God's place, assigning anyone to an eternal condition or assuming that anyone is beyond hope. Rather, the keynote of Christian discipleship is mercy.

Second, the Old Testament judge brought the strongest moral and physical judgment to bear on wrongdoers. Penalties for wrongdoing were brutal and decisive, with no appeal once judgment was published. This, too, the Christian disciple is to avoid. The ferocity of Old Testament judgment was replaced with the vulnerability of New Testament grace. Let God be Judge. Christians are to live in the light of the sovereign, loving God who makes all things new and possible.

## MATTHEW 7:21-23

### If many who call Jesus "Lord" are still without salvation, how can anyone be sure about eternity?

This is one of the most difficult warnings in the entire Bible, for we have every reason to imagine that the "Lord-Lord" sayers referred to here can be the high-profile Christian workers with impressive résumés and immaculate church credentials. Yet Jesus does not know them. If these successful Christian workers

When we accept Jesus as Savior and Lord, we are promised eternity in heaven with Him.

can't pass muster, what about those of modest skill and fewer accomplishments?

The key is found in the Sermon on the Mount, of which this warning is a part. Great Christians may build their résumés and empires, but have they mourned, suffered persecution, sought peace? Are they meek? The fruits of Christian living outlined in the Sermon on the Mount are a far cry from the accomplishments that win respect and honor in the church today. It is all but guaranteed that no Christian college will name its new residence hall after a mourner; no church will name its new wing after a meek person; no honorary degree will be given to someone unfairly defamed for Jesus—yet these are the fruits of Christian living honored in Jesus' sermon.

When the "Lord-Lord" sayers present their significant accomplishments to Jesus at the end, they will finally be confronted with the most tragic interpersonal failure described in the Bible. Their life experience did not include *knowing* Jesus, but only working for Jesus in a fashion energized by honors granted by others. We can be sure about eternity because of Jesus' promise to save us. We can know that those promises are indeed ours as we grow into obedient followers of Jesus. The accumulation of the world's honors is secondary, even unnecessary, to that process.

## MATTHEW 9:14–15

### When is fasting appropriate?

Jesus seems to reduce fasting to a minor religious practice here, in favor of a more joyous approach to God in which celebration and feasting play a prominent role. Is fasting then to be abandoned?

Not entirely. Fasting had become a standard religious practice throughout the ancient world and certainly in Judaism. All too often a fast took on the significance of religious duty and the person fasting was

to be considered a devout person indeed. When Jesus did not emphasize fasting to His disciples, some wondered how He could present Himself as a credible religious teacher. In Jesus' teaching, fasting was not to be abandoned, but neither was it to be the keynote in a relationship with God.

Fasting has its place, though the Bible remains ambiguous about precisely what place. It is often associated with prayer. Fasting should never cause a person to regard God as joyless or discipleship as an endurance test. The Christian ascetic must ask whether his or her discipline has become an end in itself. No religious exercise should become a substitute for the joy of a relationship with the living Christ. In our Western society of plenty, where most every stomach is full most of the time, fasting is a helpful reminder that true nourishment comes from fellowship with God.

## MATTHEW 9:30–31; 12:15–16

### Why did Jesus frequently instruct those He healed not to tell anyone?

Jesus did not want to be known only as a miracle worker. He also did not want His primary business—spiritual healing—to be obscured by physical healings. He knew that if word spread about His supernatural power, many would come to Him for short-term solutions to disease but miss long-term solutions to sin. They would seek physical relief prior to and exclusive of the deeper needs of the soul. Keeping still about miraculous healings would reduce sensational headlines and public acclaim and promote the God-centered ministry Jesus wanted. Jesus did not seek recognition from educational institutions, streets named in His honor, or cozy treatment from politically savvy Roman bosses. He just wanted to tell the people some very good news: The kingdom of God has come!

## MATTHEW 10:37–38

### When does loving one's children turn bad?

Loving children is only bad when it becomes an ultimate priority. Jesus' words here are some of the most puzzling in the Bible. So accustomed are we to Jesus bringing peace and harmony that we neglect to consider His own predictions concerning the family difficulties that Christian discipleship may entail. Is it all right to bypass Jesus, if becoming a Christian would anger your father? Is saying no to Jesus okay, if saying yes meant that your children would be forced out of their schools or jobs? Jesus always demands first place, no matter the sacrifice.

But be careful here. Many a Christian has spoiled both faith and family in a militant fanaticism at just this point. We should not be looking for trouble. The mind of the fanatic feeds on the trouble his overblown religious persecutions can generate.

Jesus alerts us here to His supreme place in our hearts and lives. When He is first, all other relationships work (at least, they are situated to work—some take time). In some sad cases, however, a close relationship must be sacrificed in order to worship Jesus as Lord. If so, it must be done.

might not fit neatly into a theological scheme, and theologians themselves might fail to hear this truth. In any case, the childlike listeners are those who recognize Jesus' authority, have childlike faith, and gladly follow Him. These are the people to whom God can teach His truth.

Jesus calls us all to come to Him with childlike faith and trust.

## MATTHEW 11:25

### Can only children learn about God?

Not children age-wise, but children God-wise; that is, people who are not so wrapped up in their own wisdom that God cannot speak a word to them. Perhaps Jesus had in mind the religious leadership trapped in their laws and regimen. Perhaps today Jesus' words

## MATTHEW 12:11

### Is it okay to fix your carburetor on Sunday?

Jesus could hardly believe how misguided religious leaders were on the purpose of the Sabbath. What God had given as a day of rest, renewal, and worship, men had made into a day of religious showing off. Jesus answered their rudely hypothetical catch-question with another hypothetical one—about helping a sheep out of trouble, the animal here representing all the wealth a person had.

Because Jesus is coming again, we want
to live in a manner that pleases Him.

Of *course* such a person would rescue his
sheep.

Jesus went on to explain that God's
purpose in Sabbath rest is not to impose
additional burdensome rules that define
right and wrong effort on that special day.
This is a day off! It is a day for the worker to
recover, and along with the worker, all the
worker's beasts. Modern workers do well to
give priority on Sunday to worship; then,
if tinkering under the hood is your way of
recovering from work, go ahead and enjoy
your tinkering. You have every reason to
believe that if Jesus were on earth now, He
would be glad to join you.

## MATTHEW 12:36

### Is every word we say recorded in heaven?

It's scary to think that on the day of
reckoning we will be called to account
for every single stupid thing we have ever
said. Words reveal deep-seated attitudes.
Spoken words change people's worlds.
Nothing remains the same when a guy
tells a woman, "I love you." Words have
led nations into war. Jesus' point here is to
measure one's words, suppressing the half-
baked angry ones, lest at the judgment, the

hurtful consequences of your thoughtless words require an accounting.

When using the words of love, mean them deeply. If words will lead to conflict, use words that will resolve the dispute without needless suffering. When speaking to God, don't fool around with commitments you don't mean. Words matter. By them we give meaning to everything.

## MATTHEW 12:41–42

### Why should pagans offer moral advice about anything?

One might expect that persons from pagan cultures would not be invited to render opinions at the final judgment, but just the opposite is the case. Two representatives from "the outside"—the citizens from Nineveh (the "great city" of Assyria that repented under Jonah) and the queen of Sheba (who traveled to hear Solomon) will assist in judging those who heard and rejected the gospel. If God's truth is apparent to people from "the outside," how much quicker should "insiders" repent? If the common sense of outsiders leads to right moral judgments, shouldn't the informed sense of insiders do so all the more? Jesus is telling us here not to hesitate when confronted by the truth.

## MATTHEW 13:5–6

### What's the lesson in hiking rocky terrain?

Not every person who hears the gospel will be saved, Jesus knows. Not every heart into which the gospel is sown will nurture its seed to maturity, Jesus warns. Some people will hear, accept, but not grow into disciples. They are likened to rocky soil, which provides a start to the seed lodged in its crevice. With nourishment in short supply and water quickly drained away, that seedling withers. So it will be for many who hear God's Word. The

warning is applied today to people who are distracted from God through their busyness, entertainment, or moral ambiguities. Let your life be fertile soil for God's message, Jesus urges. Then it will produce good fruit that lasts.

## MATTHEW 13:13

### How can a person hear but not hear?

The experience of sound waves crashing into the human eardrum—then nothing much happening between that point and the brain—is as common as a parent's last order to clean a bedroom. . .or a pastor's last sermon. . .or God's last word to us from the prophets or Jesus. Many sounds impressed on the eardrum are filtered from our minds long before we have considered their message. Or worse, having considered their message, we decide to ignore its truth.

Part of this verse is also a statement of the human condition: Satan has so muffled our sense of hearing that we cannot hear God's Word and respond to it. Only when God opens our ears do we hear His message. That keeps real listeners from becoming proud of their aural acuity. It keeps believers modest, even about their faith.

## MATTHEW 13:31

### When is it true that "small is better"?

This popular phrase seems counterintuitive—we like to believe that bigger is better. Yet in matters of faith and God's kingdom, preference is given to small things (modest, humble, anything but grandiose) that grow by God's grace into big things (in terms of service and faith). God's great message intends to grow from humble beginnings into something truly magnificent—from the vantage point of faith. While wealthy people might grow richer and brilliant people even more learned, the humble person growing in faith is the only growth that matters in the final accounting.

## MATTHEW 13:42

### Who gets thrown into the fire at the last judgment?

Bad people, outsiders, immoral people, we commonly think. But wait. Two kinds of people are described here. The first kind is in the middle of the church (weeds in the wheat field), not outsiders at all but insiders who never really obeyed God's Word. Instead, they "scandalized" others through maneuvering for advantage, through hurtful decisions, through callous disregard for others' spiritual welfare. Though these people seem to be integrated into the people of God, tragically, they are not. This is a warning to the church: The enemy is within, so keep faith pure. And there's a warning to religious people: Fire awaits those whose "faith" is a lie, those whose deceit hurts the real faith of others.

Fire awaits those involved in "scandal," the meaning of the Greek word used to describe those judged for hurting Jesus' cause.

## MATTHEW 13:44

### Should people sell all they own when becoming a Christian?

Jesus used this story to describe the joy of finding God. It's worth everything we have. In terms of value, nothing compares. The point of this story is joy, not poverty. Its teaching reminds us that joy fuels change, and all change is possible when the end result is finding God.

People are not instructed here to sell everything in order to find God. Poverty is not a prerequisite to spiritual life. But the joy of finding God supersedes every other consideration. Any other "find" pales in value compared to this one. So the next time you are moved by the sacrifice of missionaries or other dedicated Christians, realize that sacrifice is really joy. Knowing God is an experience full of joy.

Christ reigns above all at the Last Judgment and will judge all people according to whether they accepted Him as their Savior.

# MATTHEW 14:6

## Is dancing right or wrong?

Many Christians feel that dancing is wrong, the vertical substitute for horizontal immorality. This verse certainly speaks to the dangers of dance. Captivated by the sensuality of dance, Herod made a foolish promise that he had to keep for political reasons. John the Baptist lost his life because of a sexy dance.

Yet other examples of dance in the Bible tell of its expressiveness and joy. In 2 Samuel 6:14, David danced before the Lord "with all his might." Nothing morally questionable was attached to this demonstration of praise to God for Israel's recovery of the ark.

Apparently the rightness or wrongness of dance has everything to do with the context and meaning associated with it. When dance intends to express the virtues that enrich life, it is good. When it intends to excite passions that violate moral standards, it is wrong.

# MARK

*This book is perhaps the most straightforward of all the biographies of Jesus. Told in simple terms, the facts speak for themselves. And the story's message is compelling. Who can resist a Savior like this?*

## MARK 1:6

### Why did John the Baptist dress and act so differently from others?

John the Baptist set himself apart from the normal lifestyle of his world to do what God had called him to do. He did not drink alcohol or cut his hair. He lived in one of the harshest desert environments in the world, dressing primitively and eating simply. Yet people flocked into the desert to see this unusual man and hear his powerful message. When they arrived, they saw a man dressed like Elijah, the premier prophet of Israel hundreds of years earlier. His speech was harsh, clear, and penetrating. He called the people to repent—to turn away from their sins and to turn to God.

John the Baptist lived his message. His life in the wilderness provided solitude and focus to seek and hear the voice of God. In contrast to the religious leaders of his day, John lived in simplicity and poverty. He also lived in humility, not seeking personal fame or building his own power base. Instead, he pointed people to the coming Messiah and connected them with Jesus when He came to be baptized.

John the Baptist's unusual appearance and lifestyle not only matched his message—it was a visual protest against self-indulgent living, and it was a call to put God first.

John the Baptist dressed in clothing of camel's hair, making him look like the Old Testament prophets.

## MARK 1:11

### Is it normal for people to hear the audible voice of God?

No, it's not normal if you mean that people hear God's audible voice daily. God uses a variety of ways to communicate with us. No one can predict when God will speak in an audible voice.

God has spoken by various means throughout history. In the time of the Old Testament, God spoke to Jacob in dreams (Genesis 28:10–22), to Isaiah in visions (Isaiah 6), and audibly to Abraham (Genesis 18), Moses (Exodus 31:18), and others. God's voice was heard audibly at Jesus' baptism and on the Mount of Transfiguration (Mark 9:7), both times declaring to everyone present that Jesus was truly God's beloved Son.

Most Christians go through their entire lives without hearing the audible voice of God—but they do have clear communication with God through what is written in the Bible. That's why it is called God's *Word*. God has given us a clear record of His promises, commands, and the kind of relationship He wants to have with us. God also speaks to us through the presence of the Holy Spirit in our lives.

The Bible's existence doesn't necessarily preclude God's audible voice today. We cannot limit what God may choose to do. God may communicate miraculously in our modern world in places and circumstances where the church is not strong or where Christians do not have the Bible. And God often uses His people to be His "voice" and "arms and legs" to answer the prayers of people who are crying out to Him.

## MARK 1:14

### What is God's Good News?

The Good News that God has for people is all wrapped up in the person, life, and teachings of Jesus Christ. When Jesus started His ministry, He declared that a new time in history had arrived. The God who created this world and all its people was now on the planet in a human body. Knowing that God was not far away or disconnected from this world was good news. In Jesus, we see that God hears our cries and prayers. He knows all about us. We know God loves us and cares for us. We are not alone.

The best part of the Good News is that we can have peace with God despite our sinful nature and behavior. Although it seems too good to be true, God sent Jesus into the world to pay for our sins when He was crucified on the cross. God promises that if we believe on Jesus, we will be given everlasting life (see John 3:16). What we cannot do for ourselves, God has done for us through Jesus. Now, that's good news!

## MARK 1:35

### What would Jesus pray about—if He was God, wasn't He just talking to Himself?

Jesus could not live without prayer. When Jesus sought out solitary places for prayer, He gave a clearer picture of the three persons of

Jesus prays in the desert. Through prayer, He gains strength for the tasks He has to do on earth.

God (the Trinity)—God the Father, God the Son, and God the Holy Spirit.

Although Jesus had been present with God the Father from the creation of the world, His visit to this world in the form of a human body placed restrictions on Him that He had not known previously. Though separated physically from God the Father, He maintained contact through prayer.

Jesus knew that if He was going to meet men and women, He must first meet with God the Father. In prayer Jesus kept His mind in perfect agreement with His Father. The task of meeting the needs of the hurting people required that Jesus be full of that divine power. Prayer strengthened Him to do the work that had to be done.

on Jesus, they were even more troubled. This untrained religious leader claimed to be the fulfillment of the prophecies for the long-awaited Messiah. He declared a crippled man forgiven of his sins before He healed the man's disability. According to the religious leaders, that was blasphemy—claiming to do something only God could do.

The Jewish leaders saw Jesus as another grassroots preacher who would only lead true believers astray. They hesitated opposing Jesus for fear of losing the popularity contest with the common people, but they were looking for some action or statement that they could use to discredit Him either in religious or political matters.

## MARK 2:6–7

### If Jesus was healing and helping people, why were the Jewish leaders critical of Him?

The criticism came on two levels: professional jealousy and significant theological disagreements. The Jewish leaders were losing their popularity and influence with the people. First came John the Baptist, who drew large crowds out into the desert. His no-nonsense sincerity made the Jewish religious leaders look as though they had sold out to material comforts and status-seeking instead of preaching repentance as John was doing. When John baptized Jesus and declared Him the "Lamb of God," the Jewish leaders had another nonprofessional religious leader attracting the affections of the common people.

When Jesus spoke, His message was simple and clear. How could the Jewish leaders, with their religious rituals and limited record of miracles, compete for the loyalties and popularity of the people? They were losing their standing with the people they were supposed to lead and teach about God.

When the Jewish leaders put surveillance

## MARK 3:14

### What criteria did Jesus use to choose His disciples?

The twelve men Jesus chose represented a wide range of backgrounds and professions. It was a very mixed group with men from the extremes of society. Matthew was a tax collector and considered a sellout to the Romans. At the other end of the spectrum, Simon (called by Luke, "Simon the Zealot") was a fiery, violent nationalist seeking to overthrow the Roman oppressors. Jesus established this first Christian group with plenty of diversity as a model for the future church. The "Jesus model" is people from a variety of backgrounds and differences living together with one common focus—obeying and following the Lord.

The Bible doesn't explain specifically why these men were chosen over the many others who were following Jesus at the time. In fact, first-time readers of the Gospels would probably question the wisdom of selecting these twelve men until they read the book of Acts. The three years they spent with Jesus had a huge impression considering what these men went on to do.

Why twelve disciples? The number twelve is an important number in Jewish history. Jesus choosing exactly twelve disciples corresponds with the twelve tribes of Israel. Perhaps Jesus was trying to link the New covenant with the old system of Jewish religious practice.

## MARK 3:23–30

### How much power does Satan have in this world—and over us?

C. S. Lewis once said most people make one of two mistakes when considering Satan. Either they give him too much credit and power, or they underestimate his existence and role in this world. Satan does have great power in the world, but it is only temporary. Satan was once an angel who rebelled against God and was thrown out of heaven. Satan's power is certainly not equal to God's power. He has limited power far less than God because Satan himself was originally created by God as an angel. Satan's goal is to keep us from knowing God.

The power Satan has in this world is to tempt us to ignore or disobey God. Since the creation of Adam and Eve, Satan has been the tempter luring people away from God's truth and love. He makes what is superficial and destructive look attractive and fun. All human beings believe his lies at some point in life. He convinces us to ignore the promises of God and to exchange God's goodness to us for the lies of selfishness, greed, lust, and pride. Satan works to develop a self-centered attitude that he can manipulate for his destructive work. With Satan's subtle enticements we push God out and give ourselves permission to do whatever pleases our immediate desires.

Satan is already a defeated enemy. In Revelation 12:10–12, we read the promise of Satan's end when Christ returns to this world and destroys Satan and all his forces forever. When Jesus died on the cross and rose from the dead, He crushed Satan. Until that final judgment day we have to battle against his tricks and tactics. If we rely on God's Word and the power of the Holy Spirit, we can resist Satan. The Bible says if we resist the devil, he will flee from us (James 4:7).

## MARK 7:8–11

### Why were the Pharisees so rules oriented?

The Pharisees' desire to please God led them to build an elaborate system of man-made rules on top of God's written law. They were committed to obeying all of God's commands. Unfortunately, they treated their own religious laws with equal regard as God's holy law. In the process their focus shifted from knowing and serving God to obeying petty rules and regulations as the means of pleasing God. They came to believe that their salvation was achieved by their obedience to their law rather than by the grace and forgiveness of God.

These extra laws were developed out of

The Pharisees accuse Jesus of blasphemy and have Him arrested.

the traditions of the elders. They were not biblical or authoritative. The Pharisees' religious system pushed these petty laws more than examining the motives and desires of a person's heart. Rules were used to control behavior rather than developing a person's heart and mind to reflect what was important to God.

## MARK 8:29

### How did Peter know that Jesus was the Messiah?

Jesus asked His disciples who they thought He was. He had certainly given them plenty of evidence to believe He was the Messiah. The miracles, healings, and His power over nature added supernatural confirmation to the "Good News" message Jesus was preaching to the crowds. Still, it must have been difficult even for the disciples to declare that their new leader, Jesus, was in fact the Messiah

they had heard about all their lives.

Peter was impulsive in both his behavior and speech. So, while his fellow disciples answered Jesus' question cautiously and diplomatically, Peter boldly acknowledged what he felt in his heart. He wasn't constrained by what others thought or by their reaction to his declaration. Peter declared Jesus to be the Messiah because God had given him that truth and had opened his mouth to confess it.

## MARK 8:34

### What did Jesus mean when He said His followers must "shoulder your cross"?

Everyone living in Israel in Jesus' time knew what it meant to "shoulder your cross." The Roman empire had conquered Israel and ruled the land with its military power. Criminals and political opponents were routinely

Jesus "shoulders" His cross and carries it to Calvary.

executed by crucifixion, one of the cruelest forms of capital punishment ever practiced. The condemned were forced to carry their wooden crosses to the site of their execution. This public journey to death was a strong visual reminder that everyone was required to submit, either willingly or unwillingly, to the authority and power of Rome.

Jesus used this gruesome image both to foreshadow His future death and symbolize what it would cost for men and women to follow Him. Carrying a cross was a public display of a person's submission to Rome. Jesus called His disciples to openly identify with Him and submit to God in all issues and areas of life.

## MARK 9:23

### Can you get anything you want if you have faith?

God is not a supernatural vending machine. Jesus did not mean we can fulfill our selfish desires if we simply believe they will happen. There are some leaders and churches that teach that health and wealth are available to all Christians who have faith. That dangerous teaching not only puts the focus on the temporal comforts of life but also leads a believer to think that any shortage of health or wealth is the result of unbelief. That is not what Jesus taught.

What Jesus wants us to understand is that there are no limits to what God can do. He can heal and bless and prosper anyone and change circumstances big and small. Jesus reminds us of God's power so that we will never give up or lose hope when facing difficulties. God can come through for us and answer our prayers.

We cannot have everything we request from God. He decides what will be best for us and always gives us enough to serve and build His kingdom. We are instructed to keep asking for what will please God. "Anything is possible if a person believes."

## MARK 9:35

### What is the difference between leading people by domination and power and leading by serving?

Jesus caught His disciples arguing about who was going to be the top dog. It revealed how slow and dull the disciples were to actually understand what Jesus was teaching them. The disciples were embarrassed into silence. It gave Jesus a teachable moment with them.

Leadership by domination and power has always been the way the world operates. The bigger, stronger, smarter, more ruthless, and more attractive people get to the top. The pecking order flows down from there. Business and organizations measure greatness by high personal achievement. The disciples thought these rules were still in effect and were positioning themselves for the big moment when Jesus attained power and control of the government.

Jesus tried to explain to them the new rules—that serving others is the way to the top in God's kingdom. Desire to get ahead of others will hinder you as a disciple of Jesus. True greatness will come from being aware of the needs of others and giving service and help to them. That's how God measures true greatness. Jesus modeled this servant-leader lifestyle for the disciples. He gave of Himself to meet the needs of others even when He was weary. He did not seek recognition or honor for Himself. He washed the feet of the disciples during the last supper together before His death. He challenged them to do the same for each other.

## MARK 10:21

### Why did Jesus give such a tough command when the rich young man asked about obtaining eternal life?

When Jesus told the man to sell everything he had and follow Him, it became clear what was most important to this young man. It was a tough command from Jesus. In fact, we have no record of Jesus making such a command to anyone else. It was surprising that He would require it of someone as moral and upstanding as this young man.

Money is often a substitute for God. We all need money—but if it becomes our obsession or the basis of our security, we transform it from a necessity into an idol. Jesus wants to be first in our life. The first commandment is, "You must not have any other god but me." Giving up his money would test the young man's commitment to put following Jesus first above all else. It would also have humbled him and given him the opportunity to build his personal esteem on his service to others rather than living off the status of being rich.

The bluntness of Jesus reveals how serious a competitor money is to our worship of God. Jesus got right to the key issue and made the choice very clear. Walking away from Jesus is the last reference the Bible makes of that young man. Do you wonder if in the later years of his life he reconsidered the question and changed his answer?

## MARK 12:23

### Will we continue our relationships with family and friends in heaven?

The Bible doesn't give a clear, definitive answer to this question. There are some pieces of information, however, that we can put together to prepare ourselves for what is ahead.

We won't look the same in heaven as we do here on earth. God has promised us new, glorified bodies. Perhaps that means our new bodies will have the sensory equipment to recognize the person in the new body next to us. God has always highlighted the individuality and uniqueness of each person He created. He will not diminish that wonderful ingredient of our identity. We will be able to recognize people in some way.

Our relationships will be different. Jesus was once asked who would be married to whom in heaven, when a woman had been widowed and remarried several times over. Jesus told the questioner not to worry because there would not be any marriage in heaven. God has another plan for our relationships. We won't have the tension or competition we often feel in our earthly relationships. It will be wonderful to find out what God has planned.

## MARK 14:10

### Why did Judas betray Jesus?

The Bible doesn't give us a clear answer about the motive Judas had for betraying Jesus. Looking at the circumstances of his life as a disciple and events of the last weeks of Jesus' life, we can formulate a reasonable speculation of why it happened.

Judas Iscariot misunderstood what Jesus intended to do with the supernatural power He displayed and the following of people He had attracted. Judas wasn't alone. Most of the disciples thought Jesus was going to break out of His religious mode and make some political moves that would put Him and His disciples in charge of the nation of Israel. As Jesus and His disciples moved toward Jerusalem and the Passover celebration, Judas was growing impatient waiting for Jesus to make a move.

Judas betrays Jesus with a kiss.

When Jesus praised the woman who poured expensive perfume over Him, Judas realized Jesus was not concerned with the finances necessary to initiate a political move. So Judas talked to the enemy and hatched a plan that would force Jesus' hand. When Jesus allowed Himself to be taken without a fight, Judas had second thoughts and tried to return the money he had been paid. His remorse was so great that he hanged himself.

## What makes Jesus' prayer in the Garden of Gethsemane a model prayer for every Christian?

The major mistake we make when we pray is focusing on ourselves and our own needs. We pray "call for help" prayers and "gimme more" prayers, trying to get God to solve our immediate problems. Seldom do we pray with our mind focused on what God wants. Jesus' prayer in the garden is a helpful model for those learning how to pray.

Facing the major moment of His life, Jesus finds a solitary place to pray. He doesn't spend time talking about His crisis, avoiding it, or worrying about it—He prays about it. He takes some of His closest associates with Him and asks them to pray for Him while He slips into a solitary location. He doesn't face this moment alone. His prayer is honest. His prayer reveals His struggle and the raw emotion He is feeling. Jesus expresses His true feelings, but He does not try to get out of the situation in which His Father has placed Him. He reaffirms His desire and commitment to do God's will. Jesus is aware of the pain and suffering this will bring Him, but He seeks to please God more than having personal comfort.

We would pray better if we repeated what Jesus told the Father God—"I want your will to be done, not mine." While we will never face what Jesus faced, we can protect ourselves from temptation and bad decisions by praying as Jesus did. Read scripture and pray through what God has written about His purposes in your life and in the world. Make knowing and fulfilling God's purposes the focal point of your prayer life.

## MARK 14:71

### What made Peter ashamed to admit that he knew Jesus?

What a night it had been for Peter. Jesus had surprised them many times during their meal together by what He said and did. Judas, the treasurer, had walked out. Peter had made some big promises to Jesus and the whole group that had led to a minor confrontation with Jesus Himself. In the

Peter denies Jesus three times before the rooster crows.

garden he had fallen asleep when he should have been praying, and he had pulled a knife when he should have remained calm. Seeing Judas now connected with the enemies of Jesus really had pushed him over the edge. Jesus had intervened and somehow had kept him from being arrested or killed by the police.

Peter wasn't a coward. If he was afraid, he probably would have laid low after Jesus was taken away by Roman guards and the high priests' detail. Instead, he walked into the courtyard and risked being spotted. When a guard questioned him, Peter kept his cover by denying everything. Protecting himself when he was questioned two more times, Peter suddenly realized that Jesus' prediction about his three denials before the crowing of a rooster had come true. He remembered and his heart broke. He had failed his Lord.

## MARK 16:14

### Why were the disciples so slow to believe the reports that Jesus had risen from the dead? Didn't they want to believe that it was true?

The disciples didn't want to be fooled. They guarded themselves with cynicism. The recent events had blown away all their assumptions about life. Faced with such an incredible string of events, they retreated into the comfort zone of disbelief.

They were convinced that Jesus was going to be the conquering Messiah, freeing Israel from the oppression of Rome. They thought Jesus would use His supernatural powers to zap the Roman military might. They were prepared for a new political system and anticipated that they would be rewarded as disciples with a position of authority.

None of that happened. Jesus went willingly to His death. Rome had won again. The old religious system was still in effect. At best they were discredited; at worst they were accomplices who would be hunted down and eliminated.

In their despair, hearing the news of Jesus' empty tomb (from some emotional women) must have triggered fears of being deceived again. These men were out of hope. They didn't want to give in to some self-induced, emotional delusion. Their initial disbelief and ongoing examination of Jesus gives confidence to us as Christians separated by many centuries from Jesus' bodily experience on earth. The disciples' desire to know what was actually real, as opposed to what some wanted to believe, is similar to our modern search for truth. We can have confidence in the news these men delivered to us—Jesus Christ is risen!

# LUKE

*A physician by trade, Luke became one of our most important historians. He gave us this portrait of Jesus, and then later, in the book of Acts, he recorded the story of the early church.*

## LUKE 2:52–3:1

**Even Luke, the careful historian, skips Jesus' years between twelve and thirty. Why is nothing written about that time?**

The common assumption is that Jesus lived in Nazareth and assisted His father, Joseph, as a carpenter (see Matthew 13:55). Jesus probably experienced a life filled with the routines of any young Jewish man. If, as is commonly believed, Joseph died during this period, then Jesus as the oldest son would have helped provide for His family. Perhaps we do not have Gospel accounts of those eighteen years because Jesus' ministry had not yet begun.

Much about the life of Jesus is unreported in scripture. As John noted, "I suppose that if all the other things Jesus did were written down, the whole world could not contain the books" (John 21:25).

## LUKE 3:21–23

**Why did Jesus wait so long to begin His public ministry?**

Jesus was completely committed to doing the will of His heavenly Father (Matthew 26:39). His desire was to honor the Father (John 8:49), to please His Father (John 8:29; cf. Matthew 3:17; 17:5; Mark 1:11; Luke 3:22), to "do what the Father requires of me" (John 14:31). We must assume that Jesus did not present Himself for baptism and begin preaching the Good News until God the Father had directed Him to do so.

## LUKE 4:1–13

### When Jesus was tempted, could He have sinned? If so, how can He be fully God? If not, how can He be fully man?

That Jesus was tempted is clear (see also Matthew 4:1–11; Mark 1:12–13; Hebrews 2:18; 4:15). That Jesus never sinned is also clear (Luke 1:35; John 8:29, 46; 2 Corinthians 5:21; Hebrews 4:15; 7:26; 1 Peter 1:19; 2:22; 1 John 3:5).

For a person today to be tempted, there must be at least a momentary possibility of caving in to sin. This was not the case with Jesus; nonetheless, His temptation was real. We cannot go further, lest we diminish either Jesus' deity or His humanity.

## LUKE 8:4

### Why did Jesus speak so often in parables?

A parable is a short story that takes a familiar object or situation and gives it spiritual meaning. Parables illustrate spiritual truth by linking the common and known to the unfamiliar and hidden. A parable generally has one main point and one intended meaning.

Perhaps Jesus used parables to encourage reflection and to whet the appetites of the spiritually hungry. Listeners who were lazy and

Jesus is tempted by the devil in the desert. Satan fails and is sent away, then the angels minister to Jesus. This odd-shaped wall mural is found in a monastery in Italy.

unresponsive would not take the time or invest the effort to weigh the implications and applications of Jesus' parables. Only those who were hungry to know God and to live for Him would discover His truth and grow closer to Him. Faith is more about walking with Jesus than acquiring data to pass a test.

## LUKE 8:27

### Are demons as active today as in the time of Jesus?

There is no reason to believe and no biblical evidence to suggest that demonic activity has ceased or diminished since the time of Christ. In some corners of the world (often in primitive cultures), satanic phenomena are overt and common. In other places, demons apparently go about their evil, destructive work in more subtle, but no less real ways.

It could be theorized that the physical presence of the Son of God was in some way responsible for so many spectacular demonic encounters in the New Testament. However, it could be just as true that we are less aware of demonic activity today, since we have invented other, perhaps psychological and psychiatric, labels for it.

Christians are still engaged in spiritual warfare and must utilize "God's armor" (Ephesians 6:10–18). We have this encouragement: "The Spirit who lives in you is greater than the spirit who lives in the world" (1 John 4:4).

moments, Jesus in His glorified state (2 Peter 1:17). This brilliant revelation of the divinity of Jesus, normally veiled to the disciples, gave them a glimpse of His future glory and exposed them to the audible voice of God.

At the Transfiguration, Peter, James, and John see Jesus glorified. Moses and Elijah appear and talk with Jesus.

The experience must have encouraged the followers of Jesus, who surely were saddened by the prospect of Jesus' impending suffering and death (Luke 9:22–23).

## LUKE 9:28–36

### What purpose did the Transfiguration serve?

The Greek word translated "transfiguration" is the same word from which we get the English term *metamorphosis*. In this experience, possibly on Mount Hermon, Christ's whole appearance changed. Peter, James, and John were able to see, for a few

## LUKE 19:45–47

### What was it about Jesus and His message that so offended Israel's religious establishment?

Jesus upset the religious applecart. In His sermons and parables, He threatened long-held traditions that had become a burden to perform (Matthew 15:1–20). He openly condemned the "spiritual leaders" of Israel for their pride and hypocrisy (Matthew 23). Because of His popularity among the masses, those in power sought to squelch Him (Matthew 26:3–4; John 11:47–48). They weren't interested in truth; they merely wanted to preserve the status quo (specifically, their positions of power and prominence).

Perhaps it was inevitable that Jesus would offend religious leaders. Even today we may speculate on the number of church, seminary, and mission leaders who would not tolerate Jesus on their staffs or in their schools. People in power like to keep power and all the perks associated with it.

## LUKE 22:3–4

### Why would Jesus pick a disciple (Judas) who would betray Him?

It can be argued that all of Jesus' disciples betrayed Him. Peter denied knowing Him; the rest fled at His greatest time of need. The answer to the specific question of Judas may lie in the mysterious union of divine sovereignty and human freedom.

The betrayal of Jesus for thirty pieces of silver was both a choice Judas made (Luke 22:48) and part of the eternal plan of God (Psalm 41:9; Zechariah 11:12–13; Matthew 20:18; 26:20–25; Acts 1:16–20). That one of His select disciples would betray Him reminds us that no church is perfect. We should never assume that mere church activity constitutes true faith. It also reminds us to beware of a deal that has short-range attraction; long-range effects may be disastrous. Under any criteria, Judas made a very bad choice.

## LUKE 22:39

### What's the difference between a disciple and a Christian?

In the New Testament, a *disciple* is simply a learner, someone who subscribes to the teachings of another. A disciple of Christ, then, was one who followed Christ to learn His ways in word and deed. Outside of the Gospels, only a handful of verses in the New Testament use the word.

In the purest sense, a disciple requires the physical presence of the Master. When Christ ascended into heaven, the original disciples became known as *apostles*, and new converts were simply called *believers*, the predominant term in Acts and the Epistles. The term *Christian* was coined in Antioch (Acts 11:26). King Agrippa used this label (Acts 26:28) as did the apostle Peter (1 Peter 4:16). Practically and theologically, there is little distinction between the terms. When used in the Christian context, *disciple*, *believer*, and *Christian* all imply trust in and obedience to Jesus Christ.

## LUKE 24:39–40

### What kind of body did Jesus have after His resurrection?

It was a flesh-and-bones body like ours, recognizable to His followers (John 20:20), still scarred by the crucifixion (John 20:25–29; Revelation 5:6), and able to eat food (Luke 24:30–33, 41–43).

This resurrected body also had supernatural qualities. It could pass through walls (Luke 24:36; John 20:19) and could appear out of and disappear into thin air (Luke 24:15; John 20:19). In John's vision in Revelation 1, Christ's body retains human characteristics yet radiates heavenly glory.

According to the apostle Paul, believers will one day have resurrection bodies like Christ's (1 Corinthians 15:35–41). He was "the first of a great harvest of those who will be raised to life again. . . . For our perishable earthly bodies must be transformed into heavenly bodies that will never die" (1 Corinthians 15:20, 53).

# JOHN

*John's story of Jesus is less about the facts of our Lord's life and more about the person He is. This is an intensely personal biography, one that draws a reader to conclude that something very important is happening here.*

## JOHN 1:1

### In what way was Jesus the "Word"?

John's use of the "Word" to describe Jesus was a startling new application of a popular expression. The term was used widely by theologians and philosophers, both Jews and Greeks. It described the agent of creation (Psalm 33:6); God's message to His people through the prophets (Hosea 1:2); and God's law, His standard of holiness (Psalm 119:11). In Greek philosophy, "the Word" was the principle of reason that governed the world. John's description shows clearly that He is speaking of Jesus (John 1:14)—a human being He knew and loved, yet at the same time the Creator of the universe, the revelation of God, the living picture of God's holiness.

Use of the term held certain risks for John's Gospel. Jewish readers would hear blasphemy in calling any human person "the Word of God." Learned Greek readers would consider the "Word became human" (John 1:14) unthinkable, incomprehensible. To John and to all Christians after him, this new understanding of the Word was the gospel, the Good News of Jesus Christ.

## JOHN 2:10

### Does Jesus' miracle at Cana encourage the use of alcoholic beverages?

Conservative churches that discourage or ban use of alcoholic beverages are bewildered at the production of wine as Jesus' first miracle. Such

The wedding in Cana where Jesus performed His
first miracle by turning water into wine.

churches have sometimes insisted that the wine in John 2 was nonalcoholic, despite the wedding guests' unusual delight and appreciation of it. Surely, Jesus did make very good wine, yet no hint of alcoholic abuse clouds this account.

Everything in God's creation can be misused, including fermented beverage. Nowhere does the Bible forbid use of alcohol, only the misuse of it. Truly, this miracle of water into wine happens every growing season in the "miracle" of grapes and other crops. The miracle in John 2 came when Jesus did nature's work instantly, without the use of the natural process.

## JOHN 2:11

### Why did Jesus use miracles?

Christ did miracles to authenticate His claims to be the Messiah. John called these supernatural acts "signs"—events intended to point people to God, to signal the presence of God with His people. Who but God has authority over nature, disease, death, and evil? A carpenter from Nazareth calming a raging storm, giving sight to the blind, calling Lazarus from the tomb, and driving out demonic spirits, emphatically demonstrates that He is the Son of God. Here was the kingdom of God breaking into our lives. Here the Lord showed His heart for the needy. The miracles of Christ also point to a future when peace, health, and goodness will reign.

## JOHN 2:13-17

### How can Jesus be considered sinless when the Bible describes His anger?

All four Gospels describe Jesus clearing the money changers from the temple; none use the term "anger" as part of the description. We infer anger from the facts given and from the passion mentioned in John 2:17.

If it was indeed anger, then Jesus made good use of its strong motivating power. But He did not let anger control Him. Ephesians 4:26–27 insists that anger be short-lived. Jesus' anger in the temple market was for the honor of God's name and the sanctity of the worship place. His confrontation with those who would use such a place for commercial profit was quick, decisive, and dramatic, but nothing suggests that Jesus sustained a campaign of anger even against the persons who felt His whip that day.

## JOHN 3:5

### What did Jesus mean when He told Nicodemus that "no one can enter the Kingdom of God without being born of water and the Spirit"?

Jesus was explaining the importance of spiritual rebirth, saying that people do not enter the kingdom by living a better life but by being spiritually reborn. "Of water and the Spirit" has been taken to refer to the sequence of physical birth (water) and spiritual birth (Spirit), or regeneration by the Spirit signified by Christian baptism. Either way the need is clear: New life in Christ—eternal life—is a gift of God applied to believers in the power of the Holy Spirit.

The water may also represent the cleansing action of God's Holy Spirit (Titus 3:5). Nicodemus would have known God's promise in Ezekiel 36:25–26. Here was the fulfillment of that promise standing before him, offering all that the prophet had foretold. What a dramatic moment in Nicodemus's life. That same moment is offered to every person who hears God's Good News, the gospel of forgiveness of sins, and confesses that Jesus is Lord.

## JOHN 4:1–26

### Why did Jesus treat the Samaritan woman the way He did?

Everything in Jesus' encounter with the Samaritan woman was intended to point her to eternal life: His deep concern for her, His confronting her sin, His challenge to her shallow understanding of God. He offered her living water—spiritual life in God's holy family. In a miraculous way, Jesus offered the woman citizenship in a kingdom far different than any she belonged to. By the cultural rules of the day, none of this should have happened.

Jesus treated the Samaritan woman just like God treats all people—with deeply personal compassion and spiritual salve for the hurts that would otherwise destroy.

one that Jesus had come to fulfill: saving people from spiritual death, that is, from eternal separation from His loving heavenly Father.

Though Lazarus was raised miraculously, he did die later. So did Mary and Martha, the disciples, and all of Jesus' closest friends. Jesus did not come to spare His loved ones the experience of physical death but to show them the path to eternal life.

## JOHN 11:25–26

### What promise did Jesus make to those who believe in Him?

Jesus made the idea of a distant resurrection an immediate reality. He identified Himself as the source for all life in His stunning announcement to Martha here.

Jesus talks with the Samaritan woman at the well and tells her He will give her living water.

## JOHN 11:4–6

### Why did Jesus let Lazarus die?

No one knows. Jesus' reasons for delay are not explained here. We can only surmise that a higher purpose—higher than saving people from physical death—caused Jesus not to go with immediate haste to His friend's side. That purpose was surely the

Martha believed in a future resurrection, but she had not yet seen, in Jesus Himself, power over death. She still needed to see that death was not a barrier to Jesus' power, and because of that, death for the believer was entrance into life eternal. That is an astonishing promise indeed: that the ultimate human limitation is overcome in God's love for us. A home in heaven awaits all who follow Jesus through the door.

## JOHN 13:1-17

### Why did Jesus wash the disciples' feet?

Jesus continually surprised the people around Him, forever doing the unexpected. Yet, in every way, Jesus' actions backed up His claims. When He preached that His purpose was to serve and to give His life a ransom for many (Mark 10:45), it was not mere lip service. He

and humility. He washed their feet, illustrating an earlier statement: "Anyone who wants to be the first must take last place and be the servant of everyone else" (Mark 9:35).

## JOHN 14-16

### What does the Holy Spirit do?

The third person of the Trinity, the Holy Spirit, applies the work of Christ to each believer.

Jesus washes Peter's feet—the Master takes the form of a servant.

demonstrated His own humility by practical acts of love. As the disciples jostled among each other for the best place at the table and argued over who was greatest, Jesus quieted the competition with an ancient rite of service

During the Last Supper, Jesus described what His disciples could expect to discover about the Holy Spirit, whom they would receive shortly after His ascension. Chapters 14–16 of the Gospel of John teach that the Holy Spirit will be with believers forever. He will live with us and in us, teach us, remind us of Jesus' words, convict us of sin, show us God's righteousness, announce God's judgment on evil, guide into truth, give insight into future events, and bring glory to Christ. Many people are unaware of the Holy Spirit's activities, but to those who hear Christ's words, the Holy Spirit gives assurance of God's love and guidance for all of life.

(John 14:6), and eternal life is knowing Him (John 17:3).

On the other hand, those who do not have the Son of God have no such assurance. Like any other blessing from God, assurance belongs to each and every believer who rests in the promise of God. That's a good decision, because when God makes a promise, He keeps it.

## JOHN 20:31

### How can a person know for sure that he or she has eternal life?

John wrote his Gospel so that readers might believe in Christ (John 20:31). He wrote his epistle so that believers might be certain they possess eternal life in Christ. Though doubts occasionally shake us and we sometimes falter in faith, we do not have to worry over or wonder about our salvation. If we have the Son (through faith), we have eternal life. It is our possession, now and forevermore. Why? Because Christ is life

## JOHN 21

### Why did Peter find forgiveness, but Judas did not?

Two of the disciples stood out in their abandonment of Jesus. Judas and Peter demonstrate opposite consequences of sin. As far as we know, Judas reached the point of regret for betraying Jesus and then killed himself. Peter went beyond regret to repentance and found God's forgiveness. Jesus forgave and restored Peter for the same reason that He forgives and restores us—He has promised to do so. That's very good news, since none of us is perfect.

# ACTS

*When the Christian church was young, why didn't it fold?*
*Persecuted and dispersed, why didn't early believers cave in?*
*Shipwrecked, beaten, and rejected, why didn't early mission-*
*aries throw in the towel?*

## ACTS 2:5

### Why was Jerusalem such an international city?

Long before the events of Acts 2, the Jewish people had been dispersed as war prisoners by several nations and scattered by persecution. Nevertheless, devout Jews yearned to celebrate the holy feasts in Jerusalem.

Pentecost, an annual celebration commemorating the giving of the law on Mount Sinai fifty days after the Exodus, was celebrated each year fifty days after Passover. Jews gathered in Jerusalem from all over the Greco-Roman world. This multilingual gathering included God-fearing Jews from west of the Caspian Sea (the area of modern-day Iran, Azerbaijan, and Kurdistan), from Elam (north of the Persian Gulf) and Mesopotamia (modern-day Iraq), from Asia Minor (modern-day Turkey), from North Africa, Egypt, Libya, Rome, Crete, and possibly from the area of modern-day Yemen.

A map of old Jerusalem.

# Acts 2:17-18

## Did women take on a new role as the Christian church emerged?

In the Old Testament era, women were not allowed in leadership or priestly service. Churches today debate whether that circumstance was part of God's creation order or part of Israel's cultural apparatus. The evidence in this passage clearly shows that God's Spirit operates without respect to gender, suggesting a new way of understanding the role of women in spiritual leadership. The Spirit gives spiritual gifts to equip God's people to do His work and build up the church, the body of Christ (Ephesians 4:11–13). None of the lists of gifts (Ephesians 4, Romans 12, and 1 Corinthians 12) indicates gender as a consideration.

Several women were active ministers in the early church. Priscilla and her husband, Aquila, were coworkers in the gospel with Paul (Acts 18); Phoebe, who delivered Paul's letter to Rome, was honored as a deacon (Romans 16:2); Euodia and Syntyche are named as valuable coworkers (Philippians 4:2–3).

On the other side, 1 Timothy 2 and 1 Corinthians 14 contain instructions that seem to reduce the role women may play in the church. The issues related to interpretation and context of these passages are worth readers' further study. Books with creditable teaching are available on all sides of the question. What is clear from scripture is that both men and women are equal in terms of salvation and faith (Galatians 3:28), and that spiritual gifts are given to all in the church to carry out the work of the gospel.

# Acts 2:38

## Does baptism affect the forgiveness of sins?

Can a religious ritual trigger a spiritual result? The church throughout history has been divided on this point. Those who favor the idea believe that God honors obedient acts done by sinners whose hearts (and intentions) may not always be honorable or genuine. Those who oppose the concept believe that God wants obedience of the heart (intention, surrender of will), and outward rituals only signal internal change. Thus, the Roman Catholic Church and sacramental churches within Protestantism encourage observance of rituals as elements of obedience that carry God's blessing. Baptist churches (along with many others) reserve sacraments for those whose life is free of known sin.

So what does God want?

The Bible answers repeatedly: simple trust in Jesus Christ (He is Lord!) and eager obedience in works of love and acts of faith that God has commanded (be baptized!). In other words, both.

Mere outward show of ritual is repeatedly condemned as the gross mistake of the religiously empty—the Pharisees, for example. Inward belief not demonstrated in life is likewise condemned as fictitious faith (James 2:14).

Whenever we baptize or eat the Lord's Supper, we demonstrate obedience to God, who saves us in Christ. Those are precious moments of remembering God's great work for us and pledging ourselves anew to loyal, vigorous faith. God is pleased, and His pleasure is a blessing to us.

# Acts 4:12

## Is Jesus the only way to God?

In our eclectic, pluralistic era, it may sound arrogant to claim that God forgives sins by one way only, and that one person only— Jesus—speaks the truth about God. How can Christians be so exclusive?

Many churches today, asking that very question, have decided not to be so exclusive, and have agreed to honor and respect different faiths as valid in themselves. It's one thing to honor the faith commitments of a person, and quite another to respect that faith system as equal in value to the Bible's message. Here's the place to draw the line.

Christians surely do believe (because the Bible clearly teaches) that salvation is found in Jesus alone, and that all people are called to serve and worship Jesus as Lord. No alternatives. No second-bests.

Christians are also called to respect people of other faiths. Yes, to pray for them, serve them in love, and witness to them about the truth. But also to respect their dignity, understand their traditions, and afford them the space for decision making that genuine faith requires.

It is arrogant to reserve for Christians alone the respect, friendship, and dignity that all people deserve. It is obedient to reserve for Jesus alone the worship, dedication, and trust that He alone deserves.

## ACTS 8:13–17

### Is baptism in the name of Jesus different from baptism in the Holy Spirit?

Churches in the Pentecostal or charismatic tradition believe it is, based in part on this narrative concerning Philip. Other churches believe this story describes an emerging, young movement, holding nonetheless that Christian baptism (the one and only baptism) is normally accompanied by the presence of the Holy Spirit (Acts 2:38).

All churches affirm the necessity of the Holy Spirit in the believer's life. Differences have developed over the process by which the Spirit works, the timing of that work, and the believer's stance as trigger for the Spirit's work. No statement here can presume to be conclusive on this point, and the reader is encouraged to study the matter further,

## ACTS 5:5–10

### Isn't the death of Ananias and Sapphira harsh punishment for lying?

Yes, it is. But lying—especially to God—has consequences. Underneath the lie of Ananias and Sapphira is the deeper problem of conspiracy against God. In this case, the money was trivial, the deception monumental. This woebegone couple presumed to acquire esteem in the church, perhaps even favor with God, through a calculated act of generosity, all the while presenting themselves in a false light. Their deception brought dire consequences as a lesson in God's majesty and power—which is not to be taken lightly.

John the Baptist baptizes Jesus in preparation for His ministry.

mindful that a church's position on this matter will determine to a significant degree the kind of spiritual life that church will teach and preach as normative and good.

## ACTS 11:26

### Where did the name *Christian* come from?

Its invention is obscure. Perhaps it was coined by enemies of the church to identify a new group of enthusiastic believers who seemed bent on changing an entire way of living. Perhaps believers themselves began calling their growing population "those who belong to Christ"—*Christians*. In any case, the term was first heard around Antioch. Now, it's heard around the world.

## ACTS 16:30–31

### What does it mean to believe in Jesus Christ?

To believe is to turn the heart, mind, and body—the whole person—toward Jesus and look to Him for salvation. That turn involves four acknowledgments:

1. God is holy, righteous, and loving. He created us to be in relationship with Him forever.

2. All people have sinned; that is, all have failed to affirm that God has a claim on their lives. Instead, all have violated God's laws and are cut off from fellowship from God. No one is exempt from the crisis of sin's consequences.

3. Jesus is the answer. God Himself provided a way to restore sinners to His fellowship. The sinless Son of God, Jesus Christ, died to pay the penalty for all sin. Through His sacrifice we are restored.

4. We must personally acknowledge our sin to God and receive His gift of salvation in Christ.

To believe in Jesus Christ is to affirm these four truths and, as part of that affirmation, to surrender our lives to the care of God—to worship and serve God in gratitude and loyalty and to trust completely in His promise to save us.

## ACTS 21:11

### Why does Paul continue toward Jerusalem even though he is warned in a vision that he will be taken captive there?

With increasing clarity, Paul became aware that danger awaited him in Jerusalem. Paul's traveling companions tried to persuade him not to proceed, but the prophecies and visions did not forbid the journey—they only warned about it.

Paul seems to grow in his commitment to walk into the danger in Jerusalem, convinced that his going is for the sake of the gospel and Jesus Christ (Acts 21:13). This assurance certainly was born of prayer and much conversation. True, he might be putting himself in the cross fire of Rome's contentious paganism, but where danger held purpose, Paul never hesitated.

Paul's path from Jerusalem to Caesarea after being arrested.

# ROMANS

*No traveler through this book can fail to see the majesty of God's plan for our salvation. Along the way, Paul anticipates many of our questions and always points to the answer: God's love.*

## ROMANS 1:20

### Are people who have never heard about God, or who have never read the Bible, judged by different standards?

Put in judicial terms, is God fair to judge the faith of those who have never had the opportunity to choose true faith? The classic case is the remote tribal group detached from any contact with the church. When missionaries arrive, the key question relates to the afterlife experience of cherished ancestors.

In Romans and other New Testament letters, Paul teaches that Jesus is the only provision for reconciling sinful people to the holy God; that all people, whether they have heard the gospel or not, are guilty and deserving of God's punishment and that God's mercy extends in many directions.

For people who have never heard about Jesus, the fundamental problem is still sin. And the only solution is Jesus, who died for human sin. Whether application of that solution is made apart from cognitive faith is left to the judgment of God. Those who have heard the gospel and reject its claims are liable for their cognitive rebellion. Those who have not heard the gospel and live sinfully are liable as well. Thus, there is an imperative to evangelism: We cannot claim that remote peoples live in blissful ignorance. They must accept God's salvation. Judging the consequences and adjudicating the fairness issue are God's jobs, not ours.

## ROMANS 1:26–32

### Is homosexuality a sin?

The Bible counts homosexual behavior as sin in both New and Old Testaments (Leviticus 18:22). There appear to be no biblical considerations of homosexuality as an acceptable alternative sexual preference (with monogamous relationships similar to marriage), as a genetic trait, or as an element of public justice (a civil right).

On the first matter, biblical sexuality is celebrated always within the bounds of marriage, with mutual faithfulness the norm and procreation the expected result. Perversions of the sexual appetite—one form of which is homosexual practice—become idolatrous.

On the second count, genetic science is not the language of the Bible. In any case, genetic tendencies of many varieties—notably the sex drive itself—are constrained by divine law. Failure to curb natural drives finds no excuse in an appeal to "that's how I'm wired." Rather, persons whose unchecked sexual appetites would offend God's law are everywhere instructed to master them.

On the third count, the Bible recognizes no body of civil rights unattached to human rights, which are always under the rule of God.

Today, as in the past, homosexual practice is sin. But the treatment of the homosexual and the response of the church to the homosexual may also be sinful. The Bible gives no warrant to fear of homosexuals (homophobia), to the exclusion of them from the church (the gospel is for all), or to discrimination against those within the church who have a homosexual preference but, in obedience to God, restrain from its practice.

## ROMANS 3:22

### What does it mean to be "made right with God"?

This is surely the biggest announcement in the history of news: we are made right with God. Earning salvation by following God's law is impossible since it requires flawlessness. But God has established another way through an acquittal process similar to a court's pardon of a guilty person. Declared guilty under God's law, we face the full force of God's penalty. Yet God announced a pardon based on Jesus' payment for all sin. The sinner is set free—with no penalty at all. "Grace" is the biblical term to describe the movement of God to acquit based on Christ's work alone; "faith" is the biblical term to describe the movement of the sinner to accept God's sovereign claim on his or her life.

The term "justified by faith" in some Bible versions has a legal setting in mind. God justifies because He loves us. His justice is satisfied through Jesus' death on the cross. We respond in faith to that love. The term

expresses the thought of being right in God's sight through the only way possible—grace and faith.

## ROMANS 3:25

### Did God die on the cross?

By any measure, this idea is earthshaking. No other religion makes such a claim. No other religion even conceives of deity approaching such a situation. Yet the Bible says that Jesus, the God-Man, eternal Son of God, died on the cross as payment for the sins of all who trust in Him. Why did that happen?

When God created the world, it was perfect—fit for the Creator. But humanity's disobedience quickly created an intractable problem: a holy God cannot relate to sin.

Jesus dies on the cross. The angels mourn along with Jesus' mother, Mary, John, and Mary Magdalene.

A breach in the relationship required some form of payment.

In the Old Testament, God established a set of animal sacrifices as token payments—important indeed but not adequate to heal the breach. From the beginning, it was God's plan to heal the breach Himself, through an unprecedented action by which God Himself would satisfy His own demands for sinless perfection. Indeed, the Messiah would come to pay the price for the sins of all people.

If Jesus were merely human, a good man would have died—and that would be the end of His story, and ours. If Jesus were only divine, we would not have seen and heard Him or known firsthand about God's love. But, fully human and fully divine, Jesus told us about God and then satisfied God's own requirement. He was the sinless Son standing in the place of sinful people satisfying the perfect justice of a holy God.

That's the meaning of the amazing biblical truth of God's death for us:

◆ The purpose: our fellowship with God.

◆ The motive: God's love for us.

◆ The means: Roman crucifixion.

◆ The result: resurrection and eternal life for all who believe.

## ROMANS 6:11

### If Christians are "dead to the power of sin," why is sin still such a part of everyone's life?

To become a Christian is to turn from sin as the orientation of life to Christ as supreme Leader and Lord. That turning, the Bible teaches, is part of a completely new set of values and goals. The magnet of sin has lost its attraction; the power of the Holy Spirit has taken hold of your life. You no longer view life through the lens of self-seeking pleasure. Your glasses have been cleaned to reveal the love of God—and now everything appears different.

Oh, but wait! There's still a smudge that blurs your vision. Soon that smudge could become a smear. Then you'll really have trouble seeing.

Like that smudge, sin pesters us and sometimes gets the best of us. It's a constant irritation. Satan provokes our sense of self-preservation and stirs our old sin-loving side at every opportunity. We're not driven by sin like a whipped slave, but we're still bothered by it. Sin still nips at us, like mosquitoes drawing blood without our awareness, and we feel the results.

The solution is a constant refocus on Jesus, daily devotion to seeing the world and life through His perspective. And we must be willing to clean the lenses when they become spotted—to ask forgiveness and to humbly seek God's help to live in sync with Him.

## ROMANS 6:23

### How can salvation be called a free gift?

"There's no free lunch" speaks to the truth that things that might appear to have no cost often

Jesus' death on the cross gives us eternal life with God in heaven. We do nothing to deserve it—it's a free gift.

carry a huge price tag. Indeed, that proverb describes salvation, too. To the recipient, the gift of salvation *is* free. People cannot buy any element of salvation. No amount of good living, candle burning, charitable giving, or caregiving can contribute even a fraction to the cost. God offers the greatest gift freely to us, though at great cost to Himself—the death of His Son. The price was paid by Jesus, who bore the sins of the world on the cross, satisfying God's holy justice and winning the "free gift" for all who believe.

## ROMANS 8:28

**Outstanding promises made in the Bible seem to fall short of life experience. "God causes everything to work together for the good of those who love" Him, for example, yet very bad things happen to Christians and nonbelievers alike. Can you explain?**

Every newspaper carries stories of disasters that fall on good people and bad, rich and poor, young and old, and on people of all faiths, both pagan and Christian. We might expect a sort of subtle preferential treatment shown in such disasters, with Christians escaping the worst, at least. But, in fact, Christians die in airline accidents, Christians are hurt by muggers, and Christians get "downsized" and lose their jobs like everyone else. Where do the promises of "good" figure in?

Much happens in this life that is not God's first choice or desire. Often our accidents and disasters are caused by wrong choices made by people—perhaps even ourselves. We reap the consequences of decisions, some plainly wrong and some just poor judgment. Some of our suffering is the simple result of evil in the world—a grief to us and an offense to God.

Yet Christians know the direction they are traveling, the Leader they are following, and the promises they are claiming. Bad things will happen, but God sustains our life with a zeal to rebuild and renew. In every case of tragedy, God comforts the bereaved and converts disaster into hope. God alone can turn the worst loss into eternal gain.

Christians who have endured these experiences know how deeply personal God's consolation is. You should ask them to talk about it—and be prepared to listen for a while. Their words will tell a story of pain and love together, of wounds and healing, of fear and peace. It is the story of God overcoming evil in every corner of life, and ultimately, in heaven, for all time.

## ROMANS 13:1

**Why submit to government authority when so much of it is corrupt and morally wrong?**

This verse is a guideline, not a rule without exception. Peter and John paid no heed to government edicts in Acts 4. The Old Testament's preeminent statesman, Daniel, refused to comply with government strictures on prayer (Daniel 6). When civil law clearly contravenes divine command, biblical precedent calls for appropriate civil disobedience.

What is the point of Romans 13:1 then? Paul reminds us that government is to be respected and supported at all points possible, and that peaceful change is always the preferred choice of the Christian citizen. In some mysterious way, God sovereignly oversees the power of the state, and God's work is therefore to be supported and protected. But the state is not God, and to give full compliance to the state is to make it an idol. Rebellion and revolution should be a Christian's last option (or, as some would argue, never an option). Respectful, energetic participation in the affairs of state is part of Christian stewardship.

# 1 CORINTHIANS

*With his usual directness, the apostle Paul addressed issues in the church at Corinth. And you thought your church had problems!*

## 1 CORINTHIANS 1:2

### What was the history behind the church at Corinth?

The apostle Paul first visited Corinth on his second missionary journey (Acts 18:1–18), perhaps in the spring of A.D. 51. The ancient Greek city was notorious for its wealth and decadence, and the adjective *Corinthian* was synonymous with fornication and lewdness. Prominently featured in Corinth was the temple of Aphrodite, complete with its thousand temple prostitutes.

During Paul's initial stay in Corinth, lasting about a year and a half, he met Priscilla and Aquila, the husband-and-wife team who figured so prominently in the apostle's later ministry (Acts 18:18–28). After the founding of the Corinthian church, Paul moved on to Ephesus, leaving Apollos in charge. While in Ephesus, Paul began to hear about the numerous problems—divisiveness, immorality, questionable theology—among the Corinthian congregation. This was not a perfect place to raise children or to grow as a Christian. Yet despite difficulties, the church did grow there, as an example that the gospel should be taken as a light to the dark corners of human culture.

Ruin of the Court of Justice in Corinth where Paul preached.

# 1 Corinthians 1:11–13

## What happens when factions split a church?

The church in Corinth split probably for the same reasons modern-day churches do. Some people identified with the ministry style of Peter. Others were drawn to Paul's personality. Still others felt a connection with Apollos. We rightly learn from the insights of spiritual leaders, but crowing about one's own leader and criticizing all others is wrong, petty, and immature. The point of the message is the message itself, not the messenger. Our first allegiance is to Jesus. Leaders in the church should be respected, not used as mascots for factions.

# 1 Corinthians 5:5–13

## Should a church discipline its members?

Yes. Church discipline is that unpleasant but sometimes necessary final process in maintaining purity among the people of God. It is a radical kind of churchwide accountability that says, "We cannot and will not allow you to continue to live in sin," and "We will exert extreme pressure on you in order to get you to do what is right."

While other Bible passages speak to this issue, 1 Corinthians reveals that church discipline is reserved for believers in Christ. As a final measure, the sinning, unrepentant church member is to be expelled from the fellowship of the saints (Matthew 18:15–17). The goal of such a drastic measure is to effect change in the guilty party and to preserve the purity of the congregation. For discipline to work, the church must be united in its disapproval. The disciplined member is to be shunned (2 Thessalonians 3:14–15) until he or she repents. At that point, forgiveness and comfort are required (2 Corinthians 2:5–8), and restoration can result.

Church discipline is one way God helps us face difficult choices. When the process works as it should, it helps us make the choices that get us back to God.

# 1 Corinthians 6:1–6

## How should church members resolve disputes?

Corinthian believers filed lawsuits against each other to settle differences. Paul discouraged this shameful practice. He taught Christians to settle conflicts within the community of faith. If Christians would submit grievances against one another to church leaders (an elder board, a pastoral staff, a presbytery) and then comply with the decision rendered, they would protect the reputation of Christ and achieve better results for themselves and the church.

# 1 Corinthians 6:9–11

## Do certain sins automatically disqualify believers from heaven?

The idea that a believer can commit a certain sin that will result in the loss of his or her salvation is a doctrine that subverts the meaning of grace, makes the gospel a matter of human works, eliminates the possibility of assurance of salvation, and breeds either pride or fear.

Some Christians teach that a genuine believer will never habitually commit certain sins—usually the shocking sins of the flesh. Those who do yield to such temptations are viewed with suspicion and often condemned. It is ironic, however, that the more serious sins of the heart—pride, idolatry, failure to love—are rarely included on such lists. Indeed, if certain sins can nullify a person's salvation, who determines what those offenses are? The problems with this notion won't go away, but the notion itself should.

## 1 Corinthians 6:13-20

### Why is sexual sin such a serious issue?

God designed human sexuality. Like everything else God created, it was originally perfect and innocent. But after humans fell into sin, sex became a source of confusion and perversion.

Sexual activity affects us deeply. It is not merely a physical act—it involves deep emotion and always has spiritual ramifications. All that we are as spiritual beings we bring to our sexual experiences. We cannot park our souls outside the bedroom door.

For these reasons, God gives very careful guidelines and boundaries for sex. Within the confines of marriage, sex is portrayed in the Bible as wonderful and good. But outside marriage, sex is strongly condemned. It has the power to destroy us physically, emotionally, and even spiritually. As Christians we are to remember that God owns our bodies (1 Corinthians 6:19). By living purely, we can avoid shame, guilt, and all the other negative consequences that accompany an immoral lifestyle.

## 1 Corinthians 7

### Does 1 Corinthians teach that it is wrong for a single person to pursue marriage?

Paul speaks of the advantages of a single, celibate life. He calls it "good" and notes that those who are married have the extra problem of pleasing a spouse. Single believers, on the

A marriage ceremony in medieval times.

other hand, are free to do the Lord's work (1 Corinthians 7:32).

Paul counsels the single person who has trouble controlling his or her passions to go ahead and marry. But, he adds, speaking from a kingdom perspective, the person who can control his or her passion and doesn't marry "does even better" (1 Corinthians 7:38). This should not demote one's enthusiasm for marriage or love for the partner God has given. This is meant only to note the priority of wholehearted service to God, which marriage can sometimes obscure.

## 1 CORINTHIANS 7:15

### When is divorce allowed?

Writing to the Corinthian church, Paul tells married couples to stay together (1 Corinthians 7:10–11). Jesus also taught that marriage is permanent (Matthew 19:3–9). Paul states that having a non-Christian spouse is not a valid reason for divorce. If the unbelieving spouse deserts and will not return, Paul makes an allowance for the dissolution of the marriage. Jesus, meanwhile, listed unfaithfulness as another ground for divorce.

Throughout the Bible, marriage is meant for a lifetime. Jesus said that divorce is "a concession to [humanity's] hard-hearted wickedness" (Matthew 19:8).

## 1 CORINTHIANS 8:1

### What happens when Christians have different convictions about issues over which the Bible is silent?

Love is to be the preeminent value among Christians. Those with strong convictions should be careful not to harshly judge those with less-developed convictions. Those who feel great freedom in the Lord should not look with contempt at believers who have stricter boundaries. Pride is the insidious

enemy that seeks to divide believers over nonessential issues or traditions. On essential doctrines and behavior, we must have unity, but on matters of conscience and issues where the Bible is silent, we must respect one another and seek each other's best interests.

## 1 CORINTHIANS 8:9

### What happens when a believer causes another to stumble?

In Corinth, the big question was whether to eat meat that, before it was sold in the market, had been used in pagan sacrificial rituals. Some Christians, reasoning that idols aren't real and that pagan sacrifices are thereby meaningless, gladly bought the meat, probably at a good discount. Other Christians opposed this practice on grounds that eating the meat was tantamount to worshiping the idol itself.

Paul warned "stronger" Christians (who felt free to eat) to be careful with such freedom (1 Corinthians 8:9). The danger, according to Paul, was that a "weak Christian" might be led to violate his or her conscience. So serious was this situation that Paul determined never to consume meat if his eating hurt someone's faith.

## 1 CORINTHIANS 10:24

### Since Christ has set us free from the demands of the law, why should we voluntarily limit our freedom?

We should limit our freedom whenever our actions might injure the conscience of someone else. If a behavior has the potential to offend, it is not worth doing. Think first of the glory of God (what will bring the most honor to the Lord?) and second of the good of others. Love, not freedom, is the

Christ's death on the cross for our sins sets us free from bondage to the law. We obey because of our love for Him.

primary building block of the church, and should be our highest priority (1 Corinthians 8:1–2).

## 1 CORINTHIANS 11:3

### Why did Paul speak so much about wives submitting to their husbands?

Paul was no chauvinist. He taught the spiritual equality of women and men (Galatians 3:28) and wrote eloquently about husbands loving their wives as Christ loved the church—

sacrificially and unconditionally (Ephesians 5:25–33). But to a church in a corrupt culture where marriages were in disarray, the brave Paul argued that submission was essential for any institution—government, church, or family. Without authority, chaos reigns.

Submission of wives to husbands does not suggest inequality or inferiority. In the same way a wife is responsible to her husband, Christ is responsible to the Father. If being under authority suggests inequality, then Christ would be "inferior" to God the Father. That would contradict everything Paul ever wrote about Christ.

Submission achieves cooperation. It is not

surrender, weakness, withdrawal, or apathy. It is a choice that honors God. Authority and submission rooted in humility and love produce good (Ephesians 5:21).

# 1 CORINTHIANS 11:4–10

## Why did Paul call for women to cover their heads in worship?

Partly for reasons of reverence. Jewish women always covered their heads in worship. For a Greek woman to uncover her head in worship would create a stir as these two cultures came together in a church setting.

Partly for reasons of submission. In Corinth, a woman with short hair or an uncovered head was labeled a prostitute. Such behavior was viewed as shocking, a symbol of a rebellious spirit. By contrast, a woman who covered her head was making a nonverbal statement of submission to God-appointed authority.

# 1 CORINTHIANS 11:20–21

## What can go wrong with the Lord's Supper?

The early church often met for a fellowship meal, followed by observance of the Lord's Supper. At Corinth, the initial meal had become a drunken, disorderly feast characterized by arguments and selfishness. This ancient version of a potluck dinner did not reflect well on the person of Christ. There was little caring and no sharing. This spirit then carried over into the Lord's Supper.

Paul admonished the Corinthian believers to change their ways and make the Lord's Supper the meaningful memorial it was intended to be. During Communion, Christians are expected to soberly examine themselves and ponder the meaning of Christ's death on their behalf (1 Corinthians 11:27–34).

# 1 CORINTHIANS 12

## What should we believe about spiritual gifts?

Most Christians approach this topic from one of three viewpoints. One group sees all the gifts mentioned in Romans 12, 1 Corinthians 12, Ephesians 4, and 1 Peter 4 as still operative today. Another group says that the more spectacular, so-called "sign" gifts (prophecy, tongues, healing) were given only for the beginning era of the church (people who hold this position are called "cessationists"). Still others teach that all the gifts were temporary in nature.

Which interpretation a believer accepts today hinges on whether the book of Acts is normative (that is, what happened then should happen now), or whether Paul's letters to the churches qualify the unique period of early church experience and set a different agenda for the rest of the Christian era. These are large and difficult issues, but they must be faced.

On a more practical theme, Christians searching for spiritual gifts today must distinguish gifts from natural abilities. Natural abilities or talents are genetically derived or educationally learned. They may or may not be used for serving God and others. Generally they accrue glory to the person who possesses them.

A spiritual gift, on the other hand, is a God-given ability for building up the church. Spiritual gifts are determined by the Spirit (1 Corinthians 12:1, 11) and are apparently given when a person becomes a Christian, for that is when the Spirit indwells a new believer (see Romans 8:9; 1 Corinthians 3:16). Every Christian has at least one gift (1 Peter 4:10), but no one believer has all the gifts. The analogy of the body in 1 Corinthians 12 gives meaning to the distribution of gifts among believers.

## 1 Corinthians 15:14

### Why is the resurrection of Christ so important to Christian faith?

The resurrection of Christ is at the very heart of the Christian faith. It was prophesied in the Old Testament (Psalm 16:10; see also 1 Corinthians 15:4). Hundreds of witnesses attested to it (1 Corinthians 15:5–8). It gives the gospel its hope and power by explaining the benefits of the forgiveness of sin (1 Corinthians 15:14–15).

Furthermore, the resurrection of Jesus provides a glimpse of the future that awaits all who trust in Him (1 Corinthians 15:20–26). The day is coming when the bodies of deceased believers will also be raised, and death will be "swallowed up in victory" (1 Corinthians 15:54). The great curse of death will be undone, and life will be eternally free.

## 1 Corinthians 15:29

### What is meant by baptism "for those who are dead"?

Apparently some Corinthian believers had undergone a kind of proxy baptism on behalf of deceased family members or friends who had died unbaptized. Nothing more is known of this custom. Paul does not advocate it or expressly condemn it. He merely cites this practice as evidence for the reality of the resurrection. The Mormon Church is the only religious group that has adopted this practice today.

## 1 Corinthians 15:51–53

### What is a resurrection body?

On the day Christ returns, believers in Jesus will inherit heavenly "resurrection" bodies. Unlike earthly bodies that sicken and die, the scripture promises a transformed body like the kind Jesus has. This new body will be different, and yet—since Jesus is the model— still recognizable. Our new bodies will not be material, but spiritual, full of power, never to die or hold us back from living fully and happily.

Christ rises from the dead three days after His crucifixion. His resurrection promises that we too will be resurrected.

# 2 CORINTHIANS

*When leaders care for a church, good things happen to the people there. Every church needs leaders who care like Paul did.*

## 2 CORINTHIANS 4:8–12

### Why was Paul beaten up so much?

As the gospel confronts people with the weakness of their support systems, the futility of their wealth, and the wickedness of their hearts, it often fuels a vicious response. Paul faced that many times, but especially when he confronted the religiously and politically powerful. These two groups especially despised the notion that God had a better way. To shut Paul's mouth, they often resorted to physical violence in some form, only to discover that Paul would not be quiet for any reason, especially under duress.

Had Paul been frightened by the violence, he would have been beaten less. Had he succumbed to the threats, adjusted his rhetoric, or given up his teaching, no doubt his body would have hurt less. But passion in the soul always meets pain in the body with faith and hope. Paul did not seek the beatings and sometimes took precautionary steps to avoid them; however, he accepted pain as the price of his calling and used it to identify more fully with Jesus.

## 2 CORINTHIANS 5:17

### What changes come in the move from "old life" to "new life"?

Some have claimed that since the "old life" is typified by sin, the "new life" should be characterized by sinlessness. But experience betrays that claim every day. Rather than abruptly ceasing all sin, the Christian is cast into a new frame of reference, with new goals, new strength, and new promises. The Holy Spirit directs the Christian toward God's purposes for his or her life. Helped with divine strength, the Christian begins to run with new energy toward goals not previously in view. A new relational disposition characterizes friendships, marriages, and parent-child relationships. Instead of "me first," the orientation is toward the best interests of the other. The primary change, however, is toward God. The new-life Christian worships God in love and gratitude, whereas the old-life person acknowledged God (if at all) in fear and bewilderment.

Paul's conversion—his "new life" begins.

The full portrait of the "new life" is drawn throughout the pages of the New Testament. The eager reader is invited to add to this short account by reading the entire story of the change God brings when "new life" transforms an old one.

# 2 CORINTHIANS 6:14

### "Don't team up with. . . unbelievers." How far should we take that advice?

The warning alerts us to the problems that can arise when a Christian shares a partnership with someone whose loyalty is not to Christ, but to wealth or self-interest. Paul does not stipulate what this means precisely. Are we never to sign a contract with a nonbeliever?

Never start a business with one? Never marry one? But the principle is that the deeper your investment with someone as a team member, the more important your mutual loyalties. Thus, it is rare for the church to advise a Christian to marry outside the faith, but part-nering in a common cause across faiths on matters of public interest is entirely warranted.

Separatist Christians spoil Paul's advice by using it as an excuse never to interact with people outside their comfort zone. Likewise, a Christian who rarely seeks the company of other believers for nurture and support will miss an important source of strength. The more intimate the relationship, the stronger the emotional linkage and the greater the impact on one's life. Friendship, like all of God's gifts, should assist in the process of spiritual growth, not detract from it.

# 2 CORINTHIANS 12:7

### What was Paul's "thorn" in his flesh?

Likely some kind of physical ailment or handicap, but no one knows for sure. Some speculate that Paul's vision was impaired, that he suffered recurring malaria or epilepsy, or that he had a speech impediment. Others speculate that Paul experienced sexual temptation during his travels. Rarely did Paul report on his physical condition (see Galatians 4:13–15), and everywhere Paul fully identified himself as a man tempted like other men. Since he left no hint whatsoever concerning his "thorn," we can only say that Paul was likely not a perfect physical specimen, but that he used his ailment to depend more fully on God for strength.

# GALATIANS

*Is salvation a gift, or is it earned through a good life? People have raised that question ever since questions were invented.*

## GALATIANS 2

### Did Paul get along with the other apostles?

The relationship between Paul and the rest of the apostles bears all the marks of people living under pressure, carrying out a mission, making unprecedented decisions and some mistakes along the way, yet fully committed to the truth of their message.

There was mutual recognition of authority. Paul came to Jerusalem and met with the other leaders for their blessing. Peter affirmed Paul's writings as part of scripture (2 Peter 3:15–16). There were disagreements and confrontations. Paul describes a conflict between himself and Peter (Galatians 2:11–16) over Peter's inconsistency in treating Gentile believers as fully accepted among the believers.

Probably the most remarkable aspect of Paul's relationship with the Jerusalem church involves the change in Paul's life from being a persecutor of the church to its chief proclaimer of the gospel. There was initial suspicion, even fear, of Paul's conversion. But as Paul's life and preaching proved his new life in Christ, Christians he had previously persecuted "gave glory to God because of [him]" (Galatians 1:24).

In effect, former enemies became friends, centered on a new loyalty and love for the Savior. Personalities were different, but the mission was the same. Leaders who walked with Jesus grew to accept, respect, and acknowledge Paul as a missionary apostle under God's call to preach.

## GALATIANS 3:5–7

### What was God's plan for people who lived and died before Jesus came?

God's plan for people who lived before Jesus involved salvation by faith—just as it does for people who follow Jesus today. Jesus' atonement for sin on the cross applies backward in history as well as forward. People like Abraham placed their faith in God's promise to do something about sin, while people in the Christian era place faith in God's fulfilled promise to take care of sin—Jesus Himself.

Old Testament faith was not blind belief. It simply had fewer details than ours does today. The real children of Abraham, as Paul put it, are not those linked by ethnicity or geography, but those who put their faith in God.

# GALATIANS 5:1

## What is Christian freedom?

Paul's letter to the Galatians is history's finest statement on Christian freedom. Paul was writing to a church he had planted and to people he loved. He had introduced many of them to Christ. But recent news indicated that certain teachers were requiring Gentile Christians to submit to all the rules and regulations of Jewish legalism in order to join the church. Angered by those who would deny the gospel so blatantly, Paul was also distressed by those who believed them.

The freedom Paul talks about in Galatians is not about doing whatever you want. Rather, this freedom is freedom from sin and legalism, release from religious pressure, and the end of hopelessly trying to fulfill all the demands of God's law to win acceptance with Him.

The right way to live has not changed. God still expects obedience from those who trust Christ. He doesn't, however, want obedience in exchange for salvation. Christians are free to give obedience real attention because we do not face the threat of eternal punishment with every failure. Believers are free to live by the law's guidance because Jesus met the law's demands.

# GALATIANS 5:22-23

## How ripe is the fruit of the Spirit?

The Holy Spirit at work in a Christian's life changes rottenness to ripe fruit that is beautiful, colorful, and ready for service. Paul lists nine qualities that typify the "changed life": love, joy, peace, patience, kindness, goodness, faithfulness, gentleness, and self-control. The list sharply contrasts with what might be called the fruit of the sinful nature (Galatians 5:19–21). As a person allows the Spirit to work, the fruit of the Spirit ripen.

A dove represents the Holy Spirit. The Holy Spirit active in our lives produces the fruit of the Spirit.

# EPHESIANS

*Who saves us? What role does our decision play? Who guarantees that anyone will actually make it to heaven? Common questions for every era.*

## EPHESIANS 1:9

### Why is the gospel sometimes called a "secret" or a "mystery"?

Many of the pagan religions in Paul's day bragged about secret knowledge available only to their own members. Such claims made membership special. The same sense of mystery carries into our own day with secret or semisecret societies and even within some Christian movements where initiates pledge "not to tell" what the teacher is teaching. Paul used the term *secret*, or *mystery*, in a radically different way—to indicate that God's truth was now revealed in Christ for all the world to know.

Until Christ came, died, and rose again, who could have imagined that God's plan for saving the world would involve the death of His own Son? Now the secret is out! And the news is good! And there's nothing secret about it.

Teachers today who offer secret knowledge are continuing an age-old marketing scheme that isn't worth the price of admission—and may be dangerously misleading. Learn about your faith in the open air of genuine Christian teaching. The mystery has been revealed: Christ is Lord of all the earth!

## EPHESIANS 1:14

### How is the Holy Spirit a guarantee? Of what? For what?

The Holy Spirit in the life of each believer is God's spiritual seal, indicating that we belong to Him. Today, we prove ownership by a piece of paper called a title; in Paul's day, it was by a seal. Joe's chariot carried Joe's unique seal. Harry's toga had Harry's own seal. Believers carry God's seal, but it is visible only in the behavior that sets believers apart. It is a spiritual confirmation that the Holy Spirit is teaching, convicting, and guiding the believer's life.

The Holy Spirit is like a down payment. He assures us that faith is genuine, reminds us that we are God's children, and leads us into eternal life. The Holy Spirit communicates to us God's closeness

At Pentecost, the believers first receive the Holy Spirit, seen as "flames or tongues of fire" that settle on each of them.

and love. "For his Holy Spirit speaks to us deep in our hearts and tells us that we are God's children" (Romans 8:16). What we experience now is a mere taste of the change we will experience in eternity.

## EPHESIANS 2:8

### What is grace?

We hear the word a lot around Christian circles, sometimes referring to a prayer before a meal, sometimes to a great big idea associated with the gospel, sometimes as a girl's name. Paul used the term throughout his letters to speak of God's special favor to every person, the undeserved benefit we have of God's mercy in sending Jesus to die for our sins.

If God had not taken the initiative, we would be without hope. If God had not cared, death and separation would be our eternal plan. But we are given a very special gift, and God picked up the bill for it in terms of the pain and humiliation Jesus suffered. God's special favor to you, grace, is salvation through faith in Christ.

# EPHESIANS 2:8

## What is belief?

Faith refers to: (1) the exercise of our capacity to trust someone or something, as, for example, a rock climber has faith in his or her rope; (2) a set of beliefs, such as "Catholic faith"; (3) a deeper, very personal movement of the heart toward God that includes the first two meanings, yet moves beyond them into personal fellowship with God.

The Bible is most concerned with faith in this third sense. For example, when Jesus told Martha, "I am the resurrection and the life" (John 11:25), He did not follow up with a question about the strength of Martha's faith or about a system of beliefs, important as both are. Rather, He asked her, "Do you believe this, Martha?"

Biblical faith, or believing, is not a static system of beliefs or casual assent to the idea that God exists. Faith is not so much something we have but something we do. Biblical faith is motivated by the Holy Spirit in our minds and heart and always shows itself in acts of love that reflect God's care for all the world.

Biblical faith is always growing. It is very powerful, yet never perfect. Jesus said it could move mountains (Matthew 17:20); yet faith is often imperceptible and sometimes seems to barely "work." Biblical faith is never a matter of character strength, as if by force of will a person could make herself or himself strong in faith. It is always a matter of surrender, simple daily trust that creates in us a growing confidence of God's strategic care. "Faith" is our best term to describe the lifetime dynamic between the sovereign, eternal God and the amazing creature called the human person.

# EPHESIANS 2:9–10

## Does doing good things make us Christians?

The notion that performance of good things leads to God's approval misses one huge point about the difference between God and human beings. That simple point is that God is holy and people are not. No amount of performance overcomes that fundamental distinction.

Everywhere the Bible encourages us to do "good things." But always the good we do is an outgrowth of faith, an expression of faith, and never the basis by which we approach God to negotiate our spiritual renewal. Doing good is so important that we have reason to believe our faith is phony if we fail to do good (James 2:14). But doing good is totally unimportant (because it's so inadequate) when we approach the holy presence of God. The only "good work" adequate for our salvation is the good work of Jesus Christ, in which we trust. That good work of Jesus Christ is so life-changing that doing good will certainly follow—our small way of saying thanks for a gift we could not earn and do not deserve.

Jesus asks Martha if she believes in Him.

## EPHESIANS 4:3-6

### When Christians around the world are so obviously divided, how can the Bible insist on unity among believers?

Sadly, Christians are often divided. When division is over trivial matters, such as personal preferences, outsiders have every right to wonder if the gospel is true (John 13:35). But sometimes divisions help to accentuate different expressions of faith and life. These differences help to paint the large picture of biblical faith.

Unity among believers of different churches and denominations is still our calling and privilege. We can and should pray with each other, cooperate in common causes, and encourage each other's pursuit of truth. Paul presents several central issues that should unite all believers:

♦ awareness and acceptance that Christ makes us one body through the shared Holy Spirit

♦ our common hope of a glorious future with Christ

♦ one Lord—Jesus Himself

♦ one faith—anchored to Jesus

♦ one baptism—marking us as believers

♦ one God

Paul also teaches that God gives each believer a unique spiritual gift in Christ, which he or she brings to the body. Unity is central; variety ought to be interesting and generative, not divisive.

The Apostles' Creed, a beautiful summary of Christian faith written over the first four centuries of the church (though not by the apostles), leads all believers to make this claim: "I believe in. . .the holy catholic church." Some translations use "the holy Christian church" as a clearer reference to the church of all times and places. Though the church takes various names and emphases, the center of its faith and worship is always Jesus Christ.

## EPHESIANS 5:22-33

### How is marriage like the relationship between Christ and the church?

The Bible confronts a husband and wife with the lifelong challenge of patterning their relationship after the relationship between Jesus and the church. Certain assumptions follow:

♦ Christians will marry Christians.

♦ Christian marriage is a relationship that requires mutual submission and accountability, nurture, tenderness, and responsibility. In mutual submission, the husband and wife will exhibit the caregiving of Christ for the church, especially in terms of

Marriage is a picture of the relationship of Christ and His church.

Jesus' sacrificial devotion and sense of divine mission and call.

Some churches (now and in the past) have taught that husbands should act lordly, and wives should act worshipfully toward their lords. This approach to marriage has often been a pretext for male domination, both in the family and in the church. Clearly, husbands are not the "saviors" with the wives being the "sinners." No, both parties must come to the marriage eager for a growing relationship of service and love, each devoted to the Lord and to each other, firmly committed to the union that makes each stronger and equips each better for the life God sets before them.

## EPHESIANS 5:22

### If a wife is to submit to her husband, how much? In what areas? At what cost?

Many a marriage has fizzled because both husband and wife latch onto the notion of submission, and both are destroyed by it. The husband may like the feeling of dominance, but he discovers too late he no longer has any emotional tie with his wife. Sometimes, tragically, the husband's sense of dominance becomes perverted and hurtful. Sometimes a wife submits as a survival strategy, fails to grow as a person, loses her love for the man, questions her value as a believer, and settles into a half-life of emotional and spiritual solitude. But submission is meant to help a marriage, not hurt it. So how does it work?

First, the question is meaningless without the context. In Ephesians 5:22–33, Paul explains the wife's submission and the husband's love. In comparing a husband's relationship to his wife with Christ's relationship to the church, what might appear to be a position of power actually turns out to be a position of service and love. Christ never fails to love. In marriage, that requires an

immense amount of listening, feeling, empathy, and giving—not always a man's strongest traits.

A wife's submission is framed in an atmosphere of general submission, each to the Lord and to the other. Never is Christian marriage designed to give the first and last word to a husband and no word to a wife. But in the final accounting of the marriage, the husband has to answer: Was your union a faithful expression of love? Did it produce service to the church, raising of children, mission and calling that reflect the heart of God? No way will the husband be able to respond, "Ask her about it!"

Likewise, the wife is accountable. She won't be able to shunt responsibility for failure under the guise of submission by claiming, "Just doing what he demanded!"

As personalities differ, each couple will decide who keeps the checkbook, who decides the menu, who washes the dirty clothes. Christian marriage is not concerned with which spouse does it, but with *how* it's done: not by duty alone, certainly not in fear, never with abuse, but always in love, the kind Christ had for the church.

## EPHESIANS 6:1–4

### How should children treat parents?

The Ten Commandments remind children to honor their parents. Paul applies this command here by teaching that honor begins with obedience. Paul's reason is not that parents are always right or because children owe some debt to parents, but because obedience toward parents pleases the Lord.

On the parental side of this relationship, Paul directs fathers to avoid angering their children (probably with an eye to the social power fathers in the ancient world enjoyed) and to raise children with discipline and instruction "approved by the Lord."

A picture of the child Jesus with His parents, Mary and Joseph.

This would cover areas such as modeling a Christian lifestyle, giving children specific direction for action, and instructing them in the faith.

When each member of the family is devoted to the others' welfare and growth, children find it joyous to obey, and parents are delighted to give. Dysfunctional families can expect to struggle daily with these simple obligations.

## EPHESIANS 6:9

### Does the Bible condone slavery?

The Bible does not condone slavery but recognizes slavery as part of the social structure of the times. Rather than attacking slavery directly, biblical guidelines weakened and undermined the institution from the inside by reminding Christian masters that they had a Master and were to treat slaves as brothers (Ephesians 6:9). For slaves, the dignity that came with freedom in Christ had a powerful long-term social effect.

Today we condemn slavery as inhuman

and unjustifiable. But we forget or refuse to confront the many forms of slavelike servitude that we still impose on others to secure our own economic advantage. In these cases, too, the Bible urges treatment centered on human care, not greed. In the final analysis, more money in your pocket has nothing to do with your happiness. Your approval as a Christian worker has everything to do with loving others as Jesus would.

## EPHESIANS 6:10–17

### How does the "armor of God" protect a Christian?

The armor of God is Paul's vivid illustration of the spiritual equipment that Christ provides to those who trust Him. These pieces of armor are essential to survival and victory in the spiritual warfare that is a real (though invisible) part of each life.

Of the six pieces, the first five are protective. The only offensive piece is God's Word, the sword. When Jesus faced temptation (Matthew 4:1–11), He answered Satan not by using clever arguments but by quoting scripture. The armor reminds us always to depend on God, not on intellectual acumen or rhetorical flourish, in standing against evil and temptation. Our protection from Satan is God's business, yet rusty armor is no use to anyone. Keep faith vital by daily using all the armor.

## EPHESIANS 6:12

### What is spiritual warfare?

It is cosmic conflict between the forces of good and evil. The outcome has been determined, but the ongoing conflict still includes a great number of victories and defeats. The soul and life of each person is the battleground.

The intensity of this war may remain largely unseen, but the evidence of its reality and the tragedy of casualties lie all around us in the form of broken marriages, errant children, careers gone sour, greed run rampant, opportunities for witness lost, and even sickness, disease, and ecological devastation. Each person in God's kingdom doing real-world work—carpentry, teaching, health care, whatever—at the same time stalls the advance of evil and advances the influence of God's message.

# PHILIPPIANS

*Paul was awed at a God who gave so much. And because of God's love and mercy, we can be confident that God hangs in there with us in every circumstance—in every challenge knocking at our door.*

## PHILIPPIANS 1:7

### Is partnership or individual performance more important to spiritual development?

Individualism is the idea that personal achievement and personal blame are fundamental to a concept of the self. In Western cultures, individualism has been a reigning idea since the seventeenth century. This idea has affected how the church approaches evangelism and Christian life—as individuals responsible before God.

But Paul advances an equally strong case for community—people in relationship to others—as the primary unit of human action and responsibility. Even in this short letter, Paul cites and recites his linkage to other people in heart and mission. Not a lone crusader, Paul positions himself as part of a network that goes so deep that he refuses personal credit for his own work. Strength in community seems to be Paul's strategy for mission and spiritual growth.

## PHILIPPIANS 1:12-13

### Why was Paul in prison?

Under house arrest in Rome, Paul writes about the real reason for his imprisonment: the sake of Christ.
His extensive missionary activity ran afoul of religious and secular authorities who arrested Paul on political and religious grounds. But finally, Paul understood his experience to be ordained by God and blessed by divine call. Secular authority might claim power over Paul's movement and career, but Paul served a higher power— and in that service felt immense joy and freedom. Indeed, Paul's

Paul is arrested for preaching about Jesus.

imprisonment had resulted in the opposite of its intention. Instead of suppressing the message, it was taking hold in the heart of the Roman empire. Other believers, watching Paul's boldness and faith, were speaking out as well. State authority could restrict his movement but could not arrest his message or still his purpose.

## PHILIPPIANS 1:22

### Is it okay to be confused or indecisive?

In this instance, Paul indicates an inability to make a clear-cut decision. Two goals hold equal value for him, and to choose one requires that the other be abandoned. This Paul cannot do. Unable to make a choice, he determines to continue in the track he is in, living and preaching, until God alters the course for him.

Paul generally does not counsel this kind of passive approach to decision making. But faced with equally attractive but mutually exclusive possibilities, he leaves the decision to God while continuing to do what he knows best. This kind of faith would solve many a sleepless night for Christians worrying over which fork in the road ahead represents God's will.

## PHILIPPIANS 1:28

### How should Christians respond to terror?

Terror is the typical human response to a situation in which sudden pain or death is the likely outcome in a circumstance the individual cannot control. Paul faced such circumstances, and he knew that Christians throughout the ages will continue to face danger. The state and the bad guys own all the guns; Christians own the truth. Conflict is inevitable.

In a showdown between truth and terror, Christians are to exhibit a faith that remains calm under conditions meant to desperately excite basic survival instincts. The promise of the gospel is life with Christ. Faith under fire is a witness more profound than a thousand sermons—a sign that the triggerman who inflicts the fatal wound is the one who dies without the truth, the only real terror.

## PHILIPPIANS 2:7

### How could Jesus give up His divine privileges?

He did this by setting aside His prerogatives and privileges as a member of the Godhead, the Trinity, and becoming human. John describes the possibility of seeing the glory of God in Jesus (John 1:14), while Paul assures us that divine glory was joined to human particularity when Jesus took the form and nature of a man—and a commoner at that. Theologians still discuss the implication of this commingling of two vastly different natures: Was Jesus all-knowing, all-powerful? Was Jesus susceptible to sin? Did Jesus actually die and spend time in a place of waiting souls? But the magnitude of the claim here—God self-emptying to become human—suggests that the Incarnation is the fundamental miracle undergirding all other biblical claims.

## PHILIPPIANS 3:2

### Who are the "dogs" Paul warns about?

These were religious legalists who insisted that Christians continue to practice Old Testament Jewish rites, primarily circumcision. Pressured by conservative zealots, the "Judaizers"—keeping the Christian church under Jewish law—vigorously opposed Paul as a sectarian liberal. The gospel Paul preached was salvation by faith alone in the completed work of Jesus Christ. To Paul, a Benjamite and Pharisee himself, salvation did not require any outward ritual, nor did being a Christian require any of the old Jewish rules.

## PHILIPPIANS 3:12

### If perfection eluded the great missionary Paul, who can aspire to it?

Everyone can aspire, since perfection (maturity in faith) is God's purpose for all believers (Matthew 5:48). But the metaphor of the Christian life is a race, not a pedestal. The aspiring runner concentrates on the goal ahead. This is an action metaphor. Paul envisions discipline and effort here, not the attainment of a state of being. In Christian discipleship, imperfect people aspire toward the prize of God's blessing as a runner presses toward the finish line, bent on the best performance his or her legs will render.

## PHILIPPIANS 3:17

### Where does the class on life meet?

Students in a classroom wear down pencil points writing notes on a lecture, capturing insight and knowledge for later study and application. Take that same practice and transfer it from chemistry class to life. The class meets wherever mature Christians are running hard toward the goal, pressing toward the mark. Students in the class of life are urged to take notes on the style, form, attitude, and virtues of the senior runners—to improve their stride, to stretch their endurance, to shed the indulgences that weigh them down.

## PHILIPPIANS 3:20

### What is citizenship?

It is official membership in a community.

When the world divided into nations, citizenship became the certified recognition of privilege and accountability to the laws and leaders of the nation granting it. Paul invites Christians to think of membership in God's kingdom in the same way—a relationship of privilege and responsibility. This latter citizenship supersedes and qualifies all other memberships so that the Christian, while loyal to the state (Romans 13:1), is not unconditionally so. When the responsibilities of national citizenship conflict with biblical standards for behavior or belief, the kingdom citizen owes primary loyalty to God. Defining those conflicts and working out their solution is the ongoing task of Christian social ethics.

## PHILIPPIANS 3:21

### What happens to our bodies when we die?

The Bible says nothing about the body between the point of death and future

Because Jesus rose from the dead, those who believe in Him will also rise. He will change our bodies into glorious bodies like His own.

Ruins of a church in Philippi. The Philippian church gave Paul a
gift of money to partner with him in his ministry.

resurrection, except by occasional references
to its material disintegration. But at that
future time—often called "the day" in the
Bible—bodies of Christian believers are
raised and transformed into a glorious new
state of being.

We know nothing of the physics of this
state (how bodies are nourished, how blood
pressure is maintained, etc.), but we have
a glimpse of the result in the accounts of
the resurrected body of Jesus (see Matthew
28:9; Luke 24:30–31; John 20:19–20).
This new body will be recognizable, will
not be susceptible to aging or disease, and
likely will not have the hormonal chemistry
associated with sexual desire and activity
(Matthew 22:30).

## PHILIPPIANS 4:18

### What's so important about a gift?

Paul accepts money from the Philippian
church and thanks them for the gift. Their
gesture represents more than provision,
helpful as food and rent money can be.
Their gift represents partnership and
mutuality, the mixing of resources that says,
"I trust you with the fruit of my own labor,
and I love you with the same care I afford
myself." Paul accepts the church's gifts as a
symbol of their generous concern for him
and love for God.

Gifts are like long-term investments. The
return on a gift is the spiritual blessing of
partnership and love, a return to be valued
far above any material gain.

# COLOSSIANS

*Why did Paul go to all the trouble to help churches far away? Good question—and here's an even better answer: Because of Jesus.*

## COLOSSIANS 1:6

### How does the "Good News" actually change a person's life?

The Good News is powerful and life changing. It's the true story of Jesus Christ coming to earth as a human to give His life as a sacrifice and payment for our sins. Through Jesus we have an open door to God's forgiveness and eternal life. The Good News is full of hope, and responding to Jesus is the start of a new life. God's Holy Spirit makes us a new creation (see 2 Corinthians 5:17). We're not just turning over a new leaf; we are starting a new life and putting Jesus in charge.

The Good News rebuilds our self-esteem when we realize that God not only created us but loves us so much that He sent Jesus so we could be reconciled with Him. We learn that God is not far away or uninterested in us. We can pray and share our burdens with God because He cares for us. Our behavior is dramatically changed as God's Holy Spirit reveals changes we need to make in our lifestyle. The Holy Spirit gives us power to break the bonds of self-destructive habits. Although we will struggle with sin as long as we live on this earth, God does not give up on us. He guides us each day like a loving father and cares for us even when we fail.

The old agenda of self-advancement and competition with others is discarded. There is no reason to fear others or live in guilt because God accepts us as we are and continues to mold us into the image of Jesus. Life now has a clear purpose—to love God with all our heart, mind, and strength, and to love others as we love ourselves. Success is redefined as obeying God and becoming like Jesus. Our life focus is no longer on serving ourselves, but serving God and pleasing Him.

## COLOSSIANS 1:15

### How is Jesus Christ different from any other famous man who founded a religion?

Jesus Christ stands apart from all the other founders of major religions. The claims of His deity are extensive. He has always existed as the second person of the eternal triune God with all power and knowledge and supremacy over all things that exist. He is Lord over all creation, and in Him all things hold together. He came to earth and lived in a human body. He was God in the flesh. He was an exact reflection

Paul preached about Jesus to both Jews and Gentiles.

of the invisible God. He lived a sinless life while teaching and showing us what we need to know about God.

The ultimate purpose for Jesus' life on earth was revealed when He gave His life to be executed as a sacrifice for sin. Through His death, God made a way for people to obtain forgiveness and eternal life if they put their faith and trust in Jesus as their Savior and Lord.

This wasn't spiritual talk and premature martyrdom by Jesus Christ. He did what no other religious leader ever did. Three days after He was crucified, dead, and buried, He rose from the dead—conquering death and sin. He was seen alive by more than five hundred eyewitnesses before He ascended back into heaven.

No other religious leader can make and substantiate claims equal to the life of Jesus Christ. He stands alone as Lord over our world.

## COLOSSIANS 1:27

### Why was God's plan for the Gentiles a secret?

God wasn't playing favorites. He wasn't trying to keep the Gentiles (non-Jews) from understanding who He was and knowing the plan of salvation. It wasn't a secret like the false religious teachers promoted— that only a few people would find God. The secret Paul refers to is that God's plan was hidden until Jesus Christ came into the world. God's secret was to have His Son, Jesus Christ, live in the hearts of all believers—Jews and Gentiles. Who would have guessed that?

God gave the message first to the Jews. They had been God's chosen people for more than two thousand years. They weren't chosen because they deserved it. God wanted to show His love and mercy to the whole world through an entire nation. Of all people, the Jews should have been ready to welcome the Messiah and understand the salvation message God wanted to spread across the world. Unfortunately, most Jews were not receptive to the coming of Jesus, God's Son and chosen Messiah. Happily, some Jews—like Jesus' disciples and the apostle Paul—did recognize Jesus as God's Messiah. Then they spread the message far and wide.

## COLOSSIANS 2:13

### How can knowing Christ make you alive?

Knowing Christ makes you alive because God wakes up your spiritual nature that was previously dead. Jesus called that being "born again." Just as we were born physically and brought into the living, breathing, and moving of physical life, God wants to awaken the spiritual nature He created in each one of us. When we seek God, His Spirit breathes new life into us and we become alive in Christ.

"Alive with Christ" guarantees an eternal life that we will never lose. God created us to live beyond our time on earth. When our bodies die, God gives us new glorified bodies that will not decay. We don't know many details about these new bodies or our eternal life, but scripture promises that, "No eye has seen, no ear has heard, and no mind has imagined what God has prepared for those who love him" (1 Corinthians 2:9).

"Alive with Christ" gives us constant communion with God. Our God is personal and seeks a relationship with us even though we cannot see Him. His Word is our guide.

"Alive with Christ" awakens us to think and act like Jesus. Our actions are a visible representation of what Jesus wants to do here on earth. As we walk with God, He opens our eyes to the needs of others and gives us the resources to help them. God uses every situation to mold us into the likeness of Jesus. This process will never be completed until we get to heaven. Yet, even with all

our imperfections, the love of Jesus shines through our lives.

## COLOSSIANS 2:13

### How can your sins make you dead?

Sin is ignoring God and disobeying His commands. When we ignore God, we cut ourselves off from the God who created us and who is essential for our life.

If you put a plastic bag over your nose and mouth, you will die because you cut off your supply of oxygen. Your body was made with a specific requirement for oxygen. That's how God made you and your physical body.

God also made you with a spiritual need to be in contact with Him. Blaise Pascal wrote, "There is a God-shaped vacuum in the heart of every man which cannot be filled by any created thing, but only by God, the Creator, made known through Jesus." When you ignore or block off that God-shaped hole, you start to die spiritually. You were meant to have God in your life. Without Him you will die.

Being dead in your sins cuts off your relationship with God. He releases you to follow the foolishness of your destructive path. There is a way that seems right to you, but it leads to your destruction. When death comes, you will be alone, separated from God and everyone else. You will be dead in your sins.

## COLOSSIANS 3:2

### What do you think about when you fill your thoughts with heaven?

The goal of a Christian is to be like Jesus in thought, word, and deed. Thinking about the things of heaven is an intentional choice to see life as Jesus sees it.

Seeing other people the way Jesus sees them helps remove prejudices from our relationships. We stop judging people by the outward appearances of size, shape, beauty, or possessions. Jesus wants us to see all people as valuable and worthy of love, even if they are far from God.

Keeping heaven in our thoughts also puts a fresh perspective on material possessions and our desire to own so much of what we see. While advertisers keep telling us that we don't have enough, God wants us to remember what we do have—and to use it to help others. Jesus reminded us that possessions will rot and rust and be stolen by thieves. We are called to seek first the kingdom of God and to lay up treasures in heaven.

Looking at life through the mind of heaven helps us keep going when times are tough. In the struggle with pain and physical problems, we can be confident that God will wipe away all of our tears and sorrows in heaven. As much as life may hurt right now, God will be faithful to help us and grant us release from earth's sorrows when we see Him.

The universe reminds us that the vastness of God is bigger than our sufferings.

# 1 THESSALONIANS

*Paul cared deeply for the churches he helped to establish. He wanted them to truly experience the presence of the living Christ.*

## What does it mean to be chosen by God? Are some people not chosen?

This question has always frustrated the human mind and sometimes divided the church. How do people become part of God's family—through their own choice or through God choosing them? Another way to put it is: Given our spiritual deadness, what enables us to choose faith? Is it our choice itself, or is it God's enablement through His prior choice of us?

The Flood—only those chosen by God were saved.

Avoiding theological labels, let's characterize the two sides of the question:

(1) God chooses strongly for some, in the context of His broad choice for all. Clearly God extends His invitation to all sinners, and Christ's death covers the penalty for everyone's sin. But spiritual deadness means that no one can accept God's offer of life until God, through the Holy Spirit, enables the person's faith. In this view, we cannot even take credit for believing. God gets all the credit all the way.

(2) God chooses broadly for everyone but preferentially for no one, since that would be unfair. The offer of eternal life is available to all who know about it, and it's the church's job to get the message out. Everyone can and should believe. Don't blame God if you fail to fulfill His conditions for eternal life. Everyone within earshot of the gospel has a chance.

As you read the Bible, try to understand how your choice of faith is crucial and how God's choice of you is essential. The relationship is not cooperative, as if God needs your help; but neither is your will irrelevant, as if God would force a choice on you. Don't hesitate a moment to believe, giving credit to God for your ability to do so.

## 1 THESSALONIANS 1:10

### What are the coming "terrors"?

The Bible uses lots of descriptive word pictures to warn about God's final judgment, beyond which there is no appeal and no relief for those whom God casts away. These word pictures have inspired great literature (such as Dante's *Inferno*) and rightfully caused many souls to fear for their future.

Chief among the terrors, however, is not a burning lake or black pits, horrible as those images are. The worst terror is the complete absence of God's care and compassion. Think of your most desperate situation. It's terrible, painful, and sickening. Yet you know, down deep, there's a ray of hope—God. Now go back to that scene. Try to imagine enduring it without any ray of hope whatsoever, no caring divine presence behind the darkness. Most of us will admit that we can endure anything but hopelessness. That's complete terror—to be totally alone.

God's final judgment gathers all those in His family to the joy of heaven and all those outside His family to eternal isolation from anything good and merciful.

## 1 THESSALONIANS 2:12

### What characterizes a life that "God would consider worthy"?

First, it's a life that surrenders dependence on self and fully accepts dependence on God. To leave ego and trust completely in God is the first step. Then, just like any other experience, we need to grow in faith, not stagnating at a baby stage, but moving ahead with God, discovering His will for our lives, and depending on Him more and more for our needs and our happiness.

A life worthy of God does not mean that we earn the right through good deeds to enjoy God's favor. Rather, it means that God's message is so central to our motivation that we are living witnesses to its truth—through word and deed. To be worthy is to demonstrate to skeptics that God is good and loving, and that He has spoken to us in Jesus Christ. Oddly, God does not use loudspeakers from the heavens to speak to people today. God uses people to speak to people. To be worthy is to serve God wholeheartedly and put hands and feet to getting His message out.

## 1 THESSALONIANS 2:18

### How could Satan thwart the plans of a spiritual man like Paul?

We might imagine ourselves falling to a satanic scheme, but what about the spiritual giant, Paul? The question leads to an unexpected element of the spiritual battle between God and evil—the greater the life of faith, the stronger the opposition from the great opponent.

Compare schoolyard basketball to the level of competition in a professional game. The better the players, the tougher the game. The same apparently holds true in the spiritual life. Paul was devoted to Christ and hounded by the devil. Lesser saints may live the life of spiritual ease and comfort; the devil need not trouble them, for their faith will stir no waters and make little difference to anyone. But Paul . . .

Paul was frustrated by satanic opposition but not defeated by it. In his life was a strong sense of ultimate victory, for he knew God would see him through. He was playing in the big leagues, so to speak, and should expect trouble from the devil. But the game's outcome was never in doubt, and Paul put every effort toward playing hard until his substitute came in.

# 1 THESSALONIANS 4:3–8

### Why is sexual purity so important?

Sex is such a strong instinct that it affects every other motivation and loyalty. Biologists are just now discovering how the sex drive governs social organization in animal species from monkeys to dolphins. All animals live in hierarchies, and those hierarchies govern who mates with whom. Sex affects everything. What biologists are just discovering about animals, Hollywood entertainment producers knew long ago about people.

God has ordained heterosexual monogamous marriage as the proper setting for sexual activity. This arrangement requires considerable effort. Mere sex does not require love, but love cements mutual commitment and is our best glue for enduring marriages. Yet love is fragile, and commitment is casually broken in the interests of sexual adventure. Keeping love strong and adventurism focused on one's marriage partner is key to living by God's plan and, therefore, enjoying God's power in our lives. Men cannot flit from partner to partner and hope to care anything about God or witness to this message. Women cannot service different men and hope to understand God's will for their lives.

Spiritual power and sexual focus go hand in hand. For the single person, sexual focus means chastity. To forgo sex in obedience to God is no easier than to stay faithful throughout life to one spouse. But that's God's plan, and there's no fine print or alternatives for special cases.

Today, however, a case is being made for homosexuals. Churches are wondering how to accommodate new data concerning the causes of homosexuality and new, robust claims from homosexuals that their monogamous unions deserve the church's blessing. Many churches have accepted the fact that some individuals will feel sexually drawn to their own gender. For such people, the appropriate sexual norm is chastity.

Just as Joseph ran from Potipher's wife, God tells every person to keep away from all sexual impurity.

# 1 THESSALONIANS 4:11

## What is living quietly? Leaders are not usually recessive, passive types.

By saying "live a quiet life," it seems as if Paul is celebrating a particular personality type, making that type holier than others. We know better, however; so we must look for other explanations.

One approach is from the reverse angle: What is Paul urging believers to avoid? A loud life, one that draws attention to the self; a fix-it life, where everyone's business is ours to meddle with; a lazy life, where interdependence (people relating in the church) turns into dependence (living with reduced ambition in the shadow of greater saints). These attitudes Paul certainly would not condone.

On the positive side, Paul seems to admire here the stable Christian who lives with contentment and witnesses consistently to a small circle of personal influence. "Change the world slowly" is a respectable missions strategy here—better to walk and win than to run and faint. The fiery Christian who burns out early is no credit to the Lord and no help to the church. Not everyone is called to keep up with Paul's itinerary; some faith should grow like a plant, slow and steady, into full bloom.

# 1 THESSALONIANS 4:17

## What is the rapture and when will it happen?

Through the word *rapture* doesn't actually appear in the Bible, this verse contains the phrase ("caught up") that the Latin "rapture" derives from. The concept is widely dis-

cussed and very important to a biblical understanding of the end of history. When human history as we know it is done, a stunningly important event will lift both living and dead into the presence of the Savior. At His second coming, Christians who have died will rise first; then Christians still on earth will join them to meet Christ in the air.

Questions of the rapture's timing must be explored within broader issues of eschatology, a theological reflection on what's ahead. The major schools of thought divide on the question of when Christ will return: before a thousand years of Christ's rule on earth

All believers will one day be taken to be with Christ forever.

(premillennial thinking), at the conclusion of the church's mission in the world (amillennial thinking), or after the world has been largely converted (postmillennial thinking). Involved in this issue also is the meaning and timing of the great tribulation, whether that period is entirely in the future (following the Millennium) or representative of the present age.

Here, however, the key truth is that all Christians, living and dead, will be raised with Christ at His second coming. That is a great hope and promise.

# 1 THESSALONIANS 5:18

## Is the command to be thankful in all circumstances conditioned by certain circumstances?

It seems unnatural, even delusional, to thank God for cancer taking the life of someone dear to you. Or to be thankful for the violent brutality of a terrorist or for the destruction wrought by an F-5 tornado. Surely some circumstances absolutely refuse to lead a person into real thankfulness.

Paul's advice about thankfulness requires some context. The evil we suffer should never make us stoics (ruthlessly surrendered to fate) and never lead us to shrug off the sin around us (as the German church in the 1930s turned a deaf ear to Adolf Hitler). As Christians, we rightly oppose the effects of sin even while we are subject to them. But Paul is speaking about personal attitudes here. He is not begrudging the use of our minds to solve problems and serve humankind.

What makes the Christian so different is the strong and sure belief that nothing can happen apart from the loving care of God (Romans 8:28). When cancer strikes, it is not because God has forgotten us; therefore, we should trust God to lead and teach us as we take measures to correct the situation. And if we cannot make correction, if it's out of our control, if brutal men point rifles at us, we don't imagine God is asleep. God tracks details that we would consider quite unimportant (Matthew 10:29), so surely He cares for us at all times. Our thankfulness for that fact is all-important because the alternative is bitterness and hopelessness.

When trouble strikes, don't imagine that you're a victim of chance. Rather, thank God and seek His presence in everything you face, doing all you can for God to reduce hurt for others and bring evil to justice.

# 2 THESSALONIANS

*Many people want to know what the future holds. Paul assures us that God knows.*

## 2 THESSALONIANS 2:2

### What signs tell us that God's plan is on schedule, even if we cannot know God's timetable?

Christians are called to live obediently in light of two promises: (1) Jesus can and may return today—"You also must be ready all the time. For the Son of Man will come when least expected" (Matthew 24:44); (2) We cannot pinpoint a schedule—"No one knows the day or hour when these things will happen, not even the angels in heaven or the Son himself. Only the Father knows" (Matthew 24:36).

The Bible offers a number of "signs" that precede or accompany Christ's return (see Matthew 24; 2 Thessalonians 2; Revelation 4–22). Some of these signs are natural, such as earthquakes and other physical disasters; others are political, such as wars, rumors of war, and shifts in power leading to world domination. Still other signs are spiritual, such as growing world religious movements that reject God and the intense persecution of Christians. Some signs are positive events, such as the spread of the gospel around the world and the renewal of the Jewish nation. History demonstrates that Christians have always been able to see in their immediate context enough possible fulfillments of these signs to conclude that Jesus might come soon.

These signs can be an encouragement to faith. As long as they inspire our ongoing faithfulness, well and good. But if we use them to plot a chart of future events, we err. Paul warns here about the passion to know what no one can—the details of God's timetable for history.

## 2 THESSALONIANS 3:6

### What's wrong with idleness?

Paul warns against those who use the possibility of Christ's immediate return as an excuse for laziness. Apparently a group in Thessalonica had dropped out of daily life. They were teaching others to set aside responsibilities, quit work, and do no planning for the future.

The idea that doing nothing is an effective way to anticipate Christ's return is a damaging deception. Jesus did not command believers to stop everything and wait. Instead, he instructed them to live in obedient anticipation (Matthew 5:13–16). Idle Christians are neither modeling a life of faith nor fulfilling Jesus' command to make disciples (Matthew 28:19–20). Idleness fails to respond to God's promises with gratitude and joy.

Being lazy and idle keeps us from doing God's work and giving glory to His name.

# 1 TIMOTHY

*This first "pastoral epistle" answered many questions for a young pastor coping with a huge responsibility.*

## 1 TIMOTHY 2:12

### Should women be silent in church?

This is one of the most contested portions of the Bible today. What did Paul mean by this far-reaching restriction on women, and how does it apply now? The meaning of this passage must be drawn from its context, then from the larger biblical teaching on leadership and Christian development.

On one side of the debate are those who take this passage at face value. No women should preach or teach with men present (in some churches women are not permitted to offer intercessory prayer or read aloud the scripture on which the sermon is based). No women should be ordained to church office. Modern gender egalitarianism is irrelevant to the church, which has no biblical reason to compromise with it.

On the other side are Christians who understand this passage in the light of Galatians 3:28, which seems to open a new era in which differences of ethnicity, economy, and gender wash away. The verse in Galatians leads many to understand that the restrictions Paul placed on women were local and temporary, not binding on churches today.

Clearly, each modern church must settle this matter with policies that it believes comply with the Bible. The church—the new community in Christ—is called to be light and salt (telling the story, preserving the peace) throughout the world. Should women play only supporting roles in that mission, or does the new community witness to a new day in which traditional subordinates (women, the poor, ethnic minorities, etc.) carry a full share of responsibility? Resources on this question are abundant, and readers are urged to further study.

## 1 TIMOTHY 2:15

### How are women saved through childbearing?

This verse does not propose an alternative to salvation through faith in Christ. Women do not enjoy a gender-specific privilege foreclosed to men by nature alone. Three interpretations place this obscure verse within wider biblical teaching.

First, Paul could be referring to salvation through Mary's childbirth, the Savior Himself, Jesus.

Second, Paul may be teaching that the traditional role of birthing children is honorable, God-ordained, and worthy of high esteem.

Finally, Paul might be pointing to the curse of Eden, declaring that each woman who survived the painful birth process speaks to the power of the gospel to overcome the curse. Such a strong witness renders preaching unnecessary—the experience speaks for itself.

## 1 TIMOTHY 3:2, 12

### Must an elder or deacon be married?

No, but if they are married, they must be sexually faithful. Promiscuity cannot be tolerated in church leadership. The direction of the charge here is toward faithful support in other ways, too. Married church leaders should witness to the church of God's love through their own growing and deepening relationship.

## 1 TIMOTHY 5:23

### Why does Paul urge the use of alcoholic drink?

"A little wine" for the sake of settling a prolonged health condition is no violation of biblical directives concerning drunkenness. Paul was not affected by the modern notion that all alcoholic drink is wrong and must be studi-

ously avoided. Rather, Paul avoided the misuse of wine, but like any other food substance, he understood its proper use as well. Gluttony in any form is unhealthy and morally wrong because it spoils the body and weakens the individual. Moderate use of wine is no violation of Christian standards in Paul's eyes.

## 1 TIMOTHY 6:1–2

### Does Paul condone slavery?

Paul does three things with slavery: (1) He acknowledges its pervasive practice without comment about its morality; (2) he urges slaves to radical loyalty as an expression of faith in God's sovereign will; (3) he attacks the inequities of the system by insisting that masters and slaves become like brothers, an unprecedented notion (Philemon 16). In this passage, he wants slaves to excel in their service.

Paul's apparent social conservatism has been the subject of much misunderstanding. He would appear to give biblical sanction to the much discredited experience of the African slave trade, for example. Nothing could be further from biblical teaching, however. Nowhere does the Bible advocate slavery or present a vision of the human person or culture that gives a pro-slavery position any credence. Neither does the Bible advocate social or political revolution as a corrective.

Rather, the Bible's revolutionary language is always a matter of the heart. Change begins with the human spirit in response to God's law, energized by the Holy Spirit, and affected by the presence of the living Christ in the believer's life. That change replaces greed with love, changing the face of slavery entirely and eroding its cultural foundations. Slavery, which requires human

A woman takes grapes off the grapevine, while another woman stomps the grapes in a barrel to make wine.

exploitation in the interest of accumulating wealth, cannot survive the loss of greed enacted by God's Spirit in the heart of the believer. As Christian love always seeks to enable others, emancipation is the only possible result of the change of heart experienced in Christian conversion and discipleship.

## 1 TIMOTHY 6:10

### Is wealth immoral?

Not in itself. Wealth can be the source of great blessing when used properly. But money is indeed the world's preeminent symbol of success and, as such, a constant threat to the soul's primary loyalty. As evidence of this, we no longer question these "givens" about modern life.

♦ The company that writes your check owns your time.

♦ In any choice between work and leisure, family, or church, first priority must be given to work.

♦ Money belongs rightfully to the one who earns it or inherits it.

♦ Spending money on oneself is okay as long as you share with others, too.

Each of these "givens" is challenged by a biblical view of Christian discipleship because money easily brings opposition to God. Almost invariably, the more money a person possesses, the less faith is exercised, the less God is felt to be needed, the less patience one has toward the church, the less compassion one feels toward "have nots" (who, the thinking often goes, are poor because they are lazy). Money wars against the soul. Though many successful Christians speak about their first loyalty to God, almost none surrender their special standing in wealth. The seduction of money is best resisted by giving it away, which the Bible recognizes repeatedly as the preferred option. In relative poverty, it seems, the soul hungers for God all the more.

While wealth is considered a prerequisite for leaders in the church today (and the wealthy are fondly courted by nearly every Christian agency), nothing could be further from the biblical model. In contrast to the church's capitulation to wealth's allure, the Bible describes leaders who emerge from and gratefully remain at such levels of financial need that God's supply is their sustenance, prayer their daily vigil, and simplicity their lifestyle.

# 2 TIMOTHY

*Here is more encouragement and direction to a young leader.*

## 2 TIMOTHY 1:5

### Paul cites Timothy's mother and grandmother as people of faith. Where was Timothy's father?

Acts 16:1 informs us that Timothy's father was a Greek. Since Luke (in Acts) makes a point of indicating that Timothy's Jewish mother was a Christian, we may infer that Timothy's father was not. With respect to spiritual parentage, Timothy experienced a son-father relationship with Paul. Several times in 2 Timothy, Paul calls Timothy "my dear son."

## 2 TIMOTHY 1:7

### What overcomes fear?

Likely, Timothy was a timid person, but Paul recognized in him the qualities of a leader. Instead of urging Timothy to become more courageous, Paul wanted to plant in his heart three virtues: (1) power—the ability to act responsibly in the face of fear; (2) love—the first fruit of the Spirit (Galatians 5:22); (3) self-discipline— the last fruit of the Spirit (Galatians 5:23). Paul is reminding the young leader that fears are no match for the resources God's Spirit brings to the life of a believer.

Just like King David, we can pray for the Holy Spirit to give us what we need to overcome fear.

# 2 TIMOTHY 2:3–6

## How do soldiers, farmers, and athletes depict the exemplary Christian life?

In each of these arduous walks of life, Paul saw certain character traits and disciplines that had parallels in the Christian life. In all three cases, life is shaped by priorities and commitments. Each role involves obligations, responsibilities, and benefits. Soldiers submit to a chain of command; farmers work hard in cycles and seasons; athletes compete within the rules of their sport. Each expects to enjoy the results of victory and each pays a personal price for success.

In the same way, Christians commit to obedient service to Christ. In spiritual warfare, Christians are soldiers—fighting the good fight (2 Timothy 4:7); in evangelism, Christians are farmers—scattering seeds and harvesting (1 Corinthians 3:6–9); in purposeful living, Christians are athletes— running to the finish line (2 Timothy 4:7).

# 2 TIMOTHY 3:16

## How is the Bible inspired by God?

Through the Holy Spirit, God revealed His plan to certain people who put God's message into written language. These writings, collected into the canons of the Old and New Testaments, are unlike any other writings in authority and origin. They are "God-breathed," the literal translation of the word "inspired." While the authors of Bible books wrote from their own historical and cultural contexts, using their own minds, talents, language, and style, they wrote God's message to all people under the supervision of God. They were moved in heart and mind by a special revelatory power of God.

The Bible is completely trustworthy because God is the author of its message, while human writers framed that message as they received it. Even as we read the Bible today, it is a living Word, not a dead letter, since the Holy Spirit in a mysterious way leads us to understand, believe, and apply its truth.

God used the Holy Spirit to reveal His plan and write His Word. In this picture, the Holy Spirit fills the worshiper.

# Titus

*One of the Bible's shorter books, the letter to Titus is powerful and unforgettable.*

## Titus 1:2

### Without the capacity to lie, is God limited in His ability to speak?

The question resembles another one: Is God powerful enough to create a rock He cannot lift? Such questions use the superlative qualities of God to question those same qualities. In the case of God's ability to communicate, the question presumes that personal capacity can be detached from personal identity. God's identity is holiness. God would have no reason to lie, no inclination to lie, no regard for deception, and no attraction to gaining any advantage through deceptive means. A lying god is no God at all, but a fake. God's ability to communicate cannot be isolated from His identity. When God speaks, true words come forth always.

## Titus 1:5–9

### What qualities make a good leader?

The three letters of 1 Timothy, 2 Timothy, and Titus are also known as the "pastoral epistles" because they contain practical guidelines for the training and choosing of leaders in the church. Leadership qualities cited here include:

♦ A good reputation. Someone who has the respect of other people has already shown his or her ability to put others first.

   ♦ Marital faithfulness. Loyalty to the primary commitment of marriage usually foretells loyalty to the rest of one's commitments.

   ♦ Children who believe and act like it. Can a leader in the church hope to disciple others if those closest to him or her do not embrace the faith?

♦ Blameless living. This means not just abiding by rules but positively and consistently seeking God's way.

   ♦ No arrogance. People inflated with their self-importance leave little room for God to lead them.

      ♦ No quick temper. In a world of interpersonal violence, Christian leaders must be devoted to peace, goodwill, and self-control.

      ♦ No drunkenness. No leader can himself or herself be led by any substance.

- No violence. As violence breeds the spirit of revenge, the church needs the spirit of goodwill. The church is a community devoted to each other in God's service, not a fractured community at war.

- No greed. Leaders have access to money but cannot love it nor make decisions based on the bottom line.

- Hospitality. This means active sharing of one's personal space, enlarging one's home to people not part of the immediate family.

- Pleasure in good. Most public pleasures operate at the periphery of civic standards. Christian leaders find their recreation at the center of moral goodness.

This work is called *Religion Vanquishing Heresy*. Christians must always seek out God's truth.

- Wise living and fair judgments. This involves making good decisions based on available facts and counsel.

- Devout and disciplined. The leader is able to corral the occasional temptation to spin out of control, to binge, to flake off. He or she is someone others can depend on.

- Clear, consistent beliefs and teaching. A growing person in mind and heart, the leader is a learner and a reasonably decent communicator.

That's a long list, but leadership is a high privilege and responsibility.

# TITUS 3:10

## What is heresy?

Heresy is doctrinal deviation from God's revealed truth, as the church has come to understand that truth down through the centuries. Numerous erroneous ideas and teachings about God and the spiritual life have affected the church in every era. The apostle Paul warned Titus what to do about people who divide the church with clearly wrongheaded ideas—shun them! Peter wrote of the clever but destructive nature of such unorthodox beliefs and sadly noted that "many will follow their evil teaching" (2 Peter 2:2). Other warnings against heresy are found in Acts 20:29 and Philippians 3:2.

In 1 John, a form of Gnosticism was the heresy deceiving many naïve believers. John's counsel was for Christians to follow carefully his own apostolic teaching and the leading of the Holy Spirit rather than some seemingly attractive idea propagated by a persuasive leader.

We must be careful about accusing anyone of heresy. Heresy is a serious charge of doctrinal error and can only be applied to theological concepts that clearly violate the historic teaching of the church. Because of that, charges of heresy should only come from study teams comprised of distinguished leaders who prayerfully consider the consequences of their conclusions. Heresy charges can never arise from disgruntled individuals seeking to keep innovation from changing their church.

# PHILEMON

*How should people reconcile, especially when one is a master and the other a slave? Paul pointed Christians to a different, holy way.*

## PHILEMON 8

### Why "ask" when Paul could "demand"?

Military officers enjoy the privilege of giving orders and then being obeyed. But even military orders are to be disobeyed when they stray from military discipline and law. Paul knew that his spiritual authority included the privilege of giving "orders"—requests enforced by the conscience and ultimately by God. Yet he took a much softer approach here.

Paul's purpose was to count Philemon as a mature Christian who needed no orders to understand his duty and required no coercion to respond to that duty. By appealing to Philemon instead of commanding him, Paul set the stage for Philemon to adopt a new posture toward slaves. Paul was willing to trust the work of the Holy Spirit in Philemon's heart.

As children grow, parents seemingly lose control over their offspring. Like Paul, they must change from commanding to appealing, to signal the growth of the child's own conscience. Leaders in the church should do the same. No church operates well when motivated by coercion or guilt. Churches grow as people take personal and corporate responsibility for their attitudes and actions. Leaders who want their vision enacted immediately, and command that it be done, should be quickly dismissed as tyrants wearing the wrong uniform. They have failed to grow, and all who follow them will be stunted and small-hearted.

# HEBREWS

*This book is all about Jesus, the one way to God, superior by far to anything else we know. He is awesome in majesty, our pioneer in faith. This Savior wants our loyal service and devotion.*

## HEBREWS 1:14

### What's the typical job description for angels?

Angels apparently spend most of their career serving Christians, working as bodyguards or perhaps "spirit guards," helping Christians remain faithful throughout life. It is interesting that this type of job would be noted in the book of the Bible that describes Christians as most vulnerable to defeat and loss. Surely Jesus is the captain of all the company of the saved, but angels are the rank-and-file "coast guards," defending the spiritual perimeter against attack from the evil one.

This job function does not prevent Christians from suffering disaster or defeat, as experience clearly attests. The effectiveness of the angels' work will be known only in heaven. But the hints we have concerning these guardsmen suggest that heavenly praise to God will be all the more joyous for the help we unknowingly received from these unseen agents.

God's angels protect
His people.

## HEBREWS 2:10

### Did Jesus need to suffer to become perfect?

No other Bible book portrays the humanity of Jesus as dramatically as Hebrews. Jesus reflects God's glory and sustains the universe, yet He was also, for a time, a little lower than the angels. Then there is this quizzical note that suggests Jesus went through a developmental process in attaining a seat at the right hand of God.

As to Jesus' divine nature, no developmental process is in view. Jesus did not grow into deity or Sonship, as if God picked the man Jesus and made Him into the Christ. As to Jesus' human nature, there was development (see Luke 2:52), just as there is for every person. Jesus experienced pain, and in that pain, grew to know—as a man—the protection and presence of God, His father. The real pain Jesus endured made His death on the cross a real sacrifice for sin. Pain was the price for the fulfillment of the mission begun in the Incarnation and completed in the Resurrection.

## HEBREWS 3:15

### What is a hard heart?

It is rebelling and doing what we want to do. It is turning a deaf ear to God. It is ignoring and squandering a spiritual inheritance. It is letting the fire of faith grow cold. And it is the worst mistake a person can make.

The writer of Hebrews urges, do not harden your hearts to God. Don't squander your sensitivities to God. Do not take the advice of the devil to make your heart ash-cold. It is foolish to do so. Crazy in fact. It makes no sense. Don't do it.

## HEBREWS 4:13

### Does God respect our privacy?

Privacy protection today usually raises the ugly specter of government or business probing into data we believe they have no right to know. Basic to privacy is the notion of the sanctity of conscience. No one should be punished for thoughts, and no one should be forced to reveal thoughts. Against this common notion, God makes a startling revelation: He knows our thoughts. Instantly any claim to a right to privacy from God is declared null and void. It never existed and cannot be claimed. God knows our secrets, every one.

God does not impose His Word on the heart and mind of the person unwilling to hear and respond. In that sense, God respects privacy. But to imagine that one's mind is a safe-zone, hidden from the mind of God, is a mistake.

## HEBREWS 5:6

### Who was Melchizedek?

This verse in Hebrews is a direct quotation from Psalm 110:4, in which David is declared

Abraham acknowledges Melchizedek's standing as a man of God.

to be a priest in the order of Melchizedek. For David, that meant a privilege of priesthood higher than the Aaronic order.

Melchizedek, one of the truly mysterious characters in the Bible (see Genesis 14), had no human parentage (Hebrews 7:3). Abraham acknowledged Melchizedek's standing as a man of God, even before the people of Israel had organized a priestly class. Melchizedek represents an eternal priesthood of which David was an early participant and Jesus is the central figure. As the eternal priest, Jesus intercedes for us before God, who gladly accepts the Son's intercession and welcomes all for whom intercession is made to enter the rest—that is, God's eternal home.

## HEBREWS 6:6

### Can salvation be lost?

Can salvation, once promised, be taken back due to human failure? Plenty of Bible passages suggest that it cannot. Jesus holds Christians in His hand and will not give them up (John 10:28). Yet this passage seems to clearly warn of the danger.

Perhaps this is a hypothetical, yet real, warning: Don't carelessly abandon the race that faith requires, or you could be a dropout—with emphasis on the vast difference between "could be" and "is." Perhaps this is a warning against false faith, the "rocky soil" kind Jesus speaks about in Matthew 13:5—not real faith at all.

To the fearful and repentant believer who worries over losing his salvation over a lustful glance or white lie, the Bible assures that God's protection is strong. To the self-assured believer who boasts in the possession of a "once saved, always saved" eternal ticket that no amount of hedonistic self-indulgence can invalidate, these verses raise a sober warning: Don't drop out of the race; don't trade the truth for a lie.

## HEBREWS 7:11

### What does imperfection teach us?

It teaches us to look for something perfect. In the case of the priesthood, the imperfection of the Levites—Aaron's line of priests—points to the need for something better, which God is always eager to provide. In the case of life in general, imperfection points to the possibilities and magnificence of heaven. In the case of people, imperfection can point to all that God is doing (and will yet do) to conform us to the image of His Son Jesus. The emphasis here is on salvation. The perfect way to heaven was not found or achieved in priestly rituals. God had a better way, Jesus. Now the perfect priest has done His perfect work, all for us.

## HEBREWS 8:12

### Can God forget?

Several Bible passages warn that God's memory is complete with respect to people's sins, even with respect to their thoughts (Hebrews 4:13). However, God apparently wants to forget the sins He has forgiven; indeed, He claims to do so here.

Though God has no need to clean His mind of hurtful thoughts, we might understand this divine promise better if we compared it to washing our own minds of images and memories that cause us sadness or remind us of defeat and gloom. While we can redirect anger and melancholy, we cannot erase memories. But God apparently wants to and does so—ridding Himself of memories of the pain and wretchedness of sin.

## HEBREWS 9:22

### Why blood for forgiveness of sin?

Certain facts of life seem to be given to us, often without much negotiation or explanation. The requirement that life be lost in order for sin to be forgiven is one of those. In other words, it's a God-given rule. Perhaps a life lost better symbolizes the impossibility of sin in God's kingdom, the obliteration of imperfection that heaven requires. Nonetheless, the blood of a lost life reddens every scrap of promise that God will save us. This is a fact of life that we cannot modify.

In the older covenant, the blood of animals took the place of the blood of humans as a sacrifice for sin. The animal died as an offering of peace and in the place of the guilty. But now a perfect sacrifice has come.

The blood of Jesus now takes the place, once and for all, so that undeserving sinners need not die.

The holy God ordained that creation be perfect. The blood of Jesus recovers God's plan and saves the world from its alternate fate, annihilation.

## HEBREWS 10:24–25

### Why do Christians have to meet together?

All Christian churches encourage private devotion—prayer and scripture reading by the individual believer. But even more important is the gathering of believers for corporate worship to praise God and be encouraged in faith. People grow strong in groups as they learn together the meaning of

Following the example of the Last Supper, Christians should gather together to praise God and encourage one another in their faith.

the Bible, raise songs and prayers to God, and plan strategies for mission. Faith is a group activity. Soon that array of meetings that seems so time-consuming becomes a way of celebrating faith with the family of God and of renewing faith with brothers and sisters. To meet together is to witness to God's presence in the world and in us.

## HEBREWS 10:26–27, 31

**Some Christians teach that a "saved" person can sin all he or she wants since there is no way to lose salvation. Is this true?**

The security of salvation has long been a topic of debate among Christians. "Once saved, always saved" is a slogan that seems to reflect several parts of the Bible where believers are assured of God's promise to bring them to heaven. Yet other people believe that salvation is a treasure to protect lest it be lost.

Christians are called to live out their faith, not merely to theologize the meaning of it. The Bible calls upon Christians to live faithful to Jesus Christ, for such living pleases God. Christians who intentionally flaunt their privileges do not please God. Sinful Christians (if they can be called by that high name) treat the Bible like an irrevocable contract and treat God like a party to a contract. But God is more like the courtroom judge. And since this Judge is the final court—with no appeal to any higher—Christians do well to stay faithful in a manner the Judge prescribes.

## HEBREWS 11:1

### What does faith require?

This verse is the best and most succinct definition of faith in the Bible. Yet living by this definition is one of the most difficult tasks that God puts in front of us. We need to flesh out the definition against the biographies

included in the rest of chapter 11. How did people actually put faith into practice? Here are their stories, with all the gory details. In short, faith may bring pain, but only for a short time. Faith may bring loss, but none that God cannot resupply. Faith may bring a horrible death, but God is there, too. Faith sees beyond the immediate circumstance to God's grace and mercy, just ahead, around the next turn, where the light brightens the path. You'll get there because God will help you, no matter what stands in the way.

## HEBREWS 12:7

### How should Christians respond to God's discipline?

In the same way that muscles respond to exercise: by getting stronger through it. The breakdown of muscles invariably leads to their build-up, making them stronger. In life, breakdowns hurt. Grief is real, and mourning is part of Christian experience. Even in the worst trouble, however, God's work is secure, God's will is good, and God's strength is ours. With divine discipline, God is training a deeper faith. In severe trouble, God draws the believer into a relationship that defies all the losses and scorns any instinct toward fatalism or stoicism. Indeed, we are not subject to fate, and we need not steel ourselves against fate. We may suffer under the plague of sin that corrupts God's creation, but we never suffer out of sight of God Himself. For Christians, grief is a signal of hope, and mourning is a precursor of immense joy—God's promise.

## HEBREWS 12:29

### How is God a "devouring fire"?

This quote is part of the Bible's earliest record of God. The Hebrew people leaving Egypt understood God as a devouring fire (Exodus 24:17), especially when Moses entered the mist on top of Mount Sinai to receive God's commandments. Moses spoke of God as a devouring fire (Deuteronomy 4:24) when he explained to the people why he, their leader for forty years, could not enter the promised land with them. And the image of God as a raging fire consuming sinful enemies is common in Old Testament poetry (Psalm 97:3).

The metaphor alerts us to aspects of God's character that inspire awe and holy fear: God's jealousy (He wants priority in our lives), God's judgment (His will governs our lives), and God's power (He will prevail over enemies).

## Should Christians follow other people, or should they only follow God?

Surely they should follow God, but following God requires that we observe and follow leaders who are following God. Mature Christian mentors help our faith develop and our understanding of God's will to grow.

Leaders are those who are learning to see God in decision making, to hear God in relationship building, and to exult in God in resource sharing. Leaders are people growing in knowledge and teaching skills who have compassion for younger Christians and for people who do not yet have true faith. Leaders are people walking with God, taking steps of faith, praying for daily guidance, and growing in the ability to speak about what they know. Leaders are people who worship God joyfully, work for God when no one seems to be watching, and pray for the needs of others consistently. We do well to learn from these leaders as a way to learn about God.

Moses called God a devouring fire after his time on Mount Sinai where he received the Ten Commandments. We should be in awe of God.

# JAMES

*Let's get practical. What difference does faith make? All the difference in the world—and here's how.*

## JAMES 1:25

### How can law, which restricts and punishes, be a vehicle of liberation?

Law limits behavior and sets penalties for violating those limits. But no human law is precise enough to limit all the bad it intends to limit or promote all the good it intends to promote. That is, human law never corresponds perfectly to moral goodness. Laws against stealing, for example, erect boundaries that become morally arguable when property rights conflict or when, for example, human needs such as hunger clash with land ownership.

God's law, however, is perfect. It corresponds exactly to moral goodness since God wrote both the book on goodness and the book on divine law. No flaws or glitches in God's law punish unfairly or set arbitrary limits betrayed by human experience. To follow God's law is to follow the path of the good, which is exactly what makes life pleasurable and happy.

Liberty without law is anarchy. When everyone does whatever he or she wills, life becomes brutish and short. Law without liberty is tyranny, and life becomes fragile and monotonous. The liberty God's law brings is the freedom to live as God intended, and God's intentions are always good.

## JAMES 2:13

### Is God's judgment linked to our judgment?

Yes, in the sense that humans make decisions concerning obedience or rebellion, and those decisions carry immense consequences. God promises to bless and reward obedience and to punish rebellion. In judging the standards that govern one's life, one is choosing loyalties. God alerts us that if the one important loyalty (our loyalty to God) is neglected or refused, punishment will follow. On the other hand, if a person accepts God's lordship over life through faith in Jesus Christ, God promises to bless.

James 2:13 seems to suggest that God wavers between two impulses: to bless and to curse. Actually, God wants very much to bless and not to punish (2 Peter 3:9), but punishment awaits those who refuse His invitation to forgiveness and obedience.

# JAMES 2:14

## What gets a person into heaven— faith in God or good deeds?

"He was a good person," we often say about a departed friend, hoping that whatever heaven there is will be open to such a person, given the good deeds, on balance, that characterized the better days of his or her life. Fairness mixed with a little lenience should open heaven's gates, we hope.

But the "good person" theory is as faulty as the "faith in word only" theory of those who profess to be Christians but continue living like pagans, looking out only for themselves. Both approaches to heaven fail.

Then what unlocks those pearly gates, after all? Genuine faith—faith demonstrated by a life of obedience to God.

Faith means that we trust in Christ alone for salvation, not in anything we do or in any good works we perform. Obedience means that faith changes our priorities. That is, the change of heart that faith enacts must also change our habits and goals. The practical dimensions of faith are expressed in virtues such as generosity, patience, trustworthiness, and love. No one who claims to have faith should be absent these virtues.

If you are an old curmudgeon (or even a young one) who scorns these virtues on your drive to church every Sunday, you had better examine the faith you profess. It's probably just an empty shell that does nobody, including you, any good.

Faith in Jesus, not our good deeds, gets us into heaven.

to the truth and living in obedience to it is the key. To believe in God means to act on the truth one possesses. That simple difference separates Christian faith from demonic opposition.

## JAMES 2:24

### Can people work their way into heaven?

It might appear that by doing good things we can earn entry into heaven. Not so. No one gains the privilege of heaven apart from faith in Jesus Christ. But faith, James warns, can be mere rhetoric or play-acting or investing in something quite false. True faith always expresses itself; never does true faith remain isolated or cerebral. Is your faith genuine? Look at your behavior and see.

No, a person cannot perform enough good deeds to deserve God's forgiveness. But a good deed is required, and Jesus has done it. Through faith in His good deed—His sacrificial death on the cross—and subsequent action on that faith, we join God's family and enter into all the joy and wonder of God's own presence. Heaven awaits those who trust in Christ.

## JAMES 4:4

### What is friendship with this world?

The question concerns where we establish our loyalties. If we set life goals toward wealth, comfort, ease, status, privilege, or power, we have adopted a mind-set typical of "the world"—that is, our motivation is geared toward achieving pleasure for the self. On the other hand, if we set goals to live for God, we will invariably find ourselves acting in ways that "the world" believes to be silly, counterproductive, or wrongheaded.

The Bible often pictures our lives as spiritual battlefields. We can't live in a neutral

Satan, his demons, and the lost souls of hell.

## JAMES 2:19

### What religion do demons believe?

Demons apparently are quite intelligent about matters of theology and practice. They are monotheists (that is, they believe that one supreme God exists), though the history of demonic influence shows that they propagandize false belief in imaginary pagan deities. They hold belief in the identification of Jesus as God's Son, as shown in their confession in Matthew 8:29. They certainly believe in the existence of moral standards and in God's final judgment concerning evil. So, in many ways, demons believe biblical truth. They have seen the truth close up, and their entire job is to subvert it. You have to know the opposition, so to speak.

The demons' seemingly orthodox beliefs demonstrate that simply knowing the truth does not bring peace with God. Submitting zone; there is none. We must pitch our tent somewhere. If you've decided to be friendly with the world, look across the battlefield today. See what God's side is like. Notice the welcome sign, posted again by God's generous love toward you. Notice how powerful that side is. Then get yourself over there.

Friendship with the world is ultimately self-defeating, because "the world" consumes all its friends, chews them up, and spits them out. Pitch your tent in the camp where people grow, thrive, and make eternal friendships—where people count most because God loves them all.

## JAMES 5:15

### Can prayer cure sickness?

Yes and no. Yes, prayer *can* cure sickness. In prayer we ask God to extend help, especially when we feel helpless. God answers prayers, often providing what we ask, sometimes not, but always giving what is best—even if that answer hurts. God heals the sick. Jesus showed us that in person. Healing is a miracle, though medical science plays its part, too. It's important to remember that God, not our prayer to God, is the healing agent.

But there is a sickness God does not heal, the sickness that leads to death. We all die. Our sicknesses are not cured forever, or else we would be immortal. God reserves that ultimate healing miracle for heaven, where no sickness or death puts grief or closure on our joy together with God.

Sometimes sickness persists despite prayer. Chronic headaches never go away, cancer spreads slowly, a nervous disorder evades diagnosis. Faced with that kind of sickness, we should continue to pray in faith that God will answer powerfully. Sickness, like every other part of life, should be our proving ground of faith where we grow to depend on God's good will for us, at the same time asking for courage to endure the trials of human experience.

# 1 PETER

*In high and holy language, this book explores the meaning of belonging to God.*

## 1 PETER 1:6; 4:13

### Doesn't the Bible promise happiness to all who follow Christ?

Not happiness, but joy. It also promises trouble, as these verses testify. The hard reality of the Bible's message is that life breeds trouble and Christians are not exempt. In fact, Christians should expect more trouble, as the adversary seeks to derail faith and upset biblical promises.

It is not pessimistic, just realistic and biblical, to say that trouble is the standard and peace the exception, this side of heaven. God uses trouble to build our faith, redeeming us from all trouble through the power of the overcomer, Jesus.

## 1 PETER 1:7

### How is faith like precious metal?

A field we do not value goes to weed; a room we do not value never gets a fresh coat of paint; scrap metal is left to rust—but gold is so valued that we pass it through a refining fire to purify it.

That's what our faith is like to God. Much too valuable to go to weed, faith grows as God leads the believer through life's hardships—through the fire that burns away impurities—into heaven and peace. Faith that looks like peeling paint or rusted metal is faith that won't budge, won't step forward, won't follow. Its immovability wears away its value. Growing faith is always on the move, always a little hot from these purifying fires.

## 1 PETER 1:8–9

### Should worship be joyful?

Much formal worship seems engineered for the expression of emotions other than joy. Somber hymns, melancholy prayer, and exhortative sermons express emotions and attitudes such as humility, awe, and reverence. Yet Peter describes here that joy is welling in the hearts of the worshipers.

Perhaps charismatic worship fills the gap and gives expression to joy as a counterpoint to traditional Protestant and Catholic forms. Yet, clearly for Peter, joy is not to be repressed in worship or sequestered to one movement within the church. The joy of salvation warrants exuberant expression in all corporate worship. It need not be coaxed or fueled by gimmicks or peer pressure. Rather, joy in God should be natural and full. Worship forms need to celebrate joy as well as awe, exuberance in God as well as humility before God.

## 1 PETER 1:12

### Do angels study?

Apparently, angels have the desire to understand God's ways. The meaning of the phrase "eagerly watching" implies observing with intensity and effort. Perhaps angels study God's ways to marvel more fully at His grace and power. On this model, angels are like intelligent and gifted apprentices who eagerly seek to understand the mind of the Master.

Perhaps angels do not actually learn like we do but show an appetite for learning anyhow. If

An angel at the temptation of Christ, coming to minister to Him after He defeated Satan.

that's true, angels would be the singular element in all creation that cannot realize their purpose or potential. Such a model, while possible, fails to cohere with one of the purposes expressed in God's creative plan, that intelligence that seeks understanding is equipped to find it.

## 1 PETER 3:21

### Does baptism save us?

The ritual of baptism is not a gate of entry into God's family. Baptism is an outer ritual that recognizes the inner saving work of Jesus and pledges a life of discipleship in response. To be baptized into God's family is to obey God, but it is not salvation itself. That is effected through a person's commitment to Jesus Christ as Lord and Savior, of which baptism is a symbol.

## 1 PETER 4:3

### Why do people sin?

This is a complicated question that nearly every Bible story and chapter addresses. Here, however, sin appears to be like a constellation, and therein lies the hint of an answer to this question.

For instance, people often consider sexual sin as a primary problem. Defuse this appetite, and the problem is solved, it is thought. Yet sexual sin is described here as only a part of a bigger complex of sin, a community of sins, an environment of disobedience. Sexual sin is actually only one expression of a variety of rebellions against God. It is fed by all the others, just as it feeds all others.

People sin for many reasons, but certainly we adopt the behaviors and attitudes of communities we choose to live within. People who wish to avoid some forms of sin fall under their sway by easing their vigil on preferred sins. Resisting sexual sin, or any other kind, requires one to be vigilant all along the perimeter of his or her heart and mind.

# 2 PETER

*To be a Christian is to have a future and a hope. This book underlines the promises we all want to hear again and again.*

## 2 PETER 1:5–9

**If salvation is based on what Jesus has done for me, not on what I do, then why can't I relax and enjoy life instead of trying to change old sinful habits and develop virtues?**

Christian living is not fire insurance but a growing relationship with the holy God. This is the Christian's destiny. Imagine that God has promised you will become a virtuoso pianist some day, though you can't even tell a piano from a tuba. If you believe God's promise, what is your plan? Do you spend the day watching videos and cracking your knuckles or practicing the keyboard with the promise that your destiny is being fulfilled as you pursue it?

Being a Christian means knowing Christ better each day. God wants to produce Jesus' character in us. Peter writes that learning unselfish love for others can only be done through growing in the disciplines of trust, obedience, and self-control.

This painting depicts what are traditionally known as the seven deadly sins: pride, greed, lust, envy, gluttony, wrath, and sloth.

# 2 PETER 1:16

## How can we be sure that the stories about Jesus are true?

Eyewitnesses to Jesus' life, Peter among them, verified what really happened. We see Jesus through the eyes of Peter and other disciples who testify to the truth through stories such as the Transfiguration, where God declares Jesus to be His true Son. Peter spent three years with Jesus, observing His miracles and ingesting His teaching. When Jesus asked, "Who do you say that I am?" Peter confessed that Jesus was the Christ, the Son of the living God.

Peter was in the center of the action in the days just before Jesus' arrest and death. Peter's denial was the low point of his life, yet Jesus forgave him and chose him to be a missionary of the Good News. God used this flawed man, Peter, to establish the credibility of Jesus for future generations. Peter gives specific and clear testimony about Jesus' life and teachings. Add Peter's testimony to other Bible writers and we have detailed eyewitness accounts that serve as the foundation of our faith.

# 2 PETER 3:3–4

## Does it really matter that much if Jesus ever comes back to earth?

When Jesus makes a promise, He keeps it. Previous generations thought they would see Jesus' return, but they did not. Through this long wait, God has been faithful to His people. The church has grown. God's family is getting larger.

No one knows the time schedule of Jesus' return, so we continue to wait, just as believers waited in the early church. True believers refuse to turn to idols (immediate, though false, images of divine power) and are looking forward to that day when Jesus will surely return (1 Thessalonians 1:10).

# 2 PETER 3:16

## Peter admits that some of Paul's letters to churches are not easy to understand. If Peter was confused, how can we correctly determine what the Bible teaches?

The first step in interpreting the Bible is to find the meaning of a passage for the author. What did the statement originally intend to

The profiles of Paul and Peter, two of God's apostles who preached about Jesus and died for their faith.

communicate? This historical and linguistic study is the work of specialists and scholars, available to everyone through schools and published commentaries.

The interpreter's second job is to apply the meaning of a passage today. This is the task of teaching and preaching, available to everyone through the ministry of the local church. Parts of the Bible are historical, parts are poetic, and parts are didactic. Interpreters must recognize what is meant to be literal and what is figurative and symbolic.

One danger of Bible interpretation is to draw a far-out "truth" from one isolated passage. Rightly interpreting any one verse requires that its meaning coheres with the whole. Peter's statement about Paul's letters reveals his commitment to further study. Peter wants to know. So should we.

# 1, 2, 3 JOHN

*Here are three letters about loving God and others. In the ripples of your life's waters, you'll find the way to keep the boat afloat and the oars in the water.*

## 1 JOHN 1:1–4

### Which John wrote the New Testament letters that bear his name?

Tradition has identified the writer of these letters as John, the son of Zebedee (Mark 1:19–20), the author of the Gospel of John and Revelation. He was the disciple whom Jesus loved (John 21:20). The epistles bear a striking resemblance in style and vocabulary to the Gospel of John. The early church fathers (Irenaeus, Clement of Alexandria, Origen, and Tertullian) all pointed to the apostle John as the writer of 1, 2, and 3 John.

John was well qualified to write. In 1 John 1:1–4, John states his credentials as an eyewitness to the words and works of Jesus. Twice in these letters he mentions that he heard Christ Himself. Six times he makes reference to seeing Christ. Once he speaks of touching Jesus with his hands. Clearly John was not relating second-hand stories. He spoke with apostolic authority.

## 1 JOHN 1:1–6

### Who were the Gnostics?

The readers of John's letters were confronted with an attractive yet dangerous challenge to the truth, a religious system called Gnosticism. This term comes from the Greek word for *knowledge*. The goal of this movement was to acquire secret spiritual insight and special knowledge and thereby achieve a state of existence higher than the norm: enlightenment.

The Gnostics believed in two spheres of reality. The physical world was evil and inferior while the spirit-mind world was good and worthy. One of Gnosticism's ideas, therefore, was that Christ could not have had an actual body. To be truly good, the real Jesus was necessarily a phantom or spirit.

Gnosticism produced two kinds of followers: those who pursued an ascetic life, shunning the evil physical world with its false sensual pleasures; and others who indulged in the physical world precisely because it was inferior. For this group, physical pleasure was okay because it was irrelevant to the "real world," namely, the spiritual. Both versions of Gnosticism perverted biblical teaching about the value of material creation, the relevance of stewardship over the earth (including our bodies), and the importance of moral care. To imagine that Jesus was mere spirit was extremely dangerous to the Bible's consistent teaching that God became a man. To seek enlightenment in abstracted ideas was to direct the soul away from the personal God of love. John directed early believers to avoid this heresy, as we should today. Learn the faith from biblical Christians, not from followers of strange aberrations like this.

## 1 JOHN 1:5

### Why is God said to be "light"?

In the Bible, light indicates what is good, pure, and holy. Darkness is synonymous with sin and evil. To say that God is light is to assert that God is perfectly pure and holy. Only God is without sin. He is the standard of perfection and truth by which everything is measured.

Light reveals. Light shows the true nature of things. When confronted by God, people become painfully aware of their own failures and sin. God's "light" brings this painful crisis,

then liberates us into true freedom and joy. Like a brilliant spotlight, God guides His creatures out of the dangerous darkness of their sinful lives into a place of safety and peace. Darkness and light cannot coexist (1 John 1:5–6). To know God, we must put aside sin.

## 1 JOHN 1:6

### What does "fellowship" mean?

"Fellowship" translates the Greek word *koinonia*, meaning association, communion, and close relationship. It implies participation in a mutual task and sharing possessions. In Christ, believers are able to enjoy this kind of intimacy with God and with fellow Christians.

Fellowship goes beyond friendship. Believers worldwide enjoy fellowship, though one's range of friendship is much smaller. Because of the bonds of fellowship, Christians who will never meet still feel the joy of participating in joint projects (missionary schools, for example) and often experience quick rapport when they do meet, despite language and cultural differences.

The idea of Christian fellowship makes rivalry, interfaith warfare, and tribal suspicions nonsensical. Our bond in Christ overcomes social differences. Just as heaven will blend all God's creation, so fellowship blends and bonds people of different backgrounds into one church, one fellowship, one faith.

## 1 JOHN 2:9

### Is it okay for a Christian to intensely dislike another believer?

Several Bible passages emphasize a Christian's preeminent commitment to love—not merely a sentimental, warm feeling, but a choice of the will to put other people's welfare ahead of one's own by showing respect, considering their feelings, and praying on their behalf.

Not every Christian will enjoy a warm friendship with every other Christian. Some

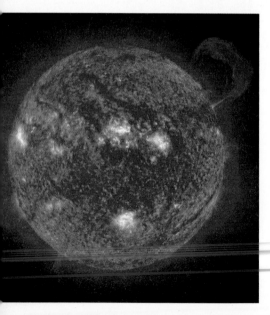

The sun—earth's source of light.

people will be irritating, quirky, and obnoxious. A few brothers and sisters in Christ will rub us the wrong way. We will always encounter fellow believers with whom our personalities clash. On the other hand, we will "click"— be naturally drawn—to some people. The Christian's goal is to choose to demonstrate love and concern regardless of warm or distant feelings, regardless of the degree of personality attachment we feel with the other. Love sees the beauty of people through God's eyes, even when our own vision is blurred by the other's apparent ugliness. Love acts to fulfill God's purpose for the other, even when the other does not seem to deserve it. That's what God did for us and calls us to do for everyone. The road to reconciliation begins when one party is willing to talk and both are willing to listen. And there's no reason why you cannot take the lead.

## 1 JOHN 2:15–18

**God loves the world, and we are to imitate God. Then we are told *not* to love the world. What does this all mean?**

Christians should love the world of people and be concerned for their eternal welfare (John 3:16). This means to have a compassionate heart. The command not to love the world in 1 John 2:15 has to do with the world of sin, the universal system organized by Satan against God and His rule. We must never become attached and devoted to the ways of the world. This is what is meant by worldliness.

## 1 JOHN 2:20, 27

### Are only certain Christians anointed by the Holy Spirit?

Some well-meaning Christians describe certain preachers, songs, worship services,

or sermons as "anointed," meaning that the person or event is able to evoke a strong sense of God's power. But to "anoint" in biblical terms means to consecrate or set apart for a special purpose. Kings and priests were anointed with oil in solemn ceremonies intended to designate them as civil and spiritual leaders.

In a similar yet figurative way, the Spirit of God anoints every believer upon

The Holy Spirit descends on believers.

conversion (1 Corinthians 12:13). Because each Christian has received this anointing, it becomes imperative to find and fulfill the special role each plays in the building of the church. All Christians have the Spirit's anointing—all are gifted and special in God's eyes.

## 1 JOHN 3:2

### Are people destined to become "gods"?

Children of God share in Christ's divine nature (2 Peter 1:4), but this does not mean that we will become little gods. God's goal is to redeem us, to make us like Christ (Romans 8:29). In heaven's glorified (but not deified) state, we will share Christ's purposes, goals, and holy character. In the words of John, "we will be like him"!

God acts on our behalf to overcome the separation that sin has created and to grant us the benefits of His heavenly, eternal, and perfect environment. The Bible gives no thought to eliminating the essential distinction between divine and human identity. In fact, the notion of people wedging into God's essence is the root of all sin, since it betrays an attitude of subversion to God as sovereign Lord.

## 1 JOHN 1:8–2:2; 3:8–9

### Do people sin naturally, like breathing (1:8–2:2), or is sin as impossible for the Christian as defying gravity (3:8–9)?

True believers won't sin habitually, as a way of life. Yet experience tells us surely that Christians do break God's laws and defy God's will. Christians may eliminate glaring and gross sins from their lives, but what about impatience, anxiety, failing to love others, anger, envy, discontentment, and lust? Honesty presents us with continuing imperfection, yet we are children of the most holy God. It seems like such a contradiction.

Perhaps the best way to understand this predicament is to say that our new nature cannot and will not sin (2 Corinthians 5:17). In our new (and true) identity as reborn people, we are dead to sin and alive to God. Sin has no power over us (Romans

6:6–7). United with Christ in His death and resurrection, we have a new capacity to say no to temptation (1 Corinthians 10:13) and yes to righteous living (Romans 6:11–14). The more we yield to the indwelling Holy Spirit, the more we realize our true identity as children of the living God.

## 1 JOHN 4:7–8

### Why did John emphasize love so much?

For the Christian, love is not an option; it is the motivating heart of all God calls us to do and become. When we love, we reveal the reality of our God, and we demonstrate our true identity as God's children. Love is a believer's calling card. It is the mark of God on us. People who do not know God sit up and take notice at this unusual freedom from fear and selfishness.

One of the great hallmarks of the early Christians was their affection for each other, prompting even their enemies to marvel. Christians have failed to love many times, as history clearly shows. The record of the church is very spotty on this lofty calling to love each other. But the obligation (truly, one of joy) is still our primary task—to show the character of God by freely sharing and caring and by building others up in God's grace. No matter what your job or how big or small your family, love is your first priority, your highest privilege and responsibility.

## 1 JOHN 4:8, 16

### What is meant by the phrase "God is love"?

John emphasized that God is the very source of love ("love comes from God," 1 John 4:7) and that "God is love" (1 John 4:16). This means that love is God's very nature. He is the fountain from which all affection flows. The supernatural, unselfish, sacrificial love that changes lives is part of the eternal existence and character of God.

This goes a long way to explain one of the biggest questions we face: Why help other people? Since everyone has personal needs and wants, why not serve the self? The answer rests in God's character. Because divine love is freely given to us, we should also freely give to others. And here's the spark plug that gets love going: God in your life!

The truth that God is love explains why the universe has hope despite its sorrow, why we give instead of clutching every morsel we can, and why we can live happily instead of fearfully. That's a lot tucked into three small words—but the reality of those words changes everything.

## 1 JOHN 4:17

### Will Christians face a day of judgment?

Believers will one day stand before Christ and be held accountable for how they have lived (2 Corinthians 5:10). Apparently believers in the first century trembled at the thought of such a judgment. Truly the thought is sobering. Yet John shows how we can drive such fear of it from our lives.

First, we must comprehend how much God loves us. Because Christ has taken the punishment we deserve, our sins are completely forgiven. When we grasp this truth—that we are fully accepted in Christ—we find a great sense of freedom.

Second, we must love others. If we spend our lives caring for others and putting their needs first, then the judgment seat of Christ will become a time for gaining, not losing, rewards. We will hear our Master say, "Well done, my good and faithful servant" (Matthew 25:21).

## 1 JOHN 5:21

### Are idols still a threat to spiritual life?

An idol need not be a carved image of some token deity. Today, more common "idols" are passions and objectives disconnected from God's purposes, such as wealth, sexual adventure, power over people, perhaps even the achievement of otherwise noble goals such as earning an advanced degree or holding elected church office. Anything that pulls a person's devotion away from God can be an idol.

An old hymn puts it this way: "Prone to wander, Lord, I feel it; prone to leave the God I love." It is a wise practice for Christians to ask themselves regularly: What are my priorities? What people, things, or events have captured my deepest affections? Do I get up in the morning to earn more dollars, to get more stuff, to achieve more power, or to love and serve God another day?

Symbols of different idols from ancient times. Many people in the world still worship idols today.

# 2 JOHN 7

## What is meant by the term *antichrist*?

The idea is opposition—hatred for God and the things of God, resentment of God's rule and reign over the world, and determination to defy God's authority and undermine God's purposes. This hostile, antichrist spirit not only affected Christians to whom John wrote, it also permeates our age and will intensify as we draw closer to the end of history.

# 3 JOHN 2

## What is a soul?

No doctor operating on a patient has ever discovered an organ called the *soul*, yet we have no better term to describe what distinguishes human beings from every other part of God's creation. Only people have the unique gift of self-consciousness, the ability to reflect on their own experience, to interpret it to others, and then to speak about it. A famous professor once said, "Dogs bark, but dogs never bark about barking." Only people speak to each other about their lives. Only people are able to know about a Being supremely good and loving and to pray to that Being. Our physical capacity for thought, speech, and prayer is lodged in our brains, but neurophysiology alone cannot explain it. That is why the elder John could write to Gaius about the health of his body and also the strength of his spirit (his soul—his uniquely human capacity for spiritual life).

When God created the world, He gave a very special gift to Adam and Eve—His own "image" (Genesis 1:26). God shared with us the ability to distinguish good from evil. This gift, however, was abused, and humans fell into sin, tainting the gift and requiring that the soul be cleansed from guilt. This Jesus did on the Cross.

The soul of each person lives forever and will someday be reunited with the body in God's heavenly kingdom. In the meantime, keep your soul healthy with lots of Bible study, prayer, and vigorous faithful service to Christ.

A picture that tries to capture the flight of the soul to heaven to be with Jesus.

# 3 JOHN 3

## How can a person live in the truth?

The elder apostle John applauds Gaius for following the truth. He commends him for walking faithfully in the truth of God's Word.

Think of living in the truth as being on a journey. You have a destination and a map. If you're distracted by a row of dazzling fast-food restaurants, an alleged shortcut through the desert, or a rest stop offering pleasures that will slow you down, you're not on course and may not make it home. But if you've packed light, are alert to the road signs, and are committed to following the directions given by your leader, you're heading toward the goal. In navigational terms, you are true to the course.

God calls each of us to faithful service, directed by the Bible, enabled by the Holy Spirit, and led by the Lord Jesus. We are true if we follow obediently, as Gaius did.

## 3 JOHN 9

### How can so-called Christian people get away with power trips?

In this case, distance gave Diotrephes a certain independence from the spiritual leadership of the church, and he used it for a "power trip" advantage. Because a lot of people never speak up about abuse in the church, egotistical people get away with power-tripping. Diotrephes had found a congregation of "sheep" who never confronted him with the truth or threatened his hold on leadership. Also, Diotrephes had learned the art of propaganda. He had turned John's attempts to correct his power trip into evidence for his own legitimacy. In so doing, he had deceived both himself and his followers, who complied with his cult-like rejection of missionary visitors.

Isolated spiritual power-trippers will one day meet with the Person who backs down to no one. Justice will be done and selfish power stripped of its pretense.

## 3 JOHN 11

### Is everyone who does "good" a Christian?

No. God's laws define the good, and many people who profess no Christian faith follow those laws. For example, the commandment to honor parents and refrain from murder (Exodus 20:12–13) are respected and observed by every human culture. In that sense, a person may be loyal to God's laws while unaware of the God who authored them.

Other people who live in what we loosely call "Christian cultures" tend to observe God's laws because they are reflected in a country's civil laws and a people's social habits. Stealing and lying are wrong, first because God condemns them, and second because governments punish the former and discourage the latter. Non-Christians who "fit in" to a Christian culture have the benefits of compliance with God's law. However, compliance with law is no substitute for faith in Jesus Christ, who alone has paid the debt for our outrageous failure to obey God.

The flip side to our question is the sad fact that many Christians fail to do good. God's people both succeed and fail to obey Him, and people without faith do the same. But God has promised to judge everyone according to Jesus' payment for sins on the cross, not on compliance with the law. Our trust in Christ alone saves us, and no one can "do" enough to make up for refusing to ask God, in humble faith, for the mercy Jesus provides.

## 3 JOHN 11

### Can only Christians do "good"?

No. The Bible points to many decisions and actions taken by pagans who, perhaps unaware, were thinking and acting in compliance with God's laws. Certainly it would be impossible to shop in a grocery store, seek care in a hospital, depend on the police force, or enjoy a sporting event if only Christians could do good. Our problem is not whether doing good is exclusively a Christian activity, but that doing good (by anyone, Christian or otherwise) is not good enough for salvation.

All people carry guilt that doing good cannot erase. Only Jesus erases the guilt that offends God. Jesus offers all people His marvelous erasure through faith—belief in His offer and surrender of our life to His purpose. Once you are born again—given spiritual life through union with Jesus Christ—the good you do is a result of God's new energy in your life and no longer a by-product of your living

### How can we know what "good" is?

We judge what's good by establishing a benchmark, which has been the task of moral philosophers since the invention of language. Several benchmarks currently compete: personal pleasure, social stability, tribal prosperity, obeying universally accepted norms ("do not inflict needless pain" is one example), following religious teaching, or obeying God.

The latter two are especially difficult. Religious teaching is so diverse, so frequently unpleasant, so prone to support the people in power that following one teaching nearly always entails disobeying or fighting another. Obeying God, however, offers these advantages. The Bible is God's Word, written for our benefit. Jesus, the divine Son of God, is our living Lord who has sent us the Holy Spirit, our ever-present helper. We acquire moral discernment as we mature in relationship with God. We come to love the good as we grow to love God, for God is good.

Granted, Christians will disagree about how God's principles for right conduct should be applied to particular problems. Solving disagreements involves continued study, prayer for insight and courage, and active discussion with people of mature faith. Christians also understand doing good as a response to God's love, not as a prerequisite for God's attention or approval. Doing good is evidence that faith is growing, never a substitute for faith itself.

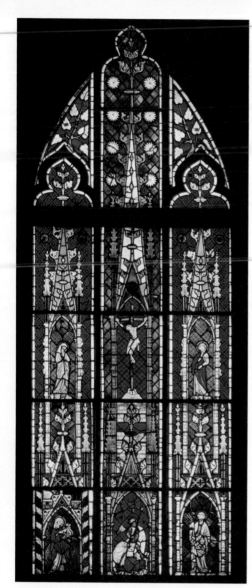

Good works can't get us into heaven. Christ's death on the cross provides our eternal salvation.

in a good place, surrounded by good people, intent on good behavior.

While all good things please God, there is special pleasure in God working His will through His people in His way. You will surely want to be part of that worldwide good thing, and you can be. Admission is through a simple prayer that accepts Jesus as Savior and trusts Him alone for all good things.

# JUDE

*The hunger for spiritual truth sometimes leads people to naïve acceptance of hurtful distortions of the truth. Know the difference between real and fake, true faith and spoof.*

## JUDE 3

### Why does the almighty, all-powerful God command Christian believers to "defend the faith"?

It seems strange that God—who needs no defense—gives Christians the job of defending the faith. If God were less patient, He might dispatch His enemies while Christians picked up the pieces, but God has a different way of accomplishing His purposes.

Christians are God's ambassadors, speaking for Him and delivering the message of forgiveness and reconciliation to everyone (2 Corinthians 5:18–21). Christians are not selected for this key role based on special intelligence or moral aptitude. In fact, quite a bit of evidence points to the need for serious remedial study in all areas of this job. Yet the best defense of the truth of God is the life of a Christian believer focused on Jesus Christ, adopting the Bible as God's authoritative Word, and loving others unselfishly. Jude warned readers to reject teachers who twist standards of right and wrong and pervert the message of salvation. Christians defend the faith when they test every idea against the central message of the Bible.

## JUDE 8

### How can a person identify a false teacher?

False teachers add or subtract from the Bible. They often have a "revelation" that allegedly supplies new data about divine matters—data that the Bible fails to reveal, so to speak. False teachers devalue the work of Jesus Christ by making Him less than God incarnate.

A carving of a teacher with his pupils.

They twist the trust about the meaning of His death or reject the truth of His resurrection.

False teachers build small empires around the three tilting towers of phony ministry—money, sex, and power. They scheme to defraud followers of money. They practice immorality and then justify sin from twisted biblical teaching. They manipulate people for selfish ends, proving again the gullibility of the human species.

False teachers cater to popular trends, designing new formulas for happiness and salvation. These formulas often promise prosperity in exchange for financial support, a contract as bogus as buying real estate in the lost city of Atlantis. Yet people still sign on.

False teachers often sound close to Christian teaching, but their mixture of truth and falsehood is hurtful, sometimes deadly. The Christian who wishes to avoid loss is advised to study the scriptures, know the history of the faith, support a sound church, and develop a network of friends whose progress in faith is trustworthy and true.

# REVELATION

*What a journey John must have taken, to see and to feel the majestic environment of heaven. But what a fearsome journey as well, to glimpse the consequences of evil.*

## REVELATION 1:1

### Is Revelation to be understood literally?

Revelation uses three types of literature. First, it is a letter written by the apostle John to seven churches in Asia Minor. Second, it is prophecy, speaking God's judgment and truth. Finally, it is apocalyptic writing, a common form of Jewish literature.

Apocalyptic literature is written to people undergoing persecution. It contains symbolic imagery and visions, and it looks to God's triumph at the end of time to convey hope to the faithful. Apocalyptic literature is not written in chronological order, but according to literary priorities. In addition, some visions or dreams contain symbols that are imaginative, powerful, and read like fantasy— a beast with seven heads and ten horns or locusts with scorpions' tails and human heads (Revelation 9:10; 13:1).

The reader of Revelation must decide whether a passage is epistolary, prophetic, or apocalyptic; then, whether its intention is literal or figurative. The details of this important interpretive process will require your further study through Bible commentaries, original language, and theological reflection.

## REVELATION 2–3

### What are the "seven churches"?

John is writing to seven churches in Asia Minor that are under growing persecution from Rome. As these churches cope with the pressure and temptations of living in a pagan culture, there remains a question whether they will faithfully serve the Lord until the end. John writes to affirm God's sovereignty and faithfulness and to encourage the churches to stand firm.

The letters contain greetings to each church, an assessment of how the church is doing, a commendation or warning, a command to persevere, and a promise. The seven letters together describe what weakens the faith of churches and individuals: losing initial passion for Jesus, losing hope, becoming tolerant of sin, compromising moral behavior, and having an inactive or lukewarm faith.

This depicts the seven stars and the names of the seven churches of Revelation.

Given the deficits of these seven churches, they are still to be "lampstands"—light illuminating the gospel of Christ to the world. They are models for present-day churches of the difficulty and responsibility of keeping faith strong under adversity.

## REVELATION 5:5

### What's at stake in the opening of the scrolls?

Only Jesus is able to break the seals on the scroll because He lived in obedience to the will of God, defeated Satan, and conquered death. He is the only Savior. Christ opens the scrolls, a symbol of God's plan for creation that was lost through human disobedience but recovered through His life, death, and resurrection. If the scrolls remain shut, the gospel story is silent. Once open, creation realizes its hope, and heavenly representatives sing with joy.

## REVELATION 7:14

### What is the great tribulation?

The meaning of this term must be integrated with other terms: the rapture, the Millennium, and the identity of the 144,000 chosen people.

Dispensational theology identifies the great tribulation as a seven-year future period of havoc and pain, Satan's last and greatest opportunity for evil before the second coming of Christ inaugurates God's heavenly kingdom. This view gained wide popularity through the *Scofield Reference Bible* and, in the 1960s, through the writings of Hal Lindsey. In this theology, the rapture occurs before the tribulation (although some allow for a rapture in the middle of the tribulation) or following it.

A more symbolic interpretation identifies the term as the period of spiritual warfare that the Christian church endures throughout its history. In great conflict with Satan, the gospel message is nevertheless carried to all the nations—God's Good News told by those who love God more than life.

## REVELATION 13:18

### What does the number 666 mean?

Either the number is a cryptic way of identifying an actual person (equal to the

complete imperfection, that is, evil. This fits the profile of the Beast described here.

Some early commentators thought that Nero, emperor of Rome (A.D. 54–68) and a persecutor of Christians, was identified in this text. The numerical value of his name in Hebrew equals 666.

## REVELATION 14:3

### Is heaven's population limited to 144,000?

The number cannot be taken literally. Even the literalism formerly taught by the Jehovah's Witnesses cult (prior to its own growth spurt) has been revised. If not a literal head count, the number must be symbolic, and likely meant to point to the completion of God's work of salvation among all the nations. The symbolic strength of the number derives from the

An artist's rendering of what heaven will be like.

sum of the numeric equivalents of the letters in a name), or it is a symbol of evil. The latter interpretation derives from the idea of perfection associated with the number seven (seven days of Creation, seven lampstands, etc.) and the idea of completion associated with the number three (the three persons of the Trinity). By these terms, the number six repeated three times would indicate

twelve tribes of Israel, multiplied by itself (the church), multiplied by one thousand (sometimes taken as a reference to millennial believers)—equaling the sum of all the earth's redeemed, those chosen and affirmed as sons and daughters of God.

# REVELATION 20:4

## What is the thousand-year reign of Christ?

Commonly called the Millennium, three positions are taken on its meaning and identity:

(1) Postmillennialists (the most popular evangelical view of a century ago) teach that the thousand-year reign occurs at the end of history when the world has turned to Christ, for the most part. Christian values dominate world cultures in a period that typifies God's original plan for creation. Christ is not literally on earth, but His message and people cover the earth. The second coming of Christ occurs as the capstone of this period.

(2) Premillennialists (a popular evangelical view today) teach a literal thousand-year reign with Christ physically present as ruler of the earth. Following the Millennium, Satan erupts from his prison for a last stand and suffers a final defeat as history ends and God's heavenly kingdom begins.

(3) Amillennialists understand the thousand-year reign to be symbolic for the new covenant era, during which Christ sits at the right hand of the Father and reigns in the hearts of His people. Satan is bound in that he cannot stop the advance of the gospel. The second coming of Christ brings human history to a close.

Important to all three views is the assurance of Christ's eventual return in glory, the reward for faithful believers, and the final disposition of Satan and all the forces of evil. The relationship of the Millennium to ecclesiology (the doctrine of the church) warrants the reader's further attention.

# REVELATION 21:1

## What will the new heaven and new earth be like?

We can hardly know. Surely it will be beyond anything we can imagine. The imagery of the Bible suggests an environment of superlative quality with no sense of diminishing resources. Competition is also eliminated, leaving no possible incentive for selfishness, hoarding, or private property, were those things even possible in the spiritual afterlife. The central focus of happiness in the biblical account, however, is not the richness of the environment but always the immediate presence of believers with the triune God.

After the final defeat of Satan and the end of death and evil, all who have believed on the Lord Jesus Christ will be forever in the presence of God. No matter how hard, hurtful, or despairing life on earth has been, those who trust in Jesus will be united with Christ for eternity.

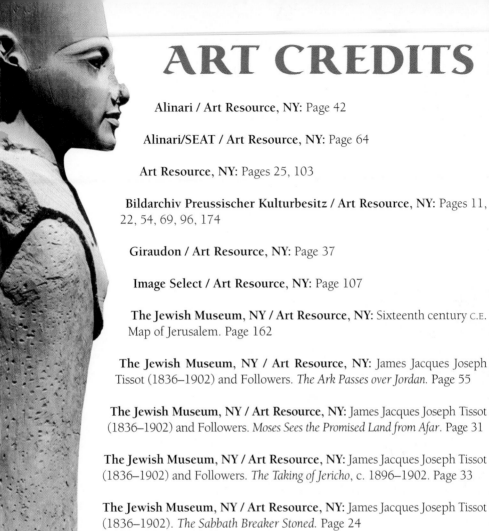

# ART CREDITS